D1572721

HISTORICAL DICTIONARIES OF U.S. DIPLOMACY
Edited by Jon Woronoff

1. *U.S. Diplomacy from the Civil War to World War I*, by Kenneth J. Blume. 2005.
2. *United States–China Relations*, by Robert Sutter, 2006.

Historical Dictionary of United States–China Relations

Robert Sutter

Historical Dictionaries of U.S. Diplomacy, No. 2

The Scarecrow Press, Inc.
Lanham, Maryland • Toronto • Oxford
2006

SCARECROW PRESS, INC.

Published in the United States of America
by Scarecrow Press, Inc.
A wholly owned subsidary of
The Rowman & Littlefield Publishing Group, Inc.
4501 Forbes Boulevard, Suite 200, Lanham, Maryland 20706
www.scarecrowpress.com

PO Box 317
Oxford
OX2 9RU, UK

British Library Cataloguing in Publication Information Available

Library of Congress Cataloging-in-Publication Data

Sutter, Robert G..
  Historical dictionary of United States–China relations / Robert Sutter.
    p. cm. — (Historical dictionaries of U.S. diplomacy ; no. 2)
  Includes bibliographical references.
  ISBN 0-8108-5502-X (hardback : alk. paper)
  1. United States—Foreign relations—China—Dictionaries. 2. China—Foreign
relations—United States—Dictionaries. I. Title. II. Series.

E183.8.C5S883 2006

327.73051'03—dc22

ACKNOWLEDGMENTS

I wish to thank Jon Woronoff, the series editor, for asking me to undertake this book, for providing guidance throughout the writing and production of the book, and for reviewing the entire manuscript and offering valuable comments. I also wish to thank Eve Cary for expert research assistance and production of appendices.

Contents

Editor's Foreword

It is sometimes claimed rather cynically that in diplomacy there are no permanent friendships and only permanent interests and that affinities should not matter anywhere near as much as realities. Well, in the case of United States–China relations, it would seem that things are the other way around. The United States is the most powerful country in the world, although it was not always, and China is the most populous country in the world and on the way to becoming at least the second or third most powerful. Yet these two countries have taken two centuries to sort out their relations and are not quite there and, during most of this trajectory, illusions and emotions clearly predominated over realities and hard facts. Otherwise, how could one explain the constant—and not really vital—antipathies and enmities, and a supposedly rational elite in Washington who repeatedly ignored the basic concerns of Beijing, while the elite in Beijing—at least the ideologically correct portion—thought it could snub the only superpower.

The long and slow progression to rationality (and even a welcome degree of cynicism) in potentially the most important bilateral relationship in the world is traced very clearly in this new volume in the U.S. Diplomacy series. It is done so almost painstakingly, step by step, in the chronology. And it is explained (explanation is certainly needed) in the introduction. Then the details, the twists and turns, the starts and stops, the advances and regressions, the concessions and compromises are laid out in greater detail in the dictionary section. This section also includes entries on the major players (presidents, prime ministers, secretaries of state, and others), the relevant state institutions and international organizations, the major issues, the conflicts and the agreements. And, of course, it provides information not only on the People's Republic of China but Taiwan (Republic of China) and Hong Kong as well. Because this is such an important relationship, readers who will want to know more should follow up the many leads in the bibliography. Still, the place to start does seem to be this *Historical Dictionary of United States–China Relations*.

The author of this volume, Robert G. Sutter, is an old hand at US–Chinese relations in many ways, having specialized in Asian affairs and US foreign policy for more than three decades. In a long and varied career, he has worked for the Department of State, the Senate Foreign Relations Committee, the Central Intelligence Agency, the Library of Congress, the Congressional Research Service, and the National Intelligence Council. For the past few years, he has been a visiting professor in the School of Foreign Services at Georgetown University. Dr. Sutter has written various posts and numcrous articles, government reports, and over a dozen books, the most recent being *The United States and East Asia: Dynamics and Implications*. Now he has repackaged the basic information for us in a concise and handy guide to the field.

Jon Woronoff
Series Editor

Reader's Note

The English-language literature on US–China relations tends to use two systems of Romanization. The Wade Giles system was in wide use until the 1970s and remains in use in Taiwan. The Pinyin system was adopted by the People's Republic of China after its establishment in 1949 and came into wide use in the 1970s. Against this background, in this book Chinese individuals, places, and other names that were commonly referred to using the Wade Giles system are referred to in that way. Chinese individuals, places, and other names that were commonly referred to using the Pinyin system are referred to in that way. For some dictionary entries, a Pinyin version has been added in parentheses to the Wade Giles version of a Chinese name. *Beijing*, the Pinyin version of the Chinese city, is used in discussions of events after 1949. References prior to 1949 use the term then in use, *Peking*.

In accord with conventional usage in China, Chinese persons are referred to using the surname first, then the given name.

In the dictionary, section items are bolded to indicate that there are entries on them, but in the case of the People's Republic of China, the Republic of China, and Taiwan, this is not done because they appear so often.

Acronyms and Abbreviations

ABM	Anti-Ballistic Missile
ADB	Asian Development Bank
AFL–CIO	American Federation of Labor–Congress of Industrial Organizations
AI	Amnesty International
AID	Agency for International Development
AIG	American International Group
AIT	American Institute in Taiwan.
APEC	Asia-Pacific Economic Cooperation
ARATS	Association for Relations Across the Taiwan Strait
ARF	Association of Southeast Asian Nations Regional Forum
ASEAN	Association of Southeast Asian Nations
CBI	China-Burma-India
CCNAA	Coordination Council for North American Affairs
CCP	Chinese Communist Party
CIA	Central Intelligence Agency
COCOM	Coordination Committee of Exports to Communist Areas
DNC	Democratic National Committee
DPP	Democratic Progressive Party
FAPA	Formosan Association for Public Affairs
FBI	Federal Bureau of Investigation
GATT	General Agreement on Tariffs and Trade
IAEA	International Atomic Energy Agency
IDA	International Development Association
IDF	Indigenous Defense Fighter
IMF	International Monetary Fund
IPR	Intellectual Property Rights

JCRR	Joint Commission on Rural Reconstruction
KMT	Kuomintang
LEGCO	Legislative Council
MFN	Most-Favored-Nation
MTCR	Missile Technology Control Regime
NPT	Non-Proliferation Treaty
NTR	Normal Trade Relations
OPIC	Overseas Private Investment Corporation
PLA	People's Liberation Army
PNTR	Permanent Normal Trade Relations
PRC	People's Republic of China
ROC	Republic of China
SACO	Sino–American Cooperation Organization
SALT	Strategic Arms Limitation Talks
SEATO	Southeast Asia Treaty Organization
SEF	Straits Exchange Foundation
TDP	Trade and Development Program
TECRO	Taipei Economic and Cultural Representative Office
TRA	Taiwan Relations Act
TMD	Theater Missile Defense
USTR	United States Special Trade Representative
VOA	Voice of America
WTO	World Trade Organization
YMCA	Young Men's Christian Association

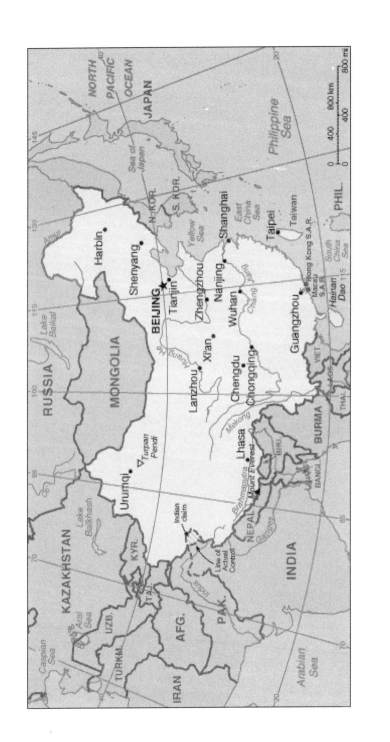

Chronology

1784   Freed from British trade restrictions, US merchants sent the ship *Empress of China* to Canton, the first American commercial vessel to engage directly in the China trade.

1821   In Canton, US merchants gave up accused murderer Francesco Terranova for Chinese trial and execution.

1824   Russell and Company, which became the most prominent US trading firm with China in the 19th century, was founded.

1837   Future Taiping rebellion leader Hung Hsiu-ch'uan spent three months studying Christianity with US missionary Issachar Roberts.

1839   The Opium War started.

1842   The US Asiatic Squadron began operations including along the China coast. The Opium War ended with the signing of the Treaty of Nanking.

1843   The United States and China signed the Treaty of Wang-hsia.

1850   The Taiping Rebellion began.

1858   Under foreign pressure, China signed in Tientsin new treaties with European powers and the United States, granting expanded foreign rights in China.

1859   Chinese forces repelled British and French envoys and accompanying forces seeking to exchange ratification of new treaties.

1860   British and French forces attacked and occupied Peking. They forced new treaties on the Chinese government that further expanded foreign, including US, rights and privileges in China.

1864   The Taiping rebellion ended.

1868 US officials and a Chinese delegation visiting the United States and led by former US envoy to China Anson Burlingame signed a treaty promoting Chinese immigration to the United States.

1870 Among early legislative steps that over the next decades would tightly restrict Chinese entry into the United States, the Page Act of 1870 banned most immigration of Chinese women to the United States.

1872 Chinese students went to the United States for study under the auspices of the Hartford Education Mission.

1879 Former President Ulysses S. Grant, encouraged by Chinese leaders, interceded with Japan on China's behalf regarding a dispute over the Liu-ch'iu/Ryukyu Islands.

1882 The Chinese Exclusion Act suspended immigration by all Chinese to the United States for 10 years.

1885 **September:** Mobs of white workers killed 28 Chinese in an outburst of burning, looting, and mayhem in the Wyoming town of Rock Springs.

1892 The Geary Act extended restrictive anti-Chinese legislation of the previous decade, stripping Chinese in the United States, whether citizens or not, of substantial legal rights.

1895 The Treaty of Shimonoseki marked China's defeat by Japan and loss of Taiwan, prompting other foreign powers to seek territory and spheres of influence at the expense of the weakened Chinese government.

1899 **September:** Responding to Japanese and European powers seeking territorial concessions and exclusive spheres of influence in China, Secretary of State John Hay sent official US messages to all foreign powers concerned with China. The Open Door Notes sought the powers' agreement that even if they established special spheres in China, they would not discriminate against foreign trade or interfere with customs collection.

1900 **June:** Anti-foreign insurgents, known as the Boxers, entered Peking. The foreign legations held out until a multinational military force arrived to crush the insurgents. **July:** Secretary of State John Hay sent a new round of Open Door Notes to foreign powers with an interest in China in which he expressed concern with preserving Chinese sovereignty.

1901 The Boxer Protocol signed by China and the concerned powers set forth Chinese obligations as a result of the Boxer uprising including an indemnity of $333 million.

1905 **July:** A boycott of American goods began in Shanghai and spread to other Chinese cities. The boycott protested American immigration and related policies and practices discriminating against Chinese. **November:** Five American missionaries were murdered in Lien-chou in southern China, marking the most serious US–China incident of the decade.

1908 **30 November:** Secretary of State Elihu Root and Japanese Ambassador Takahira Kogoro exchanged notes underlining the Theodore Roosevelt administration's intention not to challenge Japanese interests in Manchuria.

1909 The newly installed administration of President William H. Taft endeavored to use US investments—"dollar diplomacy"—to challenge Japanese and Russian dominance in Manchuria.

1912 **February:** The Qing Dynasty ended.

1915 **January:** Japan presented what came to be known as the Twenty-One Demands to the Chinese government. **May:** The Chinese government was compelled to agree to most of the Twenty-One Demands, though US Secretary of State William Jennings Bryan announced that the United States would not recognize them.

1917 Secretary of State Robert Lansing exchanged notes with Japanese envoy Ishii Kikujiro that acknowledged Japan's "special interests" in China.

1919 **4 May:** Reacting to provisions in the Versailles peace agreement ending World War I that left Japan in control of former German concessions in China's Shantung province, demonstrations in Peking saw the start of intellectual reform campaigns and radical, anti-imperialist political movements that spread throughout China in following years and became known as the May Fourth Movement.

1921   July: The Chinese Communist Party was founded. **November:** The Washington Conference, a US-organized conference of powers concerned with East Asia and the Pacific, began.

1922   February: The conclusion of the Washington Conference saw the signing of the Nine Power Treaty dealing with the territorial integrity of China and an agreement restoring Shantung Province to Chinese sovereignty.

1924   The National Origins Act marked a high point of many decades of US legal and other efforts to restrict Chinese immigration into the United States.

1925   March: Sun Yat-sen died. **30 May:** An incident in Shanghai led to an outburst of anti-imperialist, anti-foreign activity that spread to Chinese cities and into the Chinese countryside.

1926   July: The so-called Northern Expedition of forces led by Chiang Kai-shek, began.

1927   March: During the Northern Expedition, the advancing forces attacked and killed foreigners in Nanking. **April:** Chiang Kai-shek began a violent purge of Communists and other leftists in Shanghai.

1928   July: The United States signed a new tariff treaty with China, effectively recognizing the new government dominated by Chiang Kai-shek.

1931   Pearl Buck's novel, *The Good Earth,* was published.

1932   Japanese military expansion in Manchuria saw Japanese forces create, and the Japanese government recognize, Manchukuo as an independent state. The US government responded with policy statements calling on the world not to recognize the Japanese expansion.

1933   The League of Nations adopted the Lytton Commission report critical of Japan regarding Manchuria. Japan withdrew from the League of Nations.

1934   The United States passed the Silver Purchase Act, which severely disrupted Chinese currency stability and Chinese government finances.

1937   July: The Sino–Japanese War began. **October:** President Franklin D. Roosevelt responded to Japanese aggression against China and other military expansion in a speech calling for quarantine against an "epidemic of world lawlessness." **December:** The United States avoided confrontation with Japan and moved to accept Japanese apology and compensation when Japanese warplanes sank the US gunboat *Panay* and machine-gunned survivors in the Yangtze River.

1940   January: Signaling a tougher US stance against Japan over China and other issues, the United States announced it would not renew the US commercial treaty with Japan.

1941   The American Volunteer Group (also known as "The Flying Tigers") defended Chinese Nationalists' airspace against Japanese attack. **May:** China was made eligible for US Lend-Lease aid. **July:** The United States began an oil embargo against Japan. **7 December:** The Japanese attack on Pearl Harbor brought the United States into the war on the side of China against Japan.

1942   February: General Joseph Stilwell was sent as the senior US military representative in China.

1943   February: The United States and China signed a treaty ending US extraterritoriality in China. Madame Chiang Kai-shek addressed the US Congress. **October:** A major Allied declaration in Moscow affirmed China's role as one of the great powers. **December:** In Cairo, US, British, and Chinese leaders declared that territories taken from China by Japan would be restored to China.

1944   June: Vice President Henry Wallace visited China. Chiang Kai-shek was persuaded to allow American military observers to be stationed at the Chinese Communist base in Yenan. **September:** Special envoy Patrick Hurley arrived in China. **October:** Hurley's intervention resulted in the recall of General Joseph Stilwell from China. **November:** Hurley conducted negotiations with Chinese Communist leaders in Yenan.

1945   February: A secret Far Eastern Agreement reached at the Allied leaders' conference in Yalta in February laid out conditions for the Soviet Union to intervene in the war against Japan. The US embassy staff sent a message to Washington expressing grave doubts about Ambassador Patrick Hurley's one-sided support for Chiang Kai-shek. **July:** At the Allied meeting in Potsdam, the territorial provisions in the December

1943 Cairo declaration regarding the return of Japanese-held areas to China were reaffirmed. **August:** The Soviet Union and Nationalist Chinese government of Chiang Kai-shek signed a friendship treaty, Japan surrendered, and President Harry Truman issued General Order #1 commanding Japanese-controlled forces in China to surrender to Chiang Kai-shek's representatives. **September:** Peace talks between Chinese Nationalist and Chinese Communist leaders began. **November:** Ambassador Patrick Hurley abruptly resigned. **December:** President Truman appointed General George Marshall to go to China to deal with the Nationalist–Communist conflict and related issues.

1946 July: General Marshall intervened to get a cutoff of US aid in reaction to Chiang Kai-shek's 1 July order of a nationwide offensive against the Chinese Communists. **December:** The cease-fire and peace talks between the Communists and Nationalists became moribund.

1947 January: President Truman recalled General George Marshall from China. **28 February:** An incident in Taiwan led to an island-wide upheaval that was eventually crushed with military force and mass arrests and suppression of Taiwan elites. **August:** General Albert Wedemeyer was sent on a mission to assess the situation in China.

1948 April: The China Aid Act was approved. **December:** Chinese Nationalist forces were nearing defeat in the major battle at Huai Hai. Madame Chiang Kai-shek visited the United States seeking more US assistance for the Chinese Nationalists.

1949 May: US Ambassador Leighton Stuart had talks with Chinese Communist representatives. **June:** Mao Zedong signaled that the Chinese Communists would "lean to one side," the side of the Soviet Union, in the Cold War with the United States. **July:** The Chinese Nationalists began withdrawing forces from mainland China to Taiwan. **August:** The State Department released the China White Paper that endeavored to explain US policy in China up to that time. **1 October:** The Communist-led People's Republic of China (PRC) was established on the Chinese mainland. **December:** The Chinese Nationalist government evacuated to Taiwan.

1950 February: China and the Soviet Union agreed to a Sino–Soviet alliance. Senator Joseph McCarthy began his high-profile hunt for Communists and others in the US government allegedly undermining

US policy toward China. **June:** North Korean forces attacked South Korea, starting the Korean War. President Truman ordered US troops to intervene in Korea and also in the Taiwan Strait, preventing the Chinese Communists from using military force to take the island. **September:** A successful allied landing at Inchon marked the beginning of the end of the North Korean armed forces. **October–November:** Hundreds of thousands of Chinese military forces entered Korea and drove back advancing US and allied forces. A mass campaign in China, "Resist America—aid Korea," saw the removal of US non-governmental influence and personnel in China. **December:** The United States instituted a strict embargo on economic relations with China.

1951   April: General Douglas MacArthur was dismissed as US commander in the Korean War. **September:** The United States and Japan signed a security treaty.

1953   July: The armistice ending the Korean War was signed. **October:** The Committee for One Million Against the Admission of Communist China to the United Nations opened its first office.

1954   May: French forces lost the battle of Dien Bien Phu to Communist forces in Indochina. **June:** The Geneva Accords marking the end of the French war in Indochina were signed. **July:** An upsurge in Chinese political and later military pressure led to a crisis in the Taiwan Strait. **September:** The Southeast Asia Treaty Organization was established. **December:** The United States and the Republic of China on Taiwan signed a defense treaty.

1955   January: The US Congress passed the Formosa Resolution, reinforcing the US defense commitment to Taiwan. **February:** Chinese raids on the Dachen islands prompted evacuation of the islands by Chinese Nationalist forces. **April:** Chinese Premier Zhou Enlai used a conference of Afro-Asian leaders in Bandung, Indonesia, to offer a more moderate Chinese approach to the United States. **August:** The US and Chinese governments began ambassadorial-level talks in Geneva.

1958   August: Chinese forces began artillery bombardment of offshore islands, prompting a new crisis in the Taiwan Strait.

**1959   **Amid riots and Chinese troops firing on demonstrators, the Dalai Lama left Tibet, fleeing to India.

1962 The United States repeatedly warned Chiang Kai-shek against attempting to attack mainland China at a time of the collapse of the Chinese economy following the failure of China's Great Leap Forward development campaign. **July:** An international conference in Geneva ended with an agreement deferring a military crisis involving the United States and China over Laos.

1963 **December:** Assistant Secretary of State Roger Hilsman made a foreign policy speech that seemed to open the way to improved US relations with China.

1964 The Senate Foreign Relations Committee held hearings on China where advocates of more moderate and flexible US policies toward the PRC were heard.

1965 The Immigration Reform Act ended almost a century of US discrimination against Chinese people and opened the United States to immigration from Asia. The United States ended economic aid to Taiwan.

1966 The Senate Foreign Relations Committee held hearings on China in which advocates of more moderate and flexible US policies toward Chinese were heard.

1968 **August:** The Soviet Union invaded Czechoslovakia, toppled the government and replaced it with a more pro-Soviet regime. This was justified by the so-called Brezhnev Doctrine, asserting the right of Soviet leaders to intervene against other perceived deviant Communist regimes.

1969 **March:** Publicized military clashes began along the Sino–Soviet border. **July:** President Richard Nixon announced in Guam what later became known as the Nixon Doctrine, calling for reduced US military involvement throughout Asia and the reassessment of the previous US policy of containment of China. **November:** President Nixon and the Japanese prime minister signed a communiqué indicating US support for a greater Japanese role in Asian affairs and noted Japanese security interests in Korea and Taiwan. US naval forces ended previously regular patrols in the Taiwan Strait.

1970 **January:** US–Chinese ambassadorial talks resumed after a hiatus of many years. **May:** The ambassadorial talks were suspended by China on account of a US-led invasion of Cambodia.

1971 **April:** US ping-pong players received a friendly welcome by senior Chinese officials in Beijing. **April–June:** The US government took steps to ease some travel and trade restrictions involving China. **July:** National Security Adviser Henry Kissinger made a secret visit to Beijing to talk with Chinese leaders, and President Richard Nixon subsequently announced that he would be visiting China. **September:** Defense Minister Lin Biao, a critic of the opening to the United States, died in a plane crash in Mongolia. **October:** The United Nations voted to admit the People's Republic of China; Taiwan walked out.

1972 **February:** President Nixon visited China for talks with Chinese leaders. The Shanghai Communiqué at the end of his visit set forth common US and Chinese positions on the Soviet threat and marked US willingness to pull back from Taiwan. **September:** Japan and China established diplomatic relations, employing the Japanese formula that was used to guide US officials as they sought to establish official US relations with China while maintaining unofficial US relations with Taiwan.

1973 **February:** The United States and China agreed to establish official liaison offices in Beijing and Washington, staffed by senior diplomats, even though the United States continued official ambassadorial relations with Taiwan.

1974 Under terms of the Jackson–Vanik amendment of the Trade Act of 1974, conditions were established that China and other Communist countries would have to meet in order to be eligible to receive most-favored-nation tariff status from the United States. **August:** President Nixon resigned under pressure as a result of his involvement in the Watergate Scandal.

1975 **April:** Khmer Rouge forces were victorious over the US-backed government in Cambodia, and Vietnamese Communists defeated the US-backed government in South Vietnam. Chiang Kai-shek died in Taiwan. **December:** President Gerald Ford visited China for talks with Chinese leaders.

1976 **January:** Zhou Enlai died. **April:** Deng Xiaoping was purged from the Communist leadership. **September:** Mao Zedong died. **October:** Four radical Maoists in the Chinese leadership, known as the gang of four, were arrested.

1977 August: Secretary of State Cyrus Vance visited China for talks with Chinese leaders in an unsuccessful effort to move forward the normalization of US–China relations.

1978 May: National Security Adviser Zbigniew Brzezinski visited China for talks with Chinese leaders that signaled the Jimmy Carter administration's determination to move forward the normalization of US–China relations. **December:** The United States and China announced a joint communiqué establishing official US relations with China under conditions whereby the United States recognized the People's Republic of China as the government of China and acknowledged that Taiwan was part of China, ended official relations with Taiwan, and ended the US defense treaty with Taiwan. Vietnamese forces backed by the Soviet Union invaded Khmer Rouge–ruled Cambodia.

1979 1 January: The United States officially established normal diplomatic relations with China. A letter by China's National People's Congress to "compatriots" in Taiwan laid out Chinese conditions for future relations with Taiwan. **January:** Chinese leader Deng Xiaoping visited Washington and other US cities for talks with US leaders. **February–March:** Chinese armed forces carried out an invasion of Vietnamese border regions as part of Chinese efforts to punish Vietnam for its invasion of Cambodia. **March:** Chinese authorities closed down the Democracy Wall in Beijing where pro-democracy advocates had been allowed since late 1978 to place posters supporting political reform and change. Some leading dissidents were arrested. **April:** The United States approved the Taiwan Relations Act, a law to govern unofficial US relations with Taiwan. **May:** The United States and China signed a trade agreement, a step needed to allow Chinese exports to obtain most-favored-nation tariff status from the United States. **December:** A political rally and parade in the southern Taiwan city of Kaohsiung led to serious clashes with police and prompted the Taiwan government to arrest and imprison leading dissidents and political oppositionists. Soviet forces invaded Afghanistan.

1980 January: Defense Secretary Harold Brown visited China for talks with Chinese leaders focused on dealing with Soviet expansion in Afghanistan and elsewhere. **April:** China formally joined the International Monetary Fund. **May:** China formally joined the World Bank. **August:** Vice presidential candidate George H. W. Bush traveled to China for talks with Chinese officials over presidential candidate Ronald Reagan's pro-Taiwan election campaign positions.

1981   June: Secretary of State Alexander Haig traveled to China for talks with Chinese officials to deepen strategic and military cooperation in opposition to the Soviet Union and to deal with bilateral disputes focusing on Taiwan. **September:** China issued a nine-point proposal for economic and cultural exchanges across the Taiwan Strait and direct talks regarding reunification.

1982   January: The Ronald Reagan administration announced its decisions against the provision of more-advanced jet fighters for Taiwan while continuing US co-production of less-advanced jet fighter aircraft for Taiwan. **May:** Vice President George H. W. Bush traveled to China for talks with Chinese leaders to smooth differences between them and the Reagan administration. **17 August:** A communiqué between the United States and China saw the United States agree to gradually diminish US arms sales to Taiwan and China agree to emphasize a peaceful approach to dealing with Taiwan. US officials provided to Taiwan leaders private assurances, quickly made public and becoming known as the "six assurances," regarding continued US support for Taiwan.

1983   Under the leadership of recently appointed Secretary of State George Shultz, US policy shifted from the previous emphasis of Secretary of State Alexander Haig on meeting Chinese demands on Taiwan and other issues, to a less-solicitous and less-accommodating US stance toward China while giving much higher priority to US relations with Japan. **June:** Deng Xiaoping announced the "one country—two systems" formula that provided the basis of China's approach to resolving Taiwan's and Hong Kong's reunification with China.

1984   April: President Ronald Reagan visited China. **September:** China and Great Britain announced the joint declaration, an agreement governing the transfer of Hong Kong to Chinese sovereignty in 1997.

1985   July: Chinese President Li Xiannian visited the United States, marking the first time a Chinese head of state had visited the United States.

1986   February: China entered the Asian Development Bank. Taiwan, a founding member of the Bank, remained a member but with a name less offensive to Beijing. **July:** China applied for full membership into the Generalized Agreement on Tariffs and Trade, the predecessor of the World Trade Organization. **September:** Political oppositionists in Taiwan organized the Democratic Progressive Party.

1987 **September:** Martial Law ended in Taiwan.

1988 **January:** President Chiang Ching-kuo died in Taiwan. **March:** The United States and China agreed to the dispatch of US Peace Corps volunteers to China.

1989 **February:** President George H.W. Bush visited China for talks to consolidate US–China relations amid dramatically changing international circumstances brought on by the rapid thaw in the Cold War. **April:** Hu Yaobang, a popular Chinese leader whose reforms had angered Deng Xiaoping and other Communist leaders, died. His death prompted demonstrations of sympathy and support of reform in Beijing's Tiananmen Square and other parts of China. **May:** Soviet leader Mikhail Gorbachev met senior Chinese leaders in Beijing. Mass demonstrations in Beijing's Tiananmen Square and other locations continued, leading to a Chinese leadership decision to use armed military force to wipe out the demonstrators and crack down on dissent. **4 June:** The military attack on Tiananmen Square shocked US officials and the public, marking the most important turning point in US–China relations since President Nixon's opening 20 years earlier. **June–July:** While imposing sanctions on China over the Tiananmen crackdown, President Bush endeavored to keep open communications with senior Chinese leaders. **July:** President Bush sent National Security Adviser Brent Scowcroft and Deputy Secretary of State Lawrence Eagleburger on a secret mission to China. **November:** President Bush vetoed a Chinese student immigration bill, setting the stage for an acrimonious congressional effort to override the veto. **December:** President Bush sent National Security Adviser Brent Scowcroft and Deputy Secretary of State Eagleburger on a second secret mission to China. The visit became known to the media, causing an uproar of US opposition.

1990 Congressional efforts failed to override President Bush's veto of a Chinese student immigration bill, but opposition to the president's balanced policies toward China remained strong with majorities in both houses of Congress calling for stronger US measures against China.

June: The United States and the PRC reached an agreement that allowed Fang Lizhi, a prominent Chinese dissident who had taken refuge in the US embassy at the time of the Tiananmen crackdown, to leave with his wife for the United States.

1991 August: Beijing said it would sign the nuclear Non-Proliferation Treaty. Using a compromise formula, China, Taiwan, and Hong Kong joined the regional economic grouping Asia Pacific Economic Cooperation. **October:** A peace accord ending the conflict in Cambodia was agreed to by the United States, China, and other concerned powers.

1992 February: At the sidelines of an international meeting sponsored by the United Nations, Chinese Premier Li Peng met President George H. W. Bush in New York City. **April:** Great Britain appointed Christopher Patten as Hong Kong governor, beginning a period of much greater British activism to promote democracy in the territory prior to handover to China in 1997. **August:** The United States adopted the Hong Kong Policy Act, demonstrating the US government's strong interest in promoting democracy and economic development in Hong Kong as the territory moved to Chinese sovereignty. **September:** President Bush approved the sale of 150 F-16 jet fighters to Taiwan, representing the most significant US arms sale to Taiwan following the break in official relations in 1979. **November:** William Clinton won the November presidential election using sharp criticism of China and of President Bush's comparatively moderate policy toward China. **December:** US Special Trade Representative Carla Hills visited Taiwan, the first US cabinet official to do so since the break in official US relations with Taiwan in 1979.

1993 April: Ostensibly unofficial senior envoys from Taiwan and China met for talks in Singapore that were conducted in a businesslike manner. **May:** The Clinton administration issued Executive Order 128590 that established human rights factors as conditions for extension of US most-favored-nation tariff status for the PRC. **July:** The US Congress registered strong opposition to Beijing's hosting the 2000 Olympic Games. **August:** The Clinton administration imposed sanctions on China over ballistic missile transfers to Pakistan. **September:** A Chinese ship named *Yin He* was suspected of carrying chemical weapons materials to the Middle East. It was followed by US forces, forced to agree to be searched, searched, and found to contain nothing objectionable. US National Security Advisor Anthony Lake gave a foreign policy speech that placed China among those states seen at odds with international norms. The International Olympic Committee turned down Beijing's bid to host the 2000 games. **November:** Assistant Secretary of Defense Charles Freeman visited China, paving the way for resumed higher-level US–China defense contacts that were halted after the Tiananmen crackdown.

1994 **February:** State Department Assistant Secretary for Human Rights John Shattuck met recently released Chinese dissident Wei Jingsheng in Beijing. **April:** Secretary of State Warren Christopher visited Beijing for talks with Chinese leaders on disputes over human rights and other issues that appeared to block US renewal of most-favored-nation tariff treatment for China. **May:** President Clinton reversed previous policy and announced that the United States would renew most-favored-nation tariff status for China, even though China had not met human rights requirements set the year before by the US government. **September:** The Clinton administration in September announced the results of a review of Taiwan policy, which saw modest upgrades in US interchange with Taiwan.

1995 **January:** The Congress convened with Republicans controlling both houses of Congress for the first time in decades. Chinese President and party leader Jiang Zemin issued an eight-point proposal to improve relations and foster reunification with Taiwan. **May:** President Clinton bowed to strong congressional and media pressure, reversed existing US policy, and allowed Taiwan President Lee Teng-hui to visit the United States. **June:** Taiwan President Lee visited the United States and gave a speech at his alma mater Cornell University. China reacted strongly in following months, conducting ballistic missile tests and live-fire military exercises in the Taiwan Strait. **August:** China tried, convicted, and deported to the United States prominent Chinese–American human rights activist Harry Wu. **September:** Hillary Clinton gave a strong speech against international authoritarian practices at the UN Fourth Conference on Women in Beijing.

1996 **March:** A special Chinese envoy received strong warnings from US senior national security officials during meetings in the Washington area. The United States dispatched two carrier battle groups to the Taiwan area in reaction to China's provocative military exercises in the lead-up to the Taiwan presidential election. **April:** President William Clinton met the Japanese prime minister and issued a declaration strengthening the US–Japan alliance. **June:** National Security Adviser Anthony Lake visited China for talks with Chinese leaders. **October:** Defense Secretary William Perry visited China for talks with Chinese officials.

1997   October: Chinese President Jiang Zemin traveled to Washington for a summit meeting with President Clinton. China signed the International Covenant of Economic, Social and Cultural Rights. **November:** Prominent Chinese dissident Wei Jingsheng was allowed to leave China for the United States.

1998   March: Prominent Chinese dissident Wang Dan was allowed to leave China for the United States. **June:** President William Clinton traveled to China for a summit meeting with China's President Jiang Zemin and other events. While in China, President Clinton affirmed the three nos, that is, the United States does not support Taiwan independence; two Chinas or one China, one Taiwan; and Taiwan's membership in international organizations where statehood is required. **October:** China signed the International Covenant on Civil and Political Rights. A senior Taiwan envoy traveled to China for talks with Chinese President Jiang Zemin and other officials concerned with cross-strait relations. The US-led NATO air war against Yugoslavia over the Kosovo situation began, prompting strong protests from China.

1999   March: A *New York Times* story indicated that US nuclear warhead technology and designs had been acquired and used by Chinese weapons makers. Suspecting espionage, US authorities focused on an ethnic Chinese scientist at the Los Alamos Laboratory as a possible source of leaks of such information, holding him in tight confinement. **April:** Chinese Premier Zhu Rongji traveled to Washington in what turned out to be an aborted effort to reach agreement with the United States over conditions on China's entry into the World Trade Organization (WTO). Thousands of Falungong adherents demonstrated in front of the Chinese Communist Party headquarters in Beijing, alarming Chinese leaders and leading to a major Chinese crackdown on the group. **May:** US bombs fell on the Chinese embassy in Belgrade, killing three, wounding 20 and setting off demonstrations in China that saw the destruction of US diplomatic properties in China. A US congressional committee known as the Cox Committee issued a long report sharply critical of US security measures to protect nuclear weapons and other secrets in the face of Chinese spying efforts. **June:** US special envoy Thomas Pickering was dispatched to Beijing to explain and deal with consequences of the US bombing of the Chinese embassy in Belgrade. **July:** Taiwan President Lee Teng-hui added to cross-strait tensions by telling Western media that Taiwan's relations with China in his view were relations between two separate states. **November:** US and Chinese negotiators agreed on conditions governing Chinese entry into the WTO.

2000 February: The US House of Representatives passed a modified version of the Taiwan Security Enhancement Act that strengthened US support for Taiwan. **20 May:** Democratic Progressive Party leader Chen Shui-bian was inaugurated as Taiwan president amid heightened Chinese worry over perceived Taiwan moves toward greater separation and independence from China. **September:** The US Congress passed legislation granting China permanent normal trade relations status and ending the annual US government requirement to consider China's trade status.

2001 March: Senior Chinese leader Qian Qichen met with counterparts in the George W. Bush administration in Washington. **1 April:** A US reconnaissance plane and a Chinese jet fighter collided in international airspace over the South China Sea, prompting a major incident. **25 April:** President Bush said the United States would do "whatever it takes" to protect Taiwan from Chinese military attack. **July:** Beijing was selected as the site for the 2008 Olympic Games. **September:** Chinese leaders reacted with messages of sympathy and support for the United States after the 11 September terrorist attack. **December:** The PRC formally joined the World Trade Organization.

2002 April–May: Chinese Vice President Hu Jintao visited Washington and other US cities as the guest of Vice President Richard Cheney. **25 October:** Chinese President Jiang Zemin met President George W. Bush at his ranch in Crawford, Texas, in October.

2003 October: China became the third country to launch a person into space. **December:** Chinese Premier Wen Jiabao's visit to Washington saw President George W. Bush use a public meeting with the premier to register Bush's warning to Taiwan President Chen Shui-bian against further political or other actions by Taiwan that would disrupt stability in the Taiwan Strait.

2004 **April:** Vice President Richard Cheney visited China for talks with Chinese leaders. **June:** The latest round of six party talks on North Korean nuclear weapons and related issues that began in 2003 and were sponsored by China and supported by the United States ended in Beijing. **November:** George W. Bush was reelected president of the United States, defeating Senator John Kerry in an election campaign that gave little attention to issues in US–China relations. **December:** A legislative election in Taiwan marked a defeat for efforts emphasizing Taiwan's status separate from China by President Chen Shui-bian, who subsequently moderated his approach toward China.

2005 **March:** The annual meeting of China's National People's Congress saw Jiang Zemin retire from his last senior government position and consideration of a law barring Taiwan's succession from China.

Introduction

The relationship between the United States and China arguably was the most important bilateral relationship at the start of the 21st century. Its importance seemed poised to grow. US superpower status was marred by opposition to the US war in Iraq and burgeoning government spending and trade deficits. However, US military, technological, and economic leadership seemed likely to remain strong for some time to come. China's growing economy, expanding trade relations, and steadily increasing military power supported a rapidly growing Chinese influence and role in world affairs. China remained far behind the United States in economic wealth and military power, but its size and importance to world trade and economic growth were key determinants in Asia and the world.

How the US superpower and the rising China related to each other had a major impact in Asia and other parts of the world. The checkered history of US–China relations showed periods of remarkable pragmatism, with leaders on both sides putting aside ideological, historical, and cultural differences in the interests of using constructive and advantageous US–China relations. Also well in evidence were periods of sometimes protracted confrontation and conflict, with leaders of the United States and China following policies that antagonized one other and deepened mutual suspicion. US–China relations after the Cold War underlined this mixed record, with many years of tension and dispute in the 1990s, followed by comparatively smooth relations in the first few years of the 21st century.

The following is a brief review of the sometimes tortuous twists and turns in more than 200 years of US–China relations and the reasons for those turns.

PATTERNS OF AMERICAN–CHINESE
RELATIONS PRIOR TO WORLD WAR II

Throughout much of the 19th century, the United States played a limited role in Chinese affairs. It followed the lead of Great Britain, France, and other powers that used wars to compel the declining Qing dynasty (1644–1912) to grant privileges to foreigners, including Americans who did not take part in the fighting. A few American companies made significant profits in China trade, but the scope of US trade and investment there remained very small. Christian missionaries comprised the largest and most influential group of Americans in China until the start of World War II, but for much of the period, they numbered in the hundreds, not the thousands.

American diplomats, merchants, and missionaries reacted with concern as European powers (and later Japan) began at the end of the 19th century to carve up Chinese territory into exclusive spheres of influence. However, US government actions in response were mainly symbolic, using diplomatic notes, agreements, and other non-binding measures to support the principles of free access to China and Chinese territorial integrity. US importance in China also grew by default as previously active European powers withdrew forces and resources during World War I. Imperial Japan used military and other coercion to solidify Japanese control in parts of China, notably Manchuria.

Though there often was strenuous US debate, the prevailing US official position was that limited US capabilities and interests in China argued against the United States confronting increasingly dominant Japanese power in East Asia. US officials endeavored to use international agreements and political measures to persuade Japanese officials to preserve Chinese integrity and free international access to China. The US efforts were seriously complicated by political disorder in China, and by US leaders' later preoccupation with the consequences of the Great Depression. In the 1930s, Japan created a puppet state in Manchuria and continued encroachments in northern China. The United States did little apart from symbolic political posturing in response to the Japanese aggression and expansion.

The American–Chinese experience in this more than century-long period saw the emergence of patterns of behavior that influenced US and Chinese attitudes and policies toward one another. American officials and elite and popular opinion tended to emphasize what they saw as a uniquely positive role the United States played as a supporter of Chinese national interests and the well-being of the Chinese people, with some commentators seeing the emergence of a US special relationship with China. Chinese officials and elites, including a rising group of Chinese patriots in the late 19th and early 20th centuries, tended to see American policies and practices as less aggressive than other powers but of little substantive help in China's struggle for national preservation and development. Chinese officials often endeavored to manipulate American diplomacy to serve Chinese interests, but they usually were disappointed with the results. American government policies and practices were seen at bottom to serve narrow US interests, with little meaningful concern for China. Gross American discrimination and persecution of Chinese residents and Chinese immigrants in the United States underlined a perceived hypocrisy in American declarations of special concern for China.

US INTERESTS, ACTIONS, AND PERCEPTIONS

Beginning in the late 18th century, new American freedom from British rule brought American loss of access to previous British-controlled trade partners. This prompted an American search for new trading opportunities in China. Though actual US trade with China remained relatively small, the China market often loomed large in the American political and business imagination. Meanwhile, US officials sometimes sought to channel US investment in ways that would preserve American commercial opportunities in China in the face of foreign powers seeking exclusive privileges and spheres of influence.

Americans also were in the vanguard of protestant missionaries sent to China in the 19th century. US missionaries came in groups and as individuals, set to work in the treaty ports and eventually grew to many hundreds working throughout China to spread the gospel and to carry out relief, education, medical, and other works of benefit to Chinese people. Part of a well-organized network of church groups that reached deep into the United States for prayer and material support, American missionaries explained Chinese conditions to interested Americans, fostering a sense of a special bond between the United States and China.

They also served as advisers to US officials dealing with China, and sometimes became official US representatives in China. Their core interest remained unobstructed access to Chinese people for purposes of evangelization and good works carried out by the American missionaries and their foreign and Chinese colleagues.

Though commercial and missionary interests remained at the center of US interests in China well into the 20th century, a related strategic interest also had deep roots. In 1835, several years before the first US treaty with China in 1844, the United States organized the Asiatic Squadron. This US Navy group began in 1842 to maintain a regular presence along the China coast. It later was called the *Asiatic Fleet*. Initially two or three vessels, it grew to 31 vessels by 1860, before forces were recalled on account of the American Civil War. It varied in size after the Civil War, but was sufficiently strong to easily destroy the Spanish forces in Manila harbor during the Spanish American War in 1898. It protected American lives and commerce in China and throughout maritime East and South Asia, and reinforced American diplomacy in the region.

Strong American interest in commercial, missionary, and strategic access to China seemed to contrast with only episodic American diplomatic interest in China. The US government occasionally gave high-level attention to the appointment of envoys or the reception of Chinese delegations. Caleb Cushing, Anson Burlingame, and some other 19th-century US envoys to China were well connected politically. Some US envoys endeavored to use their actions in China to influence broader US policy or to advance their own political or other ambitions. US envoys sometimes came from the missionary community in China. On the other hand, the post of US minister in China often was vacant, with an interim official placed in charge in an acting capacity. Generally speaking, whenever 19th-century US envoys pushed for more assertive US policies that involved the chance of significant expenditure of US resources or political risk, Washington decision makers reflected the realities of limited US government interests in the situation in China and responded unenthusiastically. This broad pattern continued into the 20th century, though US officials from time to time took the lead in low-risk political and diplomatic efforts in support of US interests in unimpeded commercial and other access to China.

Not surprisingly, the Americans with an interest in China tended to emphasize the positive features of US policy and behavior. Thus the

United States was seen to have behaved benignly toward China, especially when compared with the European powers and Japan that repeatedly coerced and attacked China militarily. The US government repeatedly voiced support of China's territorial and national integrity. Through missionary and other activities, including education activities that brought tens of thousands of Chinese students for higher education in the United States by the 1940s, Americans also showed strong sympathy and support for the broader welfare of the Chinese people.

US officials, opinion leaders, and commentators tended to ignore or soft pedal negative features of US relations with China. Most notable was the exclusion movement that grossly discriminated against and often violently persecuted Chinese immigrants to the United States. The movement took hold in US politics beginning in the 1870s and lasted for almost a hundred years. At first centered in Western states with some significant concentrations of Chinese workers, the exclusion movement reflected widespread American prejudice and fear of Chinese workers amid sometimes difficult economic times in the United States. American elites and common people took legal and illegal actions, including riots and murder of hundreds of Chinese, to stop Chinese immigration to the United States and drive away those Chinese already in the United States. Various state governments and the national government passed an array of laws and the US courts made a variety of decisions that singled out Chinese immigrants for negative treatment and curbed the legal rights of Chinese residents and Chinese citizens of the United States. The movement eventually broadened to include all Asians. The National Origins Act of 1924 barred all new Asian immigration. US mistreatment of Chinese people in the United States became a major issue for the Chinese government, which complained repeatedly against unjust US actions, but with little effect. It was the target of a Chinese anti-American boycott in 1905.

CHINESE INTERESTS, ACTIONS, AND PERCEPTIONS

The Chinese side of the American–Chinese relationship during the more than century-long experience prior to World War II saw Chinese officials and elite opinion in the 19th and early 20th centuries remain preoccupied with massive internal rebellions and disruptions. In this context, the

United States figured secondarily in Chinese government and elite concerns. The opinion of the Chinese populace was less important in China–US relations until the anti-Christian and anti-missionary riots later in the 19th century and grassroots nationalistic actions, such as the anti-American boycott reacting to the US mistreatment of Chinese immigrants in 1905.

Qing dynasty officials often were too weak to confront foreign aggression and military pressure in the 19th and early 20th centuries. Their diplomacy frequently amounted to versions of appeasement. Forced to give ground to foreign demands, the Qing officials gave special emphasis to capitalizing on real or perceived differences among the foreign powers, hoping to use some foreign powers to fend off others. Chinese officials repeatedly tried to elicit US actions that would assist Chinese interests against other generally more aggressive and demanding powers. Although US envoys in China often would get caught up in these Chinese schemes and argue for US positions at odds with other powers in China, Washington decision makers tended to adhere to a low-risk approach that offered little of substance to support Chinese efforts.

Qing dynasty initiatives endeavoring to use possible US support against other foreign powers did not blind Chinese government officials to US interests in China that worked against Chinese government concerns. The spread of foreign missionaries throughout China as a result of treaties reached in 1860 meant that these foreign elites soon ran up against strong resistance from local Chinese elites. The latter fomented popular outbursts and riots against the foreigners and their Christian adherents. The American missionaries sought the support of their official representatives in China who backed their demands to the Chinese government for protection, punishment of Chinese malefactors, and compensation with strong diplomacy and frequent use of gunboats. This posed a very difficult dilemma for Qing officials, who needed to deal with the threats from the Americans and other foreign officials pressing for protection of missionaries and punishment of offending Chinese elites, while sustaining the support of local Chinese elites who provided key elements of Chinese governance at the local levels.

Meanwhile, American government officials were seen by Chinese officials and other elites as transparently hypocritical in demanding protection of special rights for American missionaries and other US citizens in China, while US officials and people were carrying out repeated and often violent infringements on the rights and basic safety of Chinese workers in the United States. In this context, Chinese officials tended to be sympathetic with the merchant-led and student-encouraged anti-American boycott that took hold in Chinese coastal cities in 1905 and that focused on Chinese anger over US discrimination against Chinese in immigration to the United States and poor treatment of Chinese in the United States.

With the withdrawal of the European powers to fight World War I, the United States loomed larger in the strategies of the weak Chinese governments following the end of the Qing dynasty in 1912. However, the United States remained unwilling to take substantial risks of confrontation with the now dominant power in China, imperial Japan. The US reaction to the gross Japanese infringements on Chinese sovereignty in the Twenty-One Demands of 1915 elicited statements on non-recognition and not much else from the United States. President Woodrow Wilson gravely disappointed Chinese patriots in accepting Japan's continued control of the former German leasehold in China's Shantung province at the Versailles Peace Treaty ending World War I.

The Nine Power Treaty at the US-convened Washington Conference of 1921–1922 pledged to respect Chinese territorial integrity, but when Japan took over Manchuria, creating a puppet state in the early 1930s, the US government offered little more than words of disapproval. Given this experience, Chinese patriots were not persuaded by the protestations of some American commentators that the United States had developed a special relationship with China based on concern for the well-being of the Chinese people and preservation of China's sovereignty and integrity. When Japan, after occupying Manchuria, moved in 1937 to launch an all-out war against China and the United States did little in response, Chinese patriots became even more cynical about American intentions and policies.

19TH-CENTURY ENCOUNTERS

American traders and seamen were the first from the United States to interact with China. When American traders went to China prior to the Opium War of 1839–1842, Chinese regulations under the Tribute System in foreign affairs confined them, along with most other foreign maritime traders, to Canton in southeastern China. There local officials supervised and taxed foreign trade, foreigners were required to live and work in a designated area of Canton during the trading season, and foreign interaction with Chinese was kept to a minimum; certain Chinese merchants were designated to deal with foreign merchants.

Chinese foreign relations under the Tribute System were unequal, emphasized the superiority of China, its system of governance, and the emperor. The foreigners were expected to abide by Chinese laws and regulations and to accord with Chinese instructions. As a result, although American and other foreign merchants and their foreign employees benefited from the trading opportunities at Canton, they were subject to interventions from Chinese authority that appeared unjust from a Western perspective and dangerous to those concerned.

Like their British colleagues, American merchants brought opium into China, balancing their purchases of tea and other Chinese commodities. The burgeoning trade in illegal opium entering China in the period before the Opium War was carried out mainly by British merchants, though American merchants carried Turkish opium to China and held about 10 percent of the Chinese opium market. American opium along with British opium was confiscated and destroyed by Chinese authorities in Canton in 1839, leading to Great Britain going to war. The US government took no part in the fighting.

After the British in 1842 negotiated the Treaty of Nanjing, ending the Opium War and opening five Chinese treaty ports for foreign residency and trade, the United States appointed Caleb Cushing as Commissioner to China to negotiate a US treaty with China obtaining the rights and privileges Britain had gained by force of arms. Chinese negotiator Ch'i-ying followed a general policy of trying to appease foreign demands, and the US treaty included language that Chinese concessions made to other foreign nations would apply to the United States as well. American merchants, missionaries, and others were free to settle in the five treaty ports, and Americans, like other foreigners in China, had the right of extraterritoriality. This legal system meant that foreigners and their activities in China remained governed by their own law and not Chinese law.

The upsurge of the massive Taiping Rebellion beginning in 1850 caught Chinese authorities and American and foreign observers by surprise as the rebel movement came to dominate southeastern China and most of the Yangtze River valley. Some Americans at first were attracted by Taiping leader Hung Hsiu-ch'uan's avowed Christian beliefs, but the Taiping leader's warped views of Christianity added to reasons Americans and other foreigners shied away from the radical rebel leader and his destructive activities.

Though seeing US interests resting with continued Qing dynasty rule, American officials nonetheless were ready to join with Great Britain, France, and others in pressing for treaty revisions that would open more treaty ports, allow for missionary activities outside the treaty ports, and establish foreign legations in the Chinese capital. Britain and France used military force to back up their demands, and in 1858 the Chinese government signed treaties with them and also with the Americans, who did no fighting. When British and French envoys returned in 1859 to exchange ratification, a battle resulted where the Chinese drove off the foreigners. The American envoy managed to exchange ratification, however. The British and French returned in force in 1860 and marched to Beijing before setting forth new conditions in the treaties of 1860 that also benefited the United States.

US policy in China supported stronger Chinese government efforts after 1860 that worked within the confines of the treaty system and accepted international norms while strengthening the Chinese government, economy, and military. In 1868, a visiting Chinese mission, headed by former US minister to China Anson Burlingame, signed a treaty with the United States. Among other provisions in the treaty, the United States gave Chinese immigrants the right to enter the United States, a pledge that would soon be challenged by anti-Chinese immigration advocates in the United States.

There emerged in the 1870s a broadly based exclusion movement in the United States that was a dominant feature in US relations with China for decades to come. Showing blatant prejudice against Chinese, Americans took legal and illegal actions, including riots and murder of hundreds of Chinese in the United States, to stop Chinese immigration to the United States. In September 1885, mobs of white workers attacked Chinese in Rock Springs, Wyoming, killing 28 in an outburst of burning, looting, and mayhem. In 1888, the Scott Act restricted Chinese laborers' entry and denied them reentry into the United States. In 1892, the Geary Act stripped Chinese in the United States, whether citizens or not, of substantial legal rights, and required all Chinese in the United States to obtain and carry at all times a certificate showing their right to reside in the United States. Without such proof, the punishment was hard labor and deportation.

Chinese officials in the Chinese legation in Washington protested US discrimination and persecution of Chinese and endeavored to reach agreements with the US government that would assure basic protection of Chinese rights. US mistreatment of Chinese people in the United States prompted patriotic Chinese merchants, students, and others to organize an anti-American boycott that closed several coastal Chinese cities to US goods for several months in 1905. Nevertheless, the US exclusion movement persisted and grew. It eventually broadened to include other Asians.

US–CHINA RELATIONS AMID FOREIGN DOMINATION, INTERNAL DECLINE, AND REVOLUTION IN CHINA, 1895–1941

China's unexpected defeat by Japan in the Sino-Japanese War of 1894–1895 led European powers to join Japan in seeking exclusive spheres of influence and commercial and territorial rights in China. Alarmed that US interests in free commercial access to China would be jeopardized, US officials formulated a response that led to the Open Door Notes of 1899 and 1900. The notes sought the powers' agreement that even if they established special spheres in China, they would not discriminate against foreign trade or interfere with customs collection. They underlined US interests in preserving equal commercial access to China and the preservation of the integrity of the Chinese Customs Service, a crucial source of revenue for the struggling Chinese government. Though generally unenthusiastic about the US initiative, most concerned powers offered evasive and qualified responses, but all in effect endorsed the principles in the Open Door Notes. As the United States and other foreign powers dispatched troops to crush the Boxer uprising and lift the siege of foreign legations in Peking, the United States in July 1900 sent a second round of Open Door Notes, which expressed concern for preserving Chinese sovereignty. The foreign powers went along with the notes.

US policymakers repeatedly referred to the US Open Door Policy following the issuing of the Open Door notes. The William H. Taft administration in 1910 interpreted the policy to extend beyond equal trade opportunity to include equal opportunity for investment in China. The Wilson administration in 1915 reacted to the Japanese Twenty-One Demands against China by refusing to recognize such infringements on the Open Door Policy. The related principles concerning US support for the territorial integrity of China were featured prominently in the Nine Power Treaty of the Washington Conference in the Warren Harding administration in 1922, and in the non-recognition of Japanese aggression in Manchuria during the Hoover administration in 1932. The Harry Truman administration sought Soviet Union leader Joseph Stalin's promise that the Open Door Policy would be observed in the Soviet-influenced areas of Manchuria following the Soviet military defeat of Japanese forces there in 1945. In general, American political leaders dealing with China throughout the 20th century tended to refer to the Open Door Policy in positive terms, as a US attempt to prevent China from being carved up into commercially impenetrable foreign colonies. Chinese interpretations often emphasized that Americans were more concerned about maintaining their own commercial access and were prepared to do little in practice in supporting Chinese sovereignty.

American officials also were active in the late 19th century pressing the Chinese government to protect American and other missionaries and their converts subjected to frequent attacks often fomented by Chinese local elites. The Boxer uprising in 1899–1900 added greatly to the anti-Christian attacks and implicated the Qing government in the violence. A grassroots anti-foreign, anti-dynastic insurrection in northern China, the Boxers came to receive support from some Chinese officials, and by 1899 and 1900 they was carrying out widespread attacks against foreign missionaries and Chinese Christians. The insurgents occupied Peking and Tientsin, besieging foreign legations and settlements. About 20,000 foreign troops were mustered, including thousands of Americans, to end the siege and put down the insurgents. They ended the siege of Tientsin in July 1900 and Peking in August 1900. Chinese leaders sought in vain US support in helping to moderate foreign demands in the Boxer Protocol.

The last 15 years of Qing rule also saw an erratic pattern of American business and government interest in investment in China in railway and other schemes, and erratic Chinese interest in using such US involvement in efforts to offset foreign encroachment, particularly by Japan and Russia, in Manchuria. Tang Shao-yi, a governor in Manchuria who was close to regional leader Yuan Shih-kai, encouraged the United States government and business to become more involved with railway building in Manchuria as a means to counter Japanese expansion there. Tang traveled to Washington in 1908 where he met with Secretary of State Elihu Root who underlined the Theodore Roosevelt administration's lack of interest in confronting Japan in Manchuria.

US government policy on this issue shifted markedly during the Taft administration, 1909–1913. The president and Secretary of State Philander Knox tried to use schemes involving US investment in railways to prevent Russia and Japan from dominating Manchuria. They also called for a plan to neutralize or internationalize all railway projects in Manchuria. As Japan and Russia objected, Chinese central government authorities temporized, and US investors showed little enthusiasm. The Taft administration's "dollar diplomacy" failed. The US administration subsequently adopted a more moderate stance emphasizing cooperation with European powers, and ultimately Russia and Japan, in an international consortium dealing with loans to China.

In the 30 years from the end of the Qing dynasty in early 1912 to the attack on Pearl Harbor in late 1941, US policy and practice endeavored to stake out positions and formulate political measures designed to support Chinese sovereignty and integrity. But they did so while generally avoiding the risk of confrontation with imperial Japan that emerged as the dominant power in East Asia after the pullback and weakening of European powers in the region with the start of World War I. US policymakers also were challenged by revolutionary movements and violent anti-foreign sentiment sweeping China in the 1920s. They tended to adjust to these trends pragmatically, giving way to some of the Chinese demands and eventually establishing good working relations with the Nationalist Chinese administration of Chiang Kai-shek, the dominant leader of China by the late 1920s.

Japan moved quickly to consolidate its position in China with the start of World War I. Allied with Great Britain and siding with the Allies in World War I, Japan occupied German concessions in China's Shantung province in 1914. In January 1915, Japan presented the Chinese government with five sets of secret demands that became known as the Twenty-One Demands. The demands were leaked, which compelled Japan to defer the more outrageous ones, but they resulted in May 1915 in Sino-Japanese treaties and notes confirming Japan's dominant position in China. US officials debated how to respond. Secretary of State William Jennings Bryan at first reaffirmed US support for China's territorial integrity and equal commercial access to China, but also acknowledged Japan's "special relations" with China. President Woodrow Wilson subsequently warned that the United States would not accept infringements on its rights, and Bryan said the United States would not recognize infringements on US rights, Chinese sovereignty, or the Open Door Policy. In a bid to expand US leverage, Wilson then reversed an earlier decision and supported American banks lending money to China through an international consortium as a means to balance Japanese expansion in China. Japan was not seriously deterred and maneuvered to see that its position in Shantung province was secured by the Versailles Peace Treaty ending World War I. Though US and Chinese delegations worked closely at the peace conference to free China from restrictions on her sovereignty, President Wilson in the end felt compelled to accept Japan's claim to the former German concessions, gravely disappointing Chinese patriots.

The United States after World War I took the lead in calling a major conference to include powers with interests in the western Pacific, including China but not the Soviet Union, to deal with relevant security issues. The result was the Washington Conference of 1921–1922 that saw passage of a Nine Power Treaty supporting noninterference in Chinese internal affairs. The treaty disappointed Chinese patriots because it had no enforcement mechanisms and did nothing to retrieve the rights of sovereignty China had been forced to give up over the previous 80 years

Meanwhile, US policymakers were compelled to react to repeated acts of violence against Americans and other foreigners and their interests as revolutionary political and military movements swept through China during the 1920s. Most notable was the Nanking incident, which occurred during the military advance of Nationalist Chinese forces under the leadership of Chiang Kai-shek in their Northern Expedition from Canton to reunify China under their auspices. Advancing in Nanking in March 1927, some Nationalist forces attacked foreigners and foreign property in this city, including the American, British, and

Japanese consulates. Several foreigners, including Americans, were killed. Looting and threats against foreigners did not stop until British and US gunboats began to bombard the attackers. US Secretary of State Frank Kellogg reacted with moderation and restraint to the violence and challenges to US and foreign rights in China at this time. This helped to facilitate US rapprochement with the Nationalist regime of Chiang Kai-shek once it consolidated power in 1928. In March 1928, Chiang's regime accepted American terms about the Nanking incident while the US government expressed regret about the gunboat bombardment.

US policymakers did not change their low-risk policy toward Japan, despite Tokyo's blatant grab of Manchuria in 1931–1932. President Herbert Hoover was reluctant to respond forcefully to Japan's aggression in Manchuria and favored a moral stance of "non-recognition" of the changes brought by Japan's aggression. Even when Japan engaged in all-out brutal war against China in 1937, Washington showed sympathy to China but offered little in the way of concrete support. Responding to Japanese aggression against China and other military expansion, President Franklin D. Roosevelt in a speech on 5 October 1937 called for a quarantine of an "epidemic of world lawlessness." No specific US actions in Asia followed as the US government was not prepared to stand against Japan as it ruthlessly advanced in China. Indeed, Japanese aircraft in December 1937 sank the US gunboat *Panay* and machine-gunned its survivors in the Yangtze River. US officials accepted Japan's apology and compensation, not choosing to make this an issue of confrontation with Japanese aggression in China. The US resolve to help China and oppose Japan stiffened in the year prior to Pearl Harbor and American entry into the war. That year, the American Volunteer Group (Flying Tigers) provided air defense for Nationalist Chinese areas and lend-lease aid was approved for China.

US–CHINA RELATIONS DURING WORLD WAR II, CHINESE CIVIL WAR

The Japanese attack on Pearl Harbor thrust the United States into a leadership position in China and in global affairs. Leading the Allied coalition that would eventually defeat the Axis powers, US leaders focused on fighting the massive worldwide conflict and dealing with issues that would determine the post-war international order. In this context, the complicated conditions in China, notably the bitter rivalry between Chiang Kai-shek's Nationalist forces and the Communist forces under the direction of Mao Zedong, received secondary attention. As a result, American officials tended to follow paths of least resistance as they reinforced existing proclivities to back Chiang Kai-shek's Nationalists, who enjoyed broad political support in the United States. They avoided the difficult US policy reevaluation that would have been required for US leaders to position the United States in a more balanced posture in order to deal constructively with the Chinese Communists as well as the Chinese Nationalists. The drift and bias in US policy, strengthened by interventions of US presidential envoy and Ambassador to China Patrick Hurley, foreshadowed the US failure in China once the Communists defeated the Chinese Nationalists on mainland China in 1949 and moved in early 1950 to align with the Soviet Union against the United States in the Cold War.

The China theater was a secondary concern in the overall war effort as the United States first focused on defeating Adolf Hitler in Europe. Initial expectations that China could be built up and play an active strategic role in the war effort, with Chinese armies under Chiang Kai-shek's leadership pushing back the Japanese and allowing China to become a staging area for attack on Japan, proved unrealistic. Chiang's Nationalist armies were weak and the Americans were unable to provide large amounts of military equipment because Japan cut off surface routes to Nationalist-held areas of China. US strategists turned to an approach of island hopping in the Pacific, with US-led forces coming from the south and east of Japan, taking island positions, in step-by-step progress toward the Japanese home islands. The role for the Chinese armies in this strategy mainly was to stay in the war and keep the hundreds of thousands of Japanese forces in China tied down and unable to reinforce Japanese positions elsewhere.

The United States recognized Chiang Kai-shek and the Chinese Nationalist government as China's representative in war deliberations and insisted that Chiang's China would be one of the great powers that would lead world affairs in the post-war era. US aid in China flowed exclusively to Chiang and his officials. The commanding American general in the China theater, Joseph Stilwell, was appointed as Chiang Kai-shek's chief of staff. American contact with and understanding of the rival Chinese Communists were minimal. Mao Zedong's forces were cut off from American and other contact by a blockade maintained by Nationalist Chinese forces. There were American contacts with the Chinese Communist liaison office allowed in the Chinese wartime capital of Chungking, but little of substance resulted.

Chiang Kai-shek welcomed American support but constantly complained that it was insufficient. His American chief of staff, General Stilwell, and many other US officials in China were appalled by what they saw as corrupt and self-serving Chinese Nationalist leadership, and the unwillingness of Chiang and his lieutenants to use US assistance against Japan as they focused on building capabilities to deal with the Chinese Communists. Chiang Kai-shek nonetheless maintained a positive public image in the United States, with publicists such as Henry Luce using *Time* and *Life* magazines to laud the leadership of the courageous leader of China in the face of Japanese aggression. Some US military leaders, notably General Claire Chennault of the American Volunteer Group ("Flying Tigers") and the Army Air Force collaborated with and won Chiang's support for schemes involving US use of Chinese Nationalist-defended air bases in China to attack Japanese positions and shipping. Those efforts failed when Japanese forces in 1944 overran the weakly defended airbases and expanded into Nationalist-held areas, prompting a major crisis between Chiang and Stilwell.

US presidential envoy Patrick Hurley was sent to China to mediate the conflict. He sided with Chiang Kai-shek and Stilwell was recalled. Another consequence of the crisis in 1944 was that American leaders pressed and finally received permission from Chiang Kai-shek to station a US military observer mission at the Chinese Communist headquarters in Yenan. Mao Zedong and the senior Communist leaders used the mission to appeal for a more evenhanded US policy in dealing with the Nationalist–Communist rivalry in China.

Following his appointment as US ambassador, Hurley moved to mediate the Nationalist–Communist rift in China. In November 1944, he traveled to Yenan, consulted with Mao and other Communist leaders about their conditions for reconciliation with the Nationalists, and endorsed those conditions. Returning to Chungking, he switched and sided strongly with Chiang Kai-shek in his demand that Communist forces be disbanded before the Communists could be brought into a Nationalist-led Chinese coalition administration. Much of the US embassy staff in Chungking rebelled against Hurley by sending a collective message to Washington in early 1945 warning of the dire consequences of Hurley's alienation of the Communists and bias toward Chiang's Nationalists. The ambassador disputed the charges in a meeting with President Roosevelt, who supported Hurley, leading to transfers of dissident US staff from Chungking.

US leaders worried about conditions in China and how they would affect the final stages of the war against Japan. They foresaw the inability of weak Chinese Nationalist forces to defeat the hundreds of thousands of Japanese forces in China as the war in the Pacific moved toward an end, and the danger of Nationalist–Communist civil war in China would drag in the United States and the Soviet Union on opposite sides. In the end, as a result of the so-called Far Eastern Agreement of the Allied powers at Yalta in February 1945, Soviet forces, not Chinese forces, would take on the main task of defeating Japanese armies concentrated in Manchuria and northern China. In compensation, Russian territory taken by Japan would be restored, Russian interests in Manchuria, including a naval base, would be restored, and Outer Mongolia would remain independent. The United States promised to obtain the concurrence of China's Nationalist government to provisions regarding Manchuria and Mongolia, which were claimed by China. The Soviet Union also expressed willingness to negotiate a friendship and alliance treaty with China's Nationalist government. The Far Eastern Agreement had negative implications for the Chinese Nationalist government, which was not consulted on the territorial concessions to the Soviet Union, and for the Chinese Communists, who appeared to be isolated from the Soviet Union.

The broad outlines of US policy toward China prevalent in early 1945 persisted as Harry Truman became president with the death of Franklin Roosevelt in April 1945, and as the war in the Pacific came to an unexpectedly quick end with Japan's surrender after the US atomic bomb attacks in August 1945. US policy strongly supported Chiang Kai-shek's Nationalist forces. US airplanes and other means were used to transport Nationalist forces to various parts of China to take the surrender of Japanese forces. The US government provided hundreds of millions of dollars of military equipment and other assistance. The rival Communists were urged to participate in peace talks and come to terms in a united Chinese administration under Chiang's overall leadership.

President Truman commanded that Japanese-controlled forces in China surrender their positions and arms to Chiang Kai-shek's representatives, not to Communist forces.

The Soviet army entered the war in China and defeated Japanese armies. The Soviet Union signed a friendship treaty with Chiang Kai-shek's Nationalist government, as noted in the Far Eastern Agreement at Yalta. Seemingly isolated, the Chinese Communists agreed to join peace talks in Chungking in September where Chiang, backed by US Ambassador Hurley and the Truman administration, demanded the Communists surrender their armed forces and territory as a precondition for joining a coalition government under Chiang's leadership.

There was little consideration at high levels of US policy for a more evenhanded US approach to the Nationalist–Communist rivalry in China, though some American officials warned of the danger of civil war and were uncertain how the Chinese Nationalists, weakened by years of warfare and led by often corrupt and inept officials, would fare. As the peace talks deadlocked and Communist–Nationalist armed conflict spread in northern China in late 1945, it became clear to US planners that Chiang's forces would not defeat the Chinese Communists without a substantial commitment of US military forces. Ambassador Hurley wanted such an open-ended US commitment but Washington decision makers demurred. Hurley abruptly resigned in November 1945 and President Truman appointed General George Marshall as his personal representative to salvage the deteriorating situation in China. Marshall managed a few months of shaky peace, but they were followed by frequent fighting in Manchuria as Nationalist and Communist forces vied to take control as Soviet occupiers retreated. US aid continued to go exclusively to Nationalist-held areas and increased markedly in mid-1946. On 1 July 1946, Chiang Kai-shek ordered a nationwide offensive against the Communists. Marshall intervened, got Truman to stop US arms aid to Chiang, and Chiang agreed to US–Nationalist–Communist truce teams to prevent fighting in northern China. But the fighting still spread and soon became a full-scale war.

The failure to avoid civil war in China did not lead to fundamental change in the broad framework of US policy in China. Even though the Nationalists appeared increasingly weak and inept, and seemed headed for defeat on the mainland by 1948, the Truman administration continued support for them and took no significant steps to reach out to the

Chinese Communists. In 1948, the administration supported the China Aid Act providing $125 million for the failing Nationalist government in China. This was done in large measure in order to avoid resistance from many pro-Chiang Kai-shek congressional members regarding the administration's requests for funding the Marshall Plan for Europe and Japan. Prospects for positive US relations with the Chinese Communists were soured by years of one-sided US support for the Chinese Nationalists.

Given what were seen by Truman administration officials as continued strong US congressional and other domestic constraints against abandoning Chiang Kai-shek and opening US contacts with Chiang's enemy, the Chinese Communists, the Truman administration officials allowed developments in China to settle the civil war in favor of the Chinese Communists. Over time, they hoped to find constructive ways for the United States to deal with the new Chinese Communist regime. There was strong debate in the administration as to whether the United States should allow Taiwan, the island off the Chinese coast where Chiang and his Nationalist forces retreated after their defeat on the mainland in 1949, to fall to the Communists. The policy decided upon was not to intervene to protect Taiwan. The secretary of state also instructed the US ambassador to China to make contact with Communist officials; he did so in 1949, but President Truman was unwilling to support a plan to have the ambassador travel to Peking for talks with the Communist rulers. The Chinese Communists, meanwhile, reinforced their victory in the civil war with the announcement that they would side with the Soviet Union in the emerging Cold War struggle with the United States and its noncommunist allies. Amid these grim developments for US interests in China, the administration put together a lengthy report of US documents that endeavored to explain the American failure in China in ways that placed the blame on Chiang Kai-shek and his often-corrupt and self-serving leaders and deflected attention from US policy oversights and mistakes.

CONFLICT AND CONTAINMENT

Neither the government of Mao Zedong nor the Truman administration sought or foresaw US–China war in early 1950. The Americans were surprised when North Korean forces, with the support of Soviet and Chinese leaders, launched an all-out military attack against South Korean forces in June 1950. The Chinese Communist leaders and their Korean and Soviet Communist allies apparently calculated that the better-armed North Koreans would attain victory quickly without provoking major or effective US military response. Thus, it was their turn to be surprised when the United States quickly intervened militarily in the Korean War, and also sent the US seventh fleet to prevent the Chinese Communist attack on Taiwan. US forces and their South Korean allies halted the North Korean advance and carried out an amphibious landing at Inchon in September 1950 that effectively cut off North Korean armies in the South, leading to their destruction.

The string of miscalculations continued. With UN sanction, US and South Korean forces proceeded into North Korea. The Chinese Communists warned and prepared to resist them, but US leaders thought the warnings were a bluff. By November, hundreds of thousands of Chinese Communist forces were driving the US and South Korean forces south in full retreat. Eventually, the Americans and their allies were able to sustain a line of combat roughly in the middle of the peninsula, as the two armies faced off for over two more years of combat, casualties, and destruction.

Chinese Communist leaders also launched domestic mass campaigns to root out pro-American influence and seize control of US cultural, religious, and business organizations that remained in China. The United States began wide-ranging US strategic efforts to contain the expansion of Chinese power and Chinese-backed Communist expansion in Asia. A strict US economic and political embargo against China, large US force deployments, eventually numbering between one half and one million troops, massive foreign aid allocations to US Asian allies and supporters, and a ring of US defense alliances around China were used to block Chinese expansion and to drive a wedge between China and its Soviet ally. Meanwhile, led by often irresponsible congressional advocates, notably Senator Joseph McCarthy, congressional investigators in the early 1950s took aim at US specialists on China and Asia, discrediting those with moderate and pragmatic views about the Chinese Communists and endeavoring to silence those in or out of government who were less than uniform in opposing the Chinese Communists and supporting Chiang Kai-shek and the Chinese Nationalists.

The Dwight D. Eisenhower administration used threats and negotiations in reaching an armistice agreement that stopped the fighting in Korea in 1953. American efforts to strengthen military alliances and deployments to contain Chinese Communist–backed expansion continued unabated. Defeat of US-backed French forces in Indochina led to the 1954 Geneva Conference and accords that formalized French withdrawal from Indochina. After the conference, US policy worked to support a non-Communist regime in South Vietnam, backing the regime when it resisted steps toward reunification set forth in the Geneva accords. The United States also deepened and broadened defense and other links with powers in Southeast Asia in order to check Chinese-backed Communist expansion in the region.

President Eisenhower and Secretary of State John Foster Dulles were wary of Chiang Kai-shek and Chinese Nationalist maneuvers that might drag the United States into a war with the Chinese Communists over Taiwan. At the same time, US military and economic assistance to Chiang Kai-shek and the Nationalist forces on Taiwan expanded dramatically, and Washington signed a bilateral defense treaty with Taipei in December 1954.

Mao Zedong's People's Republic of China (PRC) reacted with harsh rhetoric and military assaults against Nationalist Chinese–controlled islands off the coast of the Chinese mainland. The US administration firmly backed the Chinese Nationalists and their Republic of China (ROC), though US forces helped Nationalist forces on some exposed islands to withdraw. The Taiwan Strait crisis of 1955 raised fears of renewed US–China war.

Chinese Premier Zhou Enlai used the venue of the Afro-Asian Conference in Bandung, Indonesia, in 1955 to ease tensions and call for talks with the United States. Chinese leaders at this time attempted to engage in high-level dialogue with the United States. Secretary of State Dulles was wary that direct talks with the PRC would undermine Chiang Kai-shek's Nationalist government on Taiwan. Facing congressional and allied pressures to meet with the Chinese, Dulles agreed to low-level ambassadorial talks that began in Geneva in 1955. The two sides reached an agreement on repatriating detained personnel, but the agreement was soon disputed. The US side also pressed hard for a Chinese renunciation of force regarding Taiwan, effectively stopping progress in the talks. The talks were suspended for a time before resuming in Warsaw in 1958 where the two sides met periodically without much result. The talks did at least provide a useful line of US–PRC communication during times of crisis, as both sides strove to avoid serious military conflict.

Dulles vigorously pursued a containment policy against China, and favored a tougher US policy toward China than toward the Soviet Union. He endeavored thereby to force Beijing to rely on Moscow for economic and other needs the Soviet Union could not meet. In this and other ways, he hoped to drive a wedge between China and the USSR.

The Chinese–Soviet alliance began to unravel by the late 1950s, and 1960 saw a clear public break with the withdrawal of Soviet economic aid and advisers. US policymakers were slow to capitalize on the situation as China remained more hostile to the United States than the Soviet Union, and deepening US involvement in Vietnam exacerbated US–China frictions.

During the 1960 presidential election campaign, Senator John Kennedy criticized the "tired thinking" of the outgoing administration on issues regarding China, but said little about China once he assumed office in 1961. US domestic opposition, Chinese nuclear weapons development, Chinese aggression against India, and Chinese expansion into Southeast Asia were among factors that blocked meaningful US initiatives toward China. The administration took firm action in 1962 to block plans by Chiang Kai-shek to attack the Chinese mainland at a time of acute economic crisis in China, while it continued strong US backing of Chiang in the United Nations.

The administration of Lyndon Johnson, 1963–1969, saw US Asian policy dominated by escalating US military commitment and related difficulties in Vietnam. There was some movement within the US government for a more flexible approach to China, consistent with growing signs of congressional and US interest group advocacy of a US policy of containment without isolation toward China. But they came to little as China entered the throes of the violent and often xenophobic practices of the Cultural Revolution, and the American forces in Vietnam faced hundreds of thousands of Chinese anti-aircraft, railway, construction, and support troops sent to Vietnam. Johnson was anxious to avoid prompting full-scale military involvement of China in the Vietnam conflict. US diplomats signaled these US intentions in the otherwise moribund US–China ambassadorial talks in Warsaw, and Chinese officials made clear that China would restrain its intervention accordingly.

By early 1968, the bitter impasse in US–Chinese relations had lasted two decades and seemed unlikely to change soon. Chinese leaders were in the midst of life or death struggles for power and attendant violent mass campaigns that brought conventional Chinese diplomacy to a halt and required martial law to restore order in Chinese cities. Militant Chinese policies in support of the Vietnamese and other Communist insurgencies in Southeast Asia complemented a rigid Chinese stance on Taiwan, Korea, and other issues that had divided China and the United States. US leaders saw little prospect for any significant movement in relations with the PRC as they grappled with consuming preoccupations associated with the failing US effort against Communist insurgents in Vietnam.

RAPPROCHEMENT AND NORMALIZATION

Despite deeply rooted differences between the US government and Chinese Communist leaders on ideological, economic, and international issues, United States–Chinese Communist interchange since the start of World War II witnessed a few instances where one side or the other saw their interests served by reaching out and seeking reconciliation and better ties with the other party. The Chinese Communists in particular tried a moderate and accommodating approach to the United States in greeting the American Military Observer Group to Yenan in 1944, and in the initial ambassadorial talks following Zhou Enlai's moderate overture at Bandung in 1955. The Americans tried more tentative overtures to Beijing in 1949, and showed interest in more flexibility toward China by the 1960s. Unfortunately, these initiatives and overtures failed, as there were never occasions when both sides sought improved relations at the same time until internal and international weaknesses in 1968 and 1969 drove the United States and China closer together in a pragmatic search for means to deal with difficult circumstances.

Difficulties in the United States in 1968 began when the communist Tet offensive throughout South Vietnamese cities shattered the Johnson administration's predictions of progress in the Vietnam War and prompted US commanders to call for 200,000 more troops, in addition to the over half a million US forces in the country. Anti-war demonstrations in the United States grew in size and frequency. President

Johnson's mandate collapsed when he did poorly in the New Hampshire primary, running against an otherwise unexceptional opponent who emphasized an anti-war platform. Johnson pulled out of the race and redoubled peace efforts in talks with the Vietnamese communists in Paris.

The assassination of Martin Luther King set off a rampage of urban looting and burning that afflicted several American cities and notably closed Washington, D.C. for days as the city burned and the fire service was prevented by snipers and mob violence. Order was restored only after the imposition of martial law by elite US Army combat troops. The contentious Democratic primaries reached a conclusion in California, where Senator Robert Kennedy won, only to be assassinated just after the California victory was secured.

With Kennedy dead, anti-war advocates gathered in Chicago to protest the likely selection of Johnson's Vice President Hubert Humphrey as the Democratic standard bearer. Chicago's Mayor Richard Daley and his police officers promised tough measures to deal with unauthorized demonstrations. They delivered on their promise as American television audiences watched in shock as police officers clubbed and beat demonstrators, reporters, and others they deemed obstructing the smooth flow of the convention and nearby hotel receptions.

The Republicans at their convention later in the summer nominated Richard Nixon. On a political come-back after retreating from public life in the early 1960s, Nixon said he had a plan to deal with the Vietnam morass. He did not speak very much about an opening to China. Upon entering office, Nixon moved quickly to begin what would turn out to be the withdrawal of over 600,000 US troops from around China's periphery in Asia. In his first year in office, he announced a broad framework for Asia's future without massive US troop deployments. He also made several mainly symbolic gestures to the Chinese government while pursuing vigorous efforts in secret to develop communications with the Mao Zedong leadership.

Meanwhile, in China, Mao succeeded in removing political rivals in the early years of the Cultural Revolution, but at tremendous cost. Many urban areas were burned to the ground in violence among competing groups. Two of the three pillars of control in the PRC, the Communist Party and the government administration, were seriously disrupted. The third pillar, the army, was called in to rule the cities with de facto martial law. As order was restored, the military administrators became the core of new leaders of the reconstituted Chinese Communist Party and Chinese government administration.

Under these circumstances, China was not prepared for a national security shock. Chinese troops were engaged in domestic peacekeeping and governance. They also, for many years, followed Maoist dictates under the leadership of Defense Minister Lin Biao and eschewed professional military training in favor of ideological training and promoting popular welfare in China. Chinese military programs for developing nuclear weapons and ballistic missiles were excluded from the violence and disruption of the Cultural Revolution, but the People's Liberation Army (PLA) on the whole was poorly prepared to deal with conventional military challenges.

In August 1968, the Soviet Union invaded Czechoslovakia and removed its leadership, putting in power a regime more compatible with Soviet interests. The Soviet Union also made clear that it reserved the right to take similar actions in other deviant Communist states, a view that came to be known as the Brezhnev Doctrine, named after the Soviet party leader Leonid Brezhnev, who ruled from the mid-1960s until the early 1980s. Of course, Chinese leaders well knew that, from the Soviet perspective, there was no Communist state more deviant than China. Moreover, since Brezhnev's takeover, the Soviet Union had backed political opposition to China with increasing military muscle, deploying ever-larger numbers of forces along the Manchurian border and, as a result of a new Soviet defense treaty with Mongolia, along the Sino-Mongolian border. The Soviet forces, mainly mechanized divisions designed to move rapidly in offensive operations, were configured in a pattern used by Soviet forces when they quickly overran Japanese forces in Manchuria and northern China in the last days of World War II.

The combination of perceived greater threat and internal weakness caused a crisis and debate in the Chinese leadership. Some favored reaching out to the United States as a means to offset the Soviet threat, and the Chinese Foreign Ministry under Zhou Enlai's direction called for renewed ambassadorial talks with the newly elected Nixon administration. Others strongly opposed an opening to the United States, with Lin Biao and his lieutenants, along with the radically Maoist leadership faction, the Gang of Four, arguing in favor of continued strong Chinese opposition to both the United States and the Soviet Union.

The latter leaders held the upper hand in Chinese leadership councils during much of 1969. Chinese media rebuked and ridiculed the new US president and, at the last moment, Chinese leaders cancelled the slated ambassadorial talks in February. The Chinese authorities took the offensive in the face of Soviet military pressure along the border, ambushing a Soviet patrol on a disputed island in early March and publicizing the incident to the world. Far from being intimidated, Brezhnev's Soviet forces responded later in the month by annihilating a Chinese border guard unit, setting the stage for escalating rhetoric and military clashes that were capped by an all-day battle along the western sector of the border in August that saw the Soviets inflict hundreds of casualties on the Chinese. Soviet officials followed with warnings to Americans and other foreigners, sure to relay the warnings to the Chinese, that the Soviet Union was in the process of consulting with foreign powers to assure they would stand aside as the Soviet Union prepared all-out attack on China, including the use of nuclear weapons.

Chinese leaders were compelled to shift strategy. Zhou Enlai was brought forward to negotiate with Soviet leaders. It was clear that China would not accept Soviet demands and that Beijing now viewed the USSR as China's number one strategic threat. Zhou and others in the Chinese leadership argued that the United States was weakened by the Vietnam War, and that it was also beginning to withdraw sizeable numbers of troops from Asia and dismantle the US military containment against China. On this basis, Beijing could pursue relations with Washington as a means to deal with the Soviet threat. However, Lin Biao and others argued that both superpowers were enemies of China and in the end they would cooperate together to isolate and control China.

The debate seemed to get caught up with the broader struggle for power in this period of the Cultural Revolution. Mao Zedong came to side with the view associated with Zhou Enlai. Repeated initiatives by the Nixon administration to China ultimately succeeded in Sino–US ambassadorial talks being resumed in Warsaw in early 1970. The Nixon administration's expansion of the Vietnam War by invading Cambodia in 1970 caused China to cancel the talks and slowed forward movement. However, clandestine US–China communication continued as did the withdrawal of US forces from Vietnam and other parts of Asia. By October 1970, Mao was prepared to tell visiting US journalist Edgar Snow that Nixon could visit China.

The July 1971 announcement of Nixon's trip to China came as a surprise to most Americans, who supported the initiative; Americans watched with interest the president's February 1972 visit to China. Nixon privately indicated to Chinese leaders he would break US ties with Taiwan and establish diplomatic relations with China in his second term. In the Shanghai Communiqué signed at the end of President Nixon's historic visit to China, both sides registered opposition to "hegemony"—a codeword for Soviet expansion, laid out differences on a variety of Asian and other issues, and set forth the US intention to pull back militarily from Taiwan and to support a "peaceful settlement of the Taiwan question by the Chinese themselves." Subsequently, both sides agreed to establish US–Chinese Liaison Offices staffed with senior diplomats in Beijing and Washington in 1973, despite the fact that the United States still maintained official relations with the Chinese Nationalist government in Taipei.

Progress toward establishing formal US–Chinese relations, the so-called normalization of relations, was delayed in the mid-1970s on account of circumstances mainly involving the United States. A politically motivated break-in at the Watergate office complex in Washington, D.C. and cover-up of the crime involved President Nixon in criminal activity. As congressional investigation led toward impeachment, Nixon resigned in August 1974. His promise to normalize relations with China in his second term ended with his resignation. President Gerald Ford privately reaffirmed Nixon's pledge to shift diplomatic recognition from Taiwan to China, but then he backtracked in the face of US domestic opposition and international circumstances.

Chinese leaders for their part were preoccupied with Mao's death and the most important leadership succession struggle in the history of the People's Republic of China, and with stronger efforts by the Soviet Union to use military power and relations with allies around China's periphery, such as Vietnam and India, to contain and pressure China, mimicking the US-led containment effort against China earlier in the Cold War. Under these circumstances, Chinese leaders were prepared to wait for the United States to meet Chinese conditions on breaking all US official ties with Taiwan, including the US–Taiwan defense treaty, before moving ahead with full normalization of PRC relations with the United States.

Desiring to complete the normalization of US–China relations begun by President Nixon, President Jimmy Carter felt compelled to wait until after his success in spring 1978 in gaining Senate passage of a controversial treaty transferring control of the Panama Canal to Panama. A visit by Secretary of State Cyrus Vance to China in 1977 showed that Chinese leaders were not prepared for significant compromise on Taiwan. President Carter was aware that a complete ending of US official relations with Taiwan would alienate many in the US Senate and he needed the support of many of these senators for the two-thirds Senate vote of ratification on the Panama Canal treaty. Once the Senate approved the Panama treaty in spring 1978, Carter moved forward expeditiously with normalization with China.

National Security Adviser Zbigniew Brzezinski was in the lead in seeking rapid progress in normalizing US–China relations in 1978, and in subsequent steps to advance US–China relations as a means to counter Soviet power and expansion. Carter followed Brzezinski's advice against that of Secretary of State Cyrus Vance who gave a higher priority to US–Soviet arms control agreements. The United States–China Communiqué announced in December 1978 established official US relations with the People's Republic of China under conditions whereby the United States recognized the PRC as the government of China, acknowledged that Taiwan was part of China, ended official US relations with the Republic of China government on Taiwan, and terminated the US defense treaty with the ROC on Taiwan. Official US statements underlined US interest that Taiwan's future be settled peacefully and that the United States would continue sales of defensive arms to Taipei.

US and especially Chinese leaders used the signs of improved US–China relations in the communiqué and during Chinese leader Deng Xiaoping's widely publicized visit to the United States in January 1979 to underline Sino–US cooperation against "hegemony," notably a Soviet-backed Vietnamese military assault against Cambodia beginning in late December 1978. Returning from the United States, Deng launched a large-scale Chinese military offensive into Vietnam's northern region. Chinese forces withdrew after a few weeks, though Chinese forces maintained strong artillery attacks and other military pressure against Vietnamese border positions until the Vietnamese eventually agreed to withdraw from Cambodia 10 years later. Carter administration officials voiced some reservations about Deng's confrontational tactics against Soviet and Vietnamese expansionism, but Sino–US cooperation against the USSR and its allies increased.

In pursuing normalization of relations with China, President Carter and National Security Adviser Brzezinski followed the pattern of secret diplomacy used successfully by President Nixon and National Security Adviser Kissinger in early interactions with China. Thus, there was very little consultation with Congress, key US allies, or the Taiwan government regarding the conditions and timing of the 1978 normalization agreement. In contrast to general US congressional, media, and popular support for the surprise Nixon opening to China, President Carter and his aides notably were less successful in winning US domestic support for their initiatives. Many in Congress were satisfied with the stasis that developed in US–PRC–ROC relations in the mid-1970s and unconvinced that the United States had strategic or other need to pay the price of breaking a US defense treaty and other official ties with a loyal government in Taiwan for the sake of formalizing already existing relations with the PRC. Bipartisan majorities in Congress resisted the president's initiatives and passed laws, notably the Taiwan Relations Act (TRA), that tied the hands of the administration on Taiwan and other issues.

The Taiwan Relations Act was passed by Congress in March 1979 and signed by President Carter on 10 April 1979. The initial draft of the legislation was proposed by the Carter administration to govern US relations with Taiwan once official US ties were ended in 1979. Congress rewrote the legislation, notably adding or strengthening provisions on US arms sales, opposition to threats and use of force, economic relations, human rights, and congressional oversight. Treating Taiwan as a separate entity that would continue to receive US military and other support, the law appeared to contradict the US stance in the US–PRC communiqué of 1978 establishing official US–PRC relations. Subsequently, Chinese and Taiwan officials and their supporters in the United States competed to incline US policy toward the commitments in the US–PRC communiqué or the commitments in the TRA. US policy usually supported both, though it sometimes seemed more supportive of one set of commitments than the other.

Running against President Carter in 1980, California Governor Ronald Reagan criticized Carter's handling of Taiwan. Asserting for a time that he would restore official relations with Taipei, Reagan later backed away from this stance but still claimed he would base his policy on the Taiwan Relations Act. The Chinese government put heavy pressure on the Reagan administration. It threatened serious deterioration in relations over various issues, but especially continuing US arms sales to Taiwan. Viewing close China–US relations as a key element in US strategy against the Soviet Union, Secretary of State Alexander Haig led those in the Reagan administration who favored maintaining close China–US relations and opposed US arms sales to Taiwan that might provoke China. For a year and a half, Haig and his supporters were successful in leading US efforts to accommodate PRC concerns over Taiwan, especially US arms sales to the ROC, in the interest of fostering closer US–China cooperation against the Soviet Union. The United States ultimately signed with China the 17 August 1982 communiqué. In the communiqué, the United States agreed gradually to diminish arms sales and China agreed it would seek peaceful reunification of Taiwan with the mainland. Subsequent developments showed that the vague agreement was subject to varying interpretations. President Reagan registered private reservations about this arrangement, and his administration also took steps to reassure Taiwan's leader of continued US support.

Amid continued strong Chinese pressure tactics on a wide range of US–China disputes, US policy shifted with Haig's resignation in 1982 and the appointment of George Shultz as secretary of state. Reagan administration officers who were at odds with Haig's emphasis on the need for a solicitous US approach to China came to the fore. They were led by Paul Wolfowitz, who was chosen by Shultz as assistant secretary of state for East Asian affairs; Richard Armitage, the senior Defense Department officer managing relations with China and East Asia; and the senior National Security Council staff aide on Asian affairs and later assistant secretary of state for East Asian affairs, Gaston Sigur. While officers who had backed Haig's pro-China slant were transferred from authority over China policy, the new US leadership contingent with responsibility for Asian affairs shifted US policy toward a less solicitous and accommodating stance toward China, while giving much higher priority to US relations with Japan. There was less emphasis on China's strategic importance to the United States in American competition with the Soviet Union, and there was less concern among US policymakers about China possibly downgrading relations over Taiwan and other disputes.

The Chinese leaders grudgingly adjusted to the new US stance, viewing their interests best served by less pressure and more positive initiatives to the Reagan administration, seen notably in their warm welcome for the US president on his visit to China in 1984. Cooperative Chinese relations with the United States were crucially important to the Chinese leadership in maintaining the flow of aid, investment, and trade essential to the economic development and modernization underway in China—the linchpin of the Chinese Communist leadership's plans for sustaining their rule in China. Meanwhile, the Reagan leadership learned not to confront core Chinese interests over issues like Taiwan in overt and egregious ways, seeking to continue US military and other support for Taiwan in ways less likely to provoke strong Chinese reaction. Mutual accommodations characterized US–China relations in Reagan's second term in office that did not see repetition of the repeated China–US controversies that had marked Reagan's relations with China in his first term.

TIANANMEN, TAIWAN, AND POST–COLD WAR REALITIES

Unexpected mass demonstrations centered in Beijing's Tiananmen Square and other Chinese cities in spring 1989 represented the most serious challenge to China's post-Mao leadership. Deng Xiaoping was decisive in resolving Chinese leadership differences in favor of hard liners favoring a violent crackdown on the demonstrators and a broader suppression of political dissent that began with the bloody attack on Tiananmen Square on 4 June 1989. Reform-minded leaders were purged and punished.

Anticipating shock and disapproval to the Tiananmen crackdown from the United States and the West, Deng nonetheless argued that the negative reaction would have few prolonged negative consequences for China. The Chinese leader failed to anticipate the breadth and depth of US disapproval that would profoundly influence US policy into the 21st century. The influence was compounded by the unanticipated and dramatic collapse of communist regimes in the Soviet bloc and other areas, leading to the demise of the Soviet Union by the early 1990s. These developments undermined the perceived need for the United States to cooperate pragmatically with China despite its brutal dictatorship on account of a US strategic need for international support against the Soviet Union. Meanwhile, Taiwan's authoritarian government was moving steadily at this time to promote democratic policies and practices, marking a sharp contrast to the harsh political authoritarianism in mainland China and greatly enhancing Taiwan's popularity and support in the United States.

Taken together, these circumstances generally placed the initiative in US–China relations with US leaders. Chinese leaders at first focused on maintaining internal stability as they maneuvered to sustain workable economic relations with the United States while rebuffing major US initiatives that infringed on Chinese internal political control or territorial and sovereignty issues involving Taiwan and Tibet. As the Chinese government presided over strong economic growth beginning in 1993 and the US and other international attention that came with it, Chinese leaders reflected more confidence as they dealt with US pressures for change. However, they generally eschewed direct confrontation that would endanger the crucially important economic relations with the United States unless China was provoked by US, Taiwan, or other actions.

Effective US policy toward China proved elusive amid contentious American domestic debate over China policy during the 1990s. That debate was not stilled until the 11 September 2001 terrorist attack on America muffled continued US concerns over China amid an overwhelming American concern to deal with the immediate, serious, and broad consequences of the global war on terrorism.

RELATIONS DURING THE GEORGE H. W. BUSH ADMINISTRATION

The pattern of US policy at first saw President George H. W. Bush, with strong personal conviction in the importance of cooperative US relations with China, strive to preserve cooperative ties amid widespread American outrage and pressure for retribution and sanctions against the Chinese leaders. President Bush was the US chief executive most experienced in dealing with China. He had served as the head of the US Liaison Office in China in the mid-1970s. Bush took the lead in his own administration in 1989–1993 in dealing with severe problems in China–US relations caused by the Tiananmen crackdown and the decline in US strategic interest in China as a result of the collapse of the Soviet Bloc.

He resorted to secret diplomacy to maintain constructive communication with senior Chinese leaders, but the latter remained fairly rigid and were unable or unwilling to make many gestures to help Bush justify a continued moderate US stance toward China amid wide-ranging US skepticism and hostility in the US Congress, media, and interest groups. Although his administration officials said all high-level official contact with China would be cut off as a result of the Tiananmen crackdown, President Bush sent his national security adviser and the deputy secretary of state on secret missions to Beijing in July and December 1989. When the missions became known in December 1989, the congressional and media reaction was bitterly critical of the administration's perceived duplicity.

Bush eventually became frustrated with the Chinese leadership's intransigence, and took a tough stance on trade and other issues, though he made special efforts to ensure that the United States continued most-favored-nation tariff status for China despite opposition by a majority of the US Congress and much of the American media. Reflecting more positive US views of Taiwan, the Bush administration upgraded US interchange with ROC by sending a cabinet-level official to Taipei in 1992, the first such visit since official relations were ended in 1979. He also seemed to abandon the limits on US arms sales set in accord with the 17 August 1982 US communiqué with China by agreeing in 1992 to a sale of 150 advanced F-16 jet fighters to Taiwan worth over $5 billion.

RELATIONS DURING THE WILLIAM CLINTON ADMINISTRATION

Presidential candidate Bill Clinton used sharp attacks against Chinese government behavior, notably the Tiananmen crackdown, and President Bush's moderate approach to China to win support in the 1992 election. The presidential candidate's attacks, though probably reflecting sincere anger and concern over Chinese behavior, also reflected a tendency in the US–China debate in the 1990s to use China issues, particularly criticism of China and US policy toward China, for partisan and other ulterior purposes. The president elect, and US politicians in following years, found that criticizing China and US policy toward China provided a convenient means to pursue political and other ends. For candidate Clinton and his aides, using China issues to discredit the record of the Republican candidate, George H. W. Bush, proved to be an effective way to take votes from the incumbent. Once he won the election and was in office, President Clinton showed little interest in China policy, leaving the responsibility to subordinates.

In particular, Assistant Secretary of State for East Asia Affairs Winston Lord in 1993 played the lead administration role in working with congressional leaders, notably Senate Majority Leader George Mitchell and a House of Representative leader on China and human rights issues, Representative Nancy Pelosi, and others to establish the human rights conditions the Clinton administration would require before renewing most-favored-nation (MFN) tariff status for China. The terms he worked out were widely welcomed in the United States at the time. However, the Chinese government leaders were determined not to give in on several of the US demands and they appeared to calculate that US business interests in a burgeoning Chinese economy would be sufficient to prevent the United States from taking the drastic step of cutting MFN tariff treatment for China and risking the likely retaliation of the PRC against US trade interests. US business pressures pushed Clinton to intervene in May 1994 to reverse existing policy and allow for unimpeded US renewal of MFN status for China.

Pro-Taiwan interests in the United States, backed by US public relations firms in the pay of entities and organizations in Taiwan, took the opportunity of congressional elections in 1995, giving control of the Congress to pro-Taiwan Republican leaders to push for greater US support for Taiwan, notably a visit by ROC President Lee Teng-hui to his alma mater Cornell University. Under heavy domestic political pressure, President Clinton intervened again and allowed Taiwan's president to visit the United States.

A resulting military confrontation with China in the Taiwan Strait eventually involving two US aircraft carrier battle groups saw the Clinton administration move to a much more coherent engagement policy toward China that received consistent and high-level attention from the president and his key aides, and was marked by two US–China summit meetings in 1997 and 1998. Progress included US–China agreement on China's entry into the World Trade Organization and US agreement to provide permanent normal trade status for China. However, the new approach failed to still the vigorous US debate against forward movement in US relations with China on a wide range of strategic, economic, political, and other issues.

As in the case of Clinton's attacks on George H. W. Bush, many of the attacks on Clinton's engagement policy with China after 1996 were not so much focused on China and China issues for their own sake, as on partisan or other concerns. Most notably, as congressional Republican leaders sought to impeach President Clinton and tarnish the reputation of his administration, they endeavored to dredge up a wide range of charges regarding illegal Chinese fund-raising, Chinese espionage, and Chinese wide deviations from international norms regarding human rights, nuclear weapons, and ballistic missile proliferation and other questions in order to discredit President Clinton's moderate engagement policy toward China, and in so doing cast serious doubt on the moral integrity and competence of the President and his aides.

The Clinton policy of engagement with China also came under attack from organized labor interests within the Democratic Party, some of which used the attacks on the administration's China policy as a means to get the administration to pay more attention to broader labor interests within the Democratic Party. In a roughly similar fashion, social conservatives in the Republican Party used sharp attacks against continuation of US most-favored-nation tariff status for China (a stance often supported by congressional Republican leaders) despite Chinese coercive birth-control policies; they did this in part as a means to embarrass and pressure the Republican leaders to pay more positive attention to the various agenda issues of the social conservatives.

During the 1990s, congressional criticism of China and moderation in US policy toward China was easy to do and generally had benefits for those doing the criticism. The criticism generated positive coverage from US media strongly critical of China. It generated positive support and perhaps some fundraising and electioneering support for the congressional critics by the many interest groups in the United States that focused criticism on Chinese policies and practices at this time. The Chinese government, anxious to keep the economic relationship with the United States on an even keel, was disinclined to punish such congressional critics or take substantive action against them. More likely were Chinese invitations to the crucial congressional members for all-expenses paid trips to China in order to persuade them to change their views by seeing actual conditions in China. Finally, President Clinton, like President George H. W. Bush, often was not in a position to risk other legislative goals by punishing members critical of his China policy. In short, from a congressional perspective and a broader perspective in American politics, sharp congressional criticism of China in the 1990s became, in congressional parlance, a "free ride" with many benefits for those doing the criticizing and few perceived drawbacks.

As President Clinton and his White House staff took more control over China policy after the face-off with Chinese forces in the Taiwan Strait in 1996, they emphasized—like George H. W. Bush—a moderate policy of engagement, seeking change in offensive Chinese government practices through a gradual process involving closer Chinese integration with the world economic and political order. The US–China relationship improved but also encountered significant setbacks and resistance. The president's more activist and positive policy of engagement with China saw such high points as the China–US summits in 1997 and 1998, the Sino–US agreement on China's entry into the WTO in 1999, and passage of US legislation in 2000 granting China permanent normal trade relations status. Low points in the relationship during this time included strong congressional opposition to the president's stance against Taiwan independence in 1998; the May 1999 bombing of the Chinese Embassy in Belgrade and Chinese demonstrators trashing US diplomatic properties in China; strident congressional criticism in the so-called Cox Committee report of May 1999 charging administration officials with gross malfeasance in guarding US secrets and weaponry from Chinese spies; and partisan congressional investigations of Clinton administration political fund-raising that highlighted some illegal contributions from sources connected to the Chinese regime, and the alleged impact they had on the administration's more moderate approach to the PRC.

Chinese leaders had long sought the summit meetings with the United States. Coming in the wake of Chinese meetings with other world leaders in the aftermath of the international isolation of China caused by the Tiananmen crackdown, the summit meetings with the US president were a clear signal to audiences at home and abroad that the Communist administration of China had growing international status and that its position as the legitimate government of China now was recognized by all major world powers.

The benefits for the United States in the summit meetings were more in question, though the Clinton administration justified these steps as part of its efforts to use engagement in seeking change in offensive Chinese government practices through a gradual process involving closer Chinese integration with the world economic and political order. US and other critics failed to accept this rationale and honed their criticism on what they viewed as unjustified US concessions to Chinese leaders. Heading the list were perceived US concessions in the US president articulating limits on US support for Taiwan in the so-called three nos. Speaking in Shanghai on 29 June 1998 during his visit to China, President Clinton affirmed that the United States did not support Taiwan independence, two Chinas, or one Taiwan, one China, and that the United States does not believe Taiwan should be a member of an organization where statehood is required. The Clinton administration claimed the so-called three nos were a reaffirmation of longstanding US policy, but it was roundly criticized in the Congress and US media as a new gesture made to accommodate Beijing and undermine Taipei.

Progress in US negotiations leading to eventual agreement on China's entry into the WTO was not without serious difficulties and negative consequences. The United States took the lead among the organization's contracting parties in protracted negotiations (1986–1999) to reach agreements with China on a variety of trade-related issues before Chinese accession could move forward. Chinese Premier Zhu Rongji visited Washington in April 1999 hoping to reach agreement with the United States on China's entry into the World Trade Organization. An agreement was reached and disclosed by the Americans, only to be turned down by President Clinton. The setback embarrassed Zhu and raised serious questions in the Chinese leadership about the intentions of President Clinton and his administration. Recovering from the setback, Zhu was able to complete the US–China negotiations in November 1999, paving the way for China's entry into the WTO in 2001. After the United States agreed in late 1999 to China joining the World Trade Organization, US legislation passed granting China permanent normal trade relations (PNTR) in 2000. This ended the need for annual presidential requests and congressional reviews regarding China keeping normal trade relations tariff status, previously known as most-favored-nation tariff status.

Making such progress in US–China relations was difficult because of incidents and developments affecting US–China relations and vitriolic

US debate over the Clinton administration's China policy. Heading the list was the US bombing of the Chinese embassy in Belgrade, the most important incident in US–China relations after the Tiananmen crackdown. The reaction in China included mobs stoning the US embassy in Beijing and burning US diplomatic property in Chengtu. Both governments restored calm and dealt with some of the consequences of the bombing, but China and the United States never came to an agreement on what had happened and whether the United States explained its actions appropriately.

Lee Teng-hui added to Taiwan Strait tension that worried American policymakers when he asserted in July 1999 that Taiwan was a state separate from China and that China and Taiwan had "special state-to-state relations." Chinese leaders saw this as a step toward Taiwan independence and reacted with strong rhetoric, some military actions, and an end to cross-strait communication links.

Complementing difficulties abroad were the many challenges at home to the Clinton administration's moderate policy of engagement toward China. The US media ran repeated stories in the second term of the Clinton administration linking the president, Vice President Gore, and other administration leaders with illegal political fund-raising involving Asian donors, some of whom were said to be connected with the Chinese government. Congressional Republican Committee Chairmen, Senator Fred Thompson and Representative Dan Burton, held hearings, conducted investigations and produced information and reports regarding various unsubstantiated allegations of illegal contributions from Chinese backers in return for the Clinton administration's turning a blind eye to Chinese illegal trading practices and Chinese espionage activities in the United States.

More damaging to the administration and its engagement policy toward China was the report of the Cox Committee. Formally known as the Select Committee on US National Security and Military/Commercial Concerns with the People's Republic of China and named for its Chairman, Republican Congressman Christopher Cox, the committee released in May 1999 an 800-page unclassified version of a larger classified report. It depicted longstanding and widespread Chinese espionage efforts against US nuclear weapons facilities, allowing China to build American advanced nuclear warheads for use on Chinese missiles that were made more accurate and reliable with the assistance of US companies. It portrayed the Clinton administration as grossly negligent in protecting such vital US national security secrets. The report added substantially to congressional, media, and other concerns that the United States faced a rising security threat posed by China's rapidly expanding economic and military power.

RELATIONS DURING THE
GEORGE W. BUSH ADMINISTRATION

George W. Bush became president in 2001 with a policy toward China tougher than the policy of his predecessor. Seeking to sustain economic relations with China, the new president was wary of China's strategic intentions and took steps to deter China from using military force against Taiwan. Relations deteriorated when on 1 April 2001, a Chinese jet fighter crashed with a US reconnaissance plane, the EP-3, in international waters off the China coast. The jet was destroyed and the pilot killed. The EP-3 was seriously damaged but managed to make an emergency landing on China's Hainan Island. The US crew was held for 11 days and the US plane much longer by Chinese authorities. Weeks of negotiations produced compromises that allowed the crew and plane to return to the United States, but neither side accepted responsibility for the incident.

Many specialists predicted continued deterioration of relations but both governments worked to resolve issues and establish a businesslike relationship that emphasized positive aspects of the relationship and played down differences. The terrorist attack on America on 11 September 2001 diverted US attention away from China as a potential strategic threat. Preoccupied with leadership transition and other issues in China, Chinese leaders worked hard to moderate previous harsh rhetoric and pressure tactics in order to consolidate relations with the United States.

Some specialists were encouraged by the surprising improvement in US–China relations during the administration of President George W. Bush. They tended to emphasize greater Chinese leadership confidence and maturity as the cause for the turnabout in relations, arguing that such confidence and maturity prompted the Chinese government to deal more moderately and with restraint regarding some of the seeming challenges posed by the new US administration and its policies regarding Taiwan, weapons proliferation, ballistic missile defense, and the overall greater US assertiveness and national security power in Asian and world affairs. Another group of specialists was less convinced that US–China relations were destined to converge substantially over Asian and world affairs. These specialists emphasized the importance of what they saw as the Bush administration moving fairly rapidly from an initial toughness toward China to a stance of accommodation and compromise. The shift toward a moderate US stance prompted Chinese leaders to pursue greater moderation in turn in their overall approach to Asian and world affairs. A third view involved specialists who gave more weight to the Bush administration's firm and effective policies toward China, which were seen to have curbed assertive and potential disruptive Chinese tendencies and served to make it in China's interests to avoid confrontation, seek better US ties and avoid challenge to US interests in Asian and world affairs. This view held that it was more China than the United States that took the lead in seeking better ties in 2001, and that greater US–China cooperation in Asian affairs depended not so much on Chinese confidence and maturity as on effective US use of power and influence to keep assertive and disruptive Chinese tendencies in check and prevail upon China to limit emphasis on differences with the United States.

All three schools of thought judged that the improvement in US–China relations reinforced generally moderate Chinese tendencies in Asian and world affairs, but their differences over the causes of the US–China thaw had implications for assessing future Chinese policy and behavior. In the first instance, the key variable seemed to be Chinese confidence and maturity, which presumably would continue to grow along with Chinese development and moderation, suggesting a continued moderate Chinese approach for the next several years if not longer. The latter two views depended heavily on the United States, with the first view arguing that continued US moderation and accommodation of Chinese interest was required, as a firmer US stance presumably could lead to a more assertive and aggressive Chinese stance in the region. The second of the latter two views indicated that much depended on continued US resolve, power, and effectiveness in dealing with China. Weakness or extremism in the US stance could reverse the prevailing trend of Chinese moderation in the region and lead to a more assertive and disruptive approach.

In any event, the course of US–China relations was smoother than at any time since the normalization of US–China relations. US preoccupation with the wars in Afghanistan and Iraq and the broader war on global terrorism meant that US strategic attention to China as a threat remained a secondary consideration for American policymakers. Chinese leaders for their part continued to deal with an incomplete leadership transition and the broad problem of trying to sustain a one-party authoritarian political regime amid a vibrant economy and rapid social change. In this context, the two powers, despite a wide range of continuing differences, ranging from Taiwan and Tibet to trade issues and human rights, managed to see their interests best served by generally emphasizing the positive. In particular, they found new common ground in dealing with the crisis caused by North Korea's nuclear weapons program beginning in 2002, and the Chinese appreciated Bush's warning in December 2003 to Taiwan's leader Chen Shui-bian to avoid steps toward independence for Taiwan that could lead to conflict in the Taiwan Strait.

The Dictionary

– A –

ABORTION. *See* ONE CHILD POLICY.

ACHESON, DEAN G. (1893–1971). A prominent State Department official during the **Harry Truman** administration, Acheson served as undersecretary of state before being sworn in as secretary of state in 1949 and served in that office until 1953. Though considered an "Atlanticist" who gave US relations with Europe top priority, Acheson is known for his efforts to end US support for **Chiang Kai-shek** and his **Nationalist Party** regime. He sought publication of the famed **"China White Paper"** in 1949 that placed blame on the Chiang government and not US policy for the **Communist Party** victory on the Chinese mainland. Acheson held out hope for American reconciliation with the Chinese Communists, authorizing US Ambassador **Leighton Stuart** to approach Communist leaders in 1949. Acheson was strongly attacked by congressional and media representatives who favored continued US support for the failing Chinese Nationalist government. In early 1950, Acheson articulated an assessment of US strategic interests in East Asia in the wake of the Communist victory in China that notably excluded Taiwan, Chiang Kai-shek's last redoubt, and Korea. The Truman government reversed this view in June 1950 after North Korea attacked South Korea and US forces quickly intervened in both Korea and the **Taiwan Strait**, and the **Korean War** began.

AEGIS SEABORNE SYSTEMS. This advanced and expensive US ship-based **theater missile defense** system was considered for possible sale to Taiwan in order to counter the buildup of Chinese ballistic

1

missiles targeted at Taiwan begun in the 1990s. Chinese officials warned strongly against such US sales to Taiwan.

AFGHANISTAN. The Chinese and American governments publicly opposed the Soviet Union's occupation of this country beginning in late 1979, and they privately cooperated to support the armed resistance against it. Beijing was somewhat less supportive and somewhat more reserved than other powers in reacting to the US-led military assault toppling the terrorist-harboring Afghanistan regime following the 11 September 2001 terrorist attack on America.

AGENCY FOR INTERNATIONAL DEVELOPMENT (AID). This US government agency remained restricted in assisting China despite the normalization of official US relations with the People's Republic of China in 1979. The US government provided financial assistance through other agencies, notably **trade** financing through the **Export-Import Bank**; investment guarantees through the **Overseas Private Investment Corporation**; and trade promotional activities through the **Trade Development Program** of the US Commerce Department.

AGNEW, SPIRO (1918–1996). Elected vice president in 1968, Agnew played a small role in US China policy during the **Richard Nixon** administration. He visited Asia several times and stopped in Taiwan twice in an effort to show US support for **Chiang Kai-shek**. Reflecting his conservative views and support for Taiwan, Agnew was one of the few American politicians to respond unfavorably to the thaw in US–China relations seen during the **"ping pong diplomacy"** of the spring of 1971. He told reporters that the relaxing of relations with China was inappropriate due to the government's treatment of the citizens of China—a stance at odds with efforts by President Richard Nixon and National Security Adviser **Henry Kissinger** to improve US relations with China.

AGREED FRAMEWORK. This US–North Korean accord in 1994 froze then-known North Korean nuclear weapons development and was welcomed by China. China criticized the **George W. Bush** administration for deemphasizing the Agreed Framework as it pursued a tougher stance toward North Korea over nuclear and other issues following a US policy review in 2001. It was later revealed that North Korea engaged in secret development of nuclear weapons after the 1994 accord.

ALBRIGHT, MADELINE (1937–). As secretary of state during the second term of the **William Clinton** administration, 1997–2001, Albright supported and implemented the administration's strong emphasis on a positive **engagement policy** with China, while also raising continued differences with the Chinese government, notably over **human rights**. During this period the State Department was seen as a secondary influence in the making of administration China policy, which was decided by the president and influenced by the advice of the vice president and the White House staff.

ALLEN, HORACE N. (1858–1932). Horace Allen was the first of Protestant **missionaries** to serve in Korea and served there from 1884–1905. A medical missionary who served as a physician to the Korean king, Allen worked to promote an independent Korea. Korea during this period was at first dominated by China and then subject to advances by Japan and Russia. Allen was named the American minister to Korea in 1897.

ALLEN, RICHARD (1936–). A senior foreign policy advisor to presidential candidate **Ronald Reagan** in 1980, Allen traveled to China in mid-1980 with vice presidential candidate **George H. W. Bush** and China policy expert **James Lilley** in order to explain Reagan's policies toward China and Taiwan to Chinese leaders. After the election, Allen served as Reagan's national security advisor and worked with Lilley and others to support stronger ties with Taiwan in the face of mounting Chinese pressure against such ties.

ALSOP, JOSEPH (1910–1989). Working in China during World War II, Alsop was an aide to United States Army Air Force General **Claire Chennault**. Alsop supported Chennault in his argument that US air attacks from China on Japan and Japanese forces would be an effective strategy to help defeat Japan. He lobbied President **Franklin D. Roosevelt**, a distant relative, and White House aides, in support of Chennault's approach. This strategy was opposed by the commanding US general in China, **Joseph Stilwell**, but was supported by **Chiang Kai-shek**. It was approved by President Roosevelt, though it subsequently failed as strong Japanese ground attacks destroyed US air bases in China.

AMBASSADORIAL TALKS. Following years of war and confrontation with the United States, leaders of the People's Republic of China (PRC) by 1955 saw their interests better served by a more moderate approach to the United States that sought ways to ease tensions, improve ties, and possibly engage in high-level dialogue with the United States. The US administration led by Secretary of State **John Foster Dulles** was wary of direct talks with the PRC that would undermine US-backed efforts to isolate and pressure the PRC regime, and instead supported the **Nationalist Party** government of **Chiang Kai-shek**, the Republic of China (ROC), based on Taiwan, as the legitimate government of China. Facing congressional and Allied pressures to meet with PRC officials, Dulles agreed to low-level ambassadorial talks that began in Geneva in 1955. At the talks, the two sides reached some agreement on repatriating detained personnel, but the agreement was subsequently disputed. The US side pressed hard for a Chinese renunciation of force regarding Taiwan, effectively stopping progress in the talks. The talks were suspended for a time before resuming in Warsaw, in 1958, where the two sides met periodically without much result. The talks did provide a useful line of US–PRC communication during times of crisis, as both sides strove to avoid serious military conflict. They also were used effectively in 1970 when two sessions were held in Warsaw before being suspended on account of the US military invasion of **Cambodia** in 1970. The talks then were superseded by the various secret dialogues between **Richard Nixon** and **Mao Zedong** at that time, and were not resumed.

AMERASIA. US Foreign Service Officer **John Service** was arrested in 1945 on charges of passing classified documents critical of **Chiang Kai-shek** and US Ambassador to China **Patrick Hurley** to this leftist magazine. The charges against Service were dropped, but he was later dismissed from the State Department as a security risk.

AMERICAN ASIATIC ASSOCIATION. A coalition of US trading firms and other business interests organized this group in 1898. Its articles, petitions, and lobbying focused on the need for the US government to reaffirm a commitment to American commercial opportunities in China at a time of intensified Japanese and other foreign encroachment in China. The association and other US-organized exponents of the China **trade** grew quieter after several years as it became clearer that China was a poor market for most American finished goods and that Japan was a larger and more promising one.

AMERICAN CHINA DEVELOPMENT COMPANY. Organized in 1895 and representing US railway, banking, and investment interests, the company received from the Chinese government in 1898 a concession to build and operate a **Hankow–Canton railway** between the two Chinese cities. The company demanded and received better terms from the Chinese government in a supplementary agreement in 1900. Some American shareholders subsequently sold interest in the company to a Belgian syndicate, which by 1904 controlled five of seven seats on the company's board of directors. The Chinese government then sought to buy back the concession; and the US government encouraged efforts by American investors to restore American control to the company. In the end, American shareholders, having restored American ownership of the company, gained considerable profit by selling their interests in the railway concession back to the Chinese government in 1905.

AMERICAN COMMITTEE FOR NON-PARTICIPATION IN JAPANESE AGGRESSION. Conceived by Americans who had been **missionaries** in China, this group led efforts in the period after the Japanese attack on China in 1937 and before the Japanese attack on **Pearl Harbor** in 1941 to curb the US sales of war materials to Japan and to provide US assistance to China.

AMERICAN FEDERATION OF LABOR-CONGRESS OF INDUSTRIAL ORGANIZATIONS (AFL–CIO). This leading American labor organization was active in the 1990s in criticizing the Chinese government over **trade**, labor, and **human rights** issues. Its officials testified before Congress and lobbied in favor of imposing conditions on the annual US renewal of **most-favored-nation (MFN) tariff status** for China and imposing trade restrictions on Chinese imports.

AMERICAN INSTITUTE IN TAIWAN (AIT). AIT was established as a non-profit organization incorporated in the District of Columbia in the United States in 1979, with a board of directors appointed by the secretary of state. It undertook the duties of US official organizations maintaining relations between the United States and Taiwan following the break in official US relations with the Republic of China government of Taiwan in 1979. Headquartered in Rosslyn, Virginia, AIT established offices in Taipei and Kaohsiung. In Taiwan, AIT functioned as a US embassy. AIT personnel often were drawn from the US Foreign Service or other US offices, though these personnel assumed leave status when serving in Taiwan. Americans working for AIT were accorded "functional immunity"—meaning they could not be arrested or tried for acts carried out in connection with their duties. The budget for AIT was a line item in the State Department's budget, and it received instruction through the assistant secretary of state for East Asian and Pacific affairs. Taiwan's counterpart to AIT was known as the **Coordination Council for North American Affairs (CCNAA)**, which changed its name in 1994 to **Taipei Economic and Cultural Representational Office (TECRO)**.

AMERICAN INTERNATIONAL GROUP (AIG). The world's leading international insurance organization, AIG was active in China prior to the **Communist Party** victory on the Chinese mainland in 1949. Under the leadership of **Maurice "Hank" Greenberg**, AIG in 1992 was the first foreign company to be allowed to sell insurance in the People's Republic of China.

AMERICAN MILITARY OBSERVER GROUP (YENAN). Chiang Kai-shek reluctantly agreed in mid-1944 to allow the dispatch of this small group (about 25 people) of US military officers, technical specialists, and foreign service officers to the **Communist Party** headquarters in **Yenan**. Working with their Communist counterparts and senior Communist leaders, including **Mao Zedong**, the American officials promoted common efforts in the war against Japan. They also gained information on the Communists' capabilities and intentions. Because they were dispatched to what the ruling Chinese **Nationalist Party** viewed as "rebel" territory, the US group came to be known as the **"Dixie Mission."**

AMERICAN VOLUNTEER GROUP. Also known as the **"Flying Tigers,"** the group was established in the year prior to the Japanese attack on **Pearl Harbor**. It arose from plans by **Claire Chennault** and others that resulted in a secret presidential order allowing US military pilots to resign their commissions and sign contracts with a firm, whose operating funds came through the **lend–lease aid** program, for the purpose of flying fighter planes transferred to the Chinese government under lend–lease. The group defended Chinese airspace against Japanese attack.

AMNESTY INTERNATIONAL (AI). This **human rights** group was among the most active after the **Tiananmen crackdown** of 1989 in urging the Congress and the administration to impose conditions on the United States' granting **most-favored-nation (MFN) tariff status** to China and on the United States agreeing to China's membership in the **World Trade Organization**.

ANGELL TREATY. Named after the chief US negotiator, James G. Angell, president of the University of Michigan, this US–China treaty was signed in 1880 and ratified by the Senate in 1881. It allowed the United States to curb and suspend the entry of Chinese laborers into the United States. It was one of a series of departures from the 1868 **Burlingame Treaty** promising free **immigration** by Chinese to the United States that would see over the next few decades stringent US restrictions on Chinese immigration and on Chinese already in the United States. *See also* EXCLUSION MOVEMENT.

ANTI-AMERICAN BOYCOTT, 1905. This Chinese boycott targeted blatant US discrimination against Chinese **immigration**. It saw merchants and students lead Chinese in coastal cities like Canton and Shanghai in shunning US goods for months, damaging US trade with China.

ANTI-BALLISTIC MISSILE (ABM) TREATY. As the US government moved forward with **ballistic missile defense** programs in the 1990s, Chinese officials argued strenuously against them. They demanded that Washington adhere to the strict limits for deploying ballistic missile defenses set forth in this 1972 treaty between the United States and the Soviet Union. Chinese demands subsided as Russia decided not to resist moves by the **George W. Bush** administration to end the treaty and move ahead vigorously with ballistic missile defense programs.

ANTI-COMINTERN PACT. This agreement among Japan, Germany, and Italy in 1936 raised the specter among American and other observers of coordinated efforts at international expansion by the three fascist powers. Japan's aggression in China came to be seen as part of this global expansion, raising American concerns. *See* COMINTERN.

ARMITAGE, RICHARD (1945–). As deputy secretary of state in the **George W. Bush** administration, Armitage was influential in US policy toward China and other parts of Asia. He supported businesslike interaction with China that gave strong emphasis to US interests in relations with Japan and Taiwan, while seeking cooperation with China in a variety of areas, including in dealing with **North Korea's nuclear weapons program**. As a Defense Department Asian affairs policymaker during the **Ronald Reagan** administration, Armitage was at odds with Secretary of State **Alexander Haig** and the priority he gave to meeting Chinese concerns over Taiwan and other issues. After Haig's departure in 1982, Armitage worked closely with the State Department's new secretary, **George Shultz**, his assistant secretary for East Asia, **Paul Wolfowitz**, and the senior National Security Council staff aide on Asian affairs, **Gaston Sigur**, to shift US policy to a less solicitous and accommodating stance toward China, while giving much higher priority to US relations with Japan.

ARMS CONTROL. American concern to control China's development and proliferation of nuclear and other weapons of mass destruction and related delivery systems and technologies rose with the development of Chinese nuclear weapons in the 1960s. Beginning in the late 1960s and lasting into the 1980s, Beijing was concerned with US–Soviet arms control arrangements having potential adverse implications for China's interests in the **Strategic Arms Limitation Talks/Strategic Arms Reduction Talks (SALT I, SALT II)**. US and other foreign pressure saw China gradually conform in the 1980s and 1990s to international arms control and anti-proliferation measures seen in the **Chemical Weapons Convention**, the **Non-Proliferation Treaty (NPT)**, the **Comprehensive Nuclear Test Ban Treaty**, the **Missile Technology Control Regime (MTCR)**, and the **International Atomic Energy Agency**.

ARMSTRONG, JAMES (1794–1868). Commodore James Armstrong was the commanding officer of American naval forces in China when in November 1856 Chinese forts near Canton fired on American naval forces seeking to evacuate Americans from Canton amid intermittent fighting between Chinese and British forces. In reaction, US forces destroyed the Chinese forts. The US action came as a surprise to some Chinese officials, who had hoped to control the British through the Americans. It elicited a full apology from the local Chinese governor-general.

ASIA PACIFIC ECONOMIC COOPERATION (APEC). APEC was set up in 1989 as a loose arrangement among 12 countries: six **Association for Southeast Asian Nations** economies (Singapore, Thailand, Malaysia, Indonesia, Philippines, and Brunei) and Australia, Canada, Japan, South Korea, New Zealand, and the United States. The United States helped to engineer a compromise in 1991 allowing China, Taiwan, and **Hong Kong** to join this regional body that initially focused on economic issues but later broadened its scope to include political, security, and other issues. Annual APEC summit meetings provided opportunities for top-level US–Chinese meetings, even in periods of troubled US–Chinese relations during the 1990s.

ASIA WATCH. *See* HUMAN RIGHTS WATCH—ASIA.

ASIAN DEVELOPMENT BANK (ADB). Organized in 1967 with its headquarters in Manila, early members of the bank included Japan, the Republic of China, the United States, and a number of Asian and

European nations. As part of China's efforts to join international financial institutions, Beijing in 1983 asked to join the ADB and demanded expulsion of Taiwan, the Republic of China, a founding member of the bank. The United States supported Taiwan's continued membership in the bank. A compromise was reached where China entered the bank and Taiwan officials also participated in bank functions under the title "Taipei, China."

ASIAN ECONOMIC CRISIS. Beginning in 1997, this crisis severely damaged South Korea, Thailand, Indonesia, Malaysia, and several other Asian economies and threaten the stability of regional development. Chinese and US leaders consulted closely to limit the damage caused by the negative contagion flowing from collapsing financial arrangements in several Asian states. With US encouragement, Chinese officials retained the existing exchange rate for the Chinese currency, avoiding a devaluation that would have worsened conditions for other Asian economies and made recovery from the crisis more difficult for all concerned.

ASIATIC SQUADRON. Officially organized in 1835, this US Navy group began in 1842 to maintain a regular presence along the China coast. Initially consisting of two or three vessels, it grew to 31 vessels by 1860. It protected American lives and commerce in China and throughout maritime East and South Asia, and reinforced American diplomacy in the region. It was later known as the Asiatic Fleet.

ASSOCIATION FOR RELATIONS ACROSS THE TAIWAN STRAIT (ARATS). An ostensibly private organization established in China in the early 1990s to manage contacts with Taiwan, ARATS and its Taiwan counterpart, the **Straits Exchange Foundations (SEF)**, held numerous consultations and meetings in the 1990s that were welcomed by the US government as a means to ease tensions in relations across the **Taiwan Strait**. The contacts were halted by China in 1999 amid tensions featuring strong Chinese opposition to Taiwan President **Lee Teng-hui**'s public assertion that Taiwan was a state separate from China and that China and Taiwan had **"special state-to-state" relations.**

ASSOCIATION OF SOUTHEAST ASIAN NATIONS (ASEAN) REGIONAL FORUM (ARF). China joined this regional security group formed in the 1990s with a membership of over 20 Asian and Pacific countries. The forum provided an opportunity for discussions with US and other regional leaders on security issues of common concern. Specific accomplishments of the group were limited, but most participants valued the opportunity for dialogue, improved communication, and enhanced mutual understanding.

ATKINSON, BROOKS (1894–1984). A reporter for the *New York Times*, Atkinson along with some other US journalists was allowed into the Chinese **Communist Party** zone by **Chiang Kai-shek** in 1944. Like many of the other US journalists, Atkinson was positively impressed by the Communist soldiers and general living conditions. This favorable opinion in their news dispatches led to Chiang's denial of further journalistic visits.

17 AUGUST 1982 COMMUNIQUE. This US–China communiqué came after two years of discord that saw heavy Chinese pressure on Washington to curb and stop arms sales to Taipei, and debate in the United States on how far to go in meeting the Chinese demands. In the communiqué, the United States agreed gradually to diminish arms sales, and China agreed it would seek peaceful reunification of Taiwan with the mainland. Subsequent developments showed that the vague agreement was subject to varying interpretations. Notably, President **George H. W. Bush** agreed in 1992 to sell 150 F-16 fighters to Taiwan, a deal worth over five times the value of US arms sales to Taiwan in 1982.

– B –

BAKER, JAMES A. III (1930–). As secretary of state in the **George H. W. Bush** administration, Baker, a personal friend of the president, understood well the president's strong interest in US policy toward China. He and the State Department followed the lead of the president and his senior White House advisors in dealing with the American outrage over the **Tiananmen crackdown** of 1989 and the concurrent international transformation caused by the collapse of the Soviet Bloc and subsequent decline in American interest in using China as a counterweight to the Soviet Union. Baker felt that little was accomplished through secret missions and other US initiatives to Chinese leaders, who seemed unable or unwilling to modify Beijing's hard political line flowing from the Tiananmen crackdown and the collapse of world communism. *See also* HUMAN RIGHTS.

BALLISTIC MISSILE DEFENSE. As the US government moved forward with ballistic missile defense programs in the 1990s, Chinese officials argued strenuously against them. They demanded that the United States adhere to the strict limits for deploying ballistic missile defenses set forth in the 1972 **Anti-Ballistic Missile (ABM) Treaty** between the United States and the Soviet Union. Chinese opposition subsided as Russia decided not to resist moves by the **George W. Bush** administration to end the treaty and move ahead vigorously with ballistic missile defense programs, though Chinese officials still saw the US missile defense programs as a serious challenge to the ability of Chinese missiles to strike at the United States. They also opposed US efforts to develop and deploy **theater missile defense** systems in East Asia, and to share these systems with Japan and Taiwan.

BANDUNG CONFERENCE. This conference of Afro-Asian leaders was hosted by Indonesia in April 1955. Chinese Premier **Zhou Enlai** used it to offer a more moderate Chinese approach to the United States following years of hostility and months of military action and threats in the **Taiwan Strait**. His approach led the way to the start of US–China **ambassadorial talks** in Geneva in summer 1955.

BARNETT, A. DOAK (1921–1999). A journalist, teacher, and scholar, Barnett remained one of the top US specialists on China throughout the Cold War. Called upon repeatedly to advise US administrations, to testify before congressional committees, and to pursue public policy studies seeking new approaches to US policy toward China, Barnett sought to deepen Sino–American understanding, build closer interchange between the two estranged countries, and pursue balanced and moderate approaches in American relations toward China.

BARSHEFSKY, CHARLENE (1951–). As the US special trade representative in the second term of the **William Clinton** administration, Barshefsky was the lead US negotiator with China over conditions governing China's entry into the **World Trade Organization.** The US–China agreement reached in late 1999 paved the way for US legislation in 2000 granting China **permanent normal trade relations (PNTR)** trading status.

BATTLE ACT. This act was one of several pieces of legislation passed during the **Korean War** that severely restricted US and other countries' trade and other relations with China. The act threatened penalties against any country that sold a wide variety of products to China.

BAYARD, THOMAS (1828–1898). As secretary of state in the **Grover Cleveland** administration, Bayard negotiated a treaty with China in 1888 regarding restrictions on Chinese **immigration** to the United States and American protection for Chinese in the United States. The treaty failed to get Chinese government approval while President Cleveland moved to support US legislation requiring a tougher approach to Chinese immigration. *See also* EXCLUSION MOVEMENT.

BELGRADE, US BOMBING OF CHINESE EMBASSY. During US-led air attacks in a war against the former Yugoslavia in 1999, two US planes on 7 May 1999 dropped guided gravity bombs on various targets. One target was misidentified by American forces and turned out to be the Chinese embassy. It was hit by three bombs, killing three, wounding 20, and causing great damage to the building. The reaction in China included mobs stoning the US embassy in Beijing and burning US diplomatic property in Chengtu. Both governments restored calm and dealt with some of the consequences of the bombing, but Beijing and Washington never came to an agreement on what had happened and whether the United States had explained its actions appropriately. It was the most serious incident in US–China relations in the years following the **Tiananmen crackdown** of 1989.

BENTSEN, LLOYD (1921–). As secretary of the treasury in the first term of the **William Clinton** administration, Bentsen advised the president in early 1994 against continuing a policy supported by the State Department that linked US granting **most-favored-nation tariff status** to China with Chinese government improvements in human rights policy and practice. The president decided to abandon the policy in May 1994.

BEREUTER, DOUGLAS (1939–). A Republican congressman from Nebraska, Bereuter chaired the US House of Representatives subcommittee dealing with East Asia affairs in the mid-late 1990s, proposing and passing legislation that allowed strong congressional criticism of China, passage of continued **most-favored-nation tariff status** for China, and passage of **permanent normal trade relations** for China. He also chaired or helped to establish congressional oversight bodies assessing China's policies and behavior toward **Hong Kong** and Chinese **human rights**, labor, and democracy practices.

BERGER, SAMUEL (1945–). Berger's promotion from deputy national security adviser to national security adviser at the start of the second term of the **William Clinton** administration formalized his predominance as the president's closest and most influential foreign policy adviser. In the second term of the Clinton administration, China policy in general was made by the president and the vice president and their close White House advisers. Berger supported the president's more activist and positive **engagement policy** with China through such high points as the China–US summits in 1997 and 1998, the Sino–US agreement on China's entry into the **World Trade Organization** in 1999, and passage of US legislation in 2000 granting China **permanent normal trade relations**; and through such low points as the intense congressional debate over the president's stance against Taiwan independence (the **three nos**) in 1998, the May 1999 bombing of the Chinese Embassy in **Belgrade**, and strident congressional criticism in the **Cox Committee** report of May 1999 charging administration officials with gross malfeasance in guarding US secrets and weaponry from Chinese spies.

BLUE SHIRTS. Dai Li was selected by **Chiang Kai-shek** in 1934 to lead a fascist-style police force within the **Kuomintang (KMT)**, known as the Blue Shirts. The group modeled itself on the private party armies created by Adolf Hitler and Benito Mussolini to suppress dissent. Some American officials cooperated with Dai Li and his secret police, though the police also reinforced American views of Chiang Kai-shek's regime as a fascist regime.

BOEING. With over half the jetliners in the growing China market coming from Boeing by the end of the 20th century, the US company was a strong advocate of constructive economic and **trade** relations with China despite US differences with China over political, security, and other issues.

BORODIN, MICHAEL (1884–1951). Sent by the **Comintern** to Canton in 1923, Borodin became **Sun Yat-sen**'s adviser, moved the **Nationalist Party** closer to the model of the Soviet Communist Party, and gave Sun's followers lessons in mobilizing mass support. He fled China amid the **White Terror** of 1927 as **Chiang Kai-shek** established his leadership and moved the Nationalist regime closer to the United States and the West.

BOSNIA. The Chinese government supported the sovereignty and integrity of Yugoslavia and strongly disagreed with US and Western sanctions and military intervention in Bosnia, then a disputed part of Yugoslavia, in the 1990s. *See also* BELGRADE, US BOMBING OF CHINESE EMBASSY.

BOWLES, CHESTER (1901–1986). A high-ranking diplomat during the **John Kennedy** administration, Bowles along with **Adlai Stevenson** and others felt that Kennedy's firm stance against the Chinese government was unwarranted. He argued that China's threats were largely empty words, unable to be carried out by the Chinese. He felt that nationalism was the key to preventing the spread and consolidation of communism and judged that the United States should adjust policies to be more in accord with Chinese nationalism.

BOXER INDEMNITY. The United States government remitted to China for use in **education** some of the funds it received from China, about $25 million, as compensation for the costs associated with the **Boxer uprising** of 1899–1900.

BOXER PROTOCOL. This agreement of September 1901 between China and the concerned foreign powers, including the United States, mandated among other things punishments China would carry out against officials who supported the **Boxer uprising**, foreign garrisons to guarantee security of foreign legations, and a Chinese indemnity of $333 million. *See* BOXER INDEMNITY.

BOXER UPRISING. A grassroots anti-foreign insurrection in northern China, known as the Boxers, came to receive support from some Chinese officials, and by 1899 and 1900 it was carrying out widespread attacks against foreign **missionaries** and Chinese Christians. As the movement grew, it received the support of the **Qing dynasty** court, though regional leaders in most of China did not support the Boxers. The insurgents occupied Peking and Tientsin, besieging foreign legations and settlements. About 20,000 foreign troops were mustered, including thousands of Americans, to end the siege and put down the insurgents. They ended the siege of Tientsin in July and Peking in August. Many troops stayed, carrying out punitive expeditions.

BRAINWASHING. Chinese officials were accused by Americans of using strenuous thought reform techniques common in China in the early years of **Communist Party** rule to win over American and Allied prisoners of war to the Communist cause during the **Korean War**. The Americans called this Chinese action brainwashing.

BREWSTER, OWEN (1888–1961). Brewster served as US senator from Maine from 1941–1952. He spoke out against President **Harry Truman**'s policy of restricted aid to China, claiming that more support was needed for **Chiang Kai-shek** and his **Nationalist Party** government. However, he did not believe that American troops should be sent to assist the Nationalists in their armed struggle against the **Communist Party**.

BREZHNEV DOCTRINE. Named after Soviet leader **Leonid Brezhnev** following his orders for Soviet troops to invade Czechoslovakia to topple what was seen as a deviant Communist government in August 1968, this doctrine gave the Soviet Union the right to intervene against other such regimes. The Chinese viewed this as a threat, especially in light of the buildup of Soviet forces along the Chinese border since the start of Brezhnev's leadership in 1964. This situation prompted Chinese leaders to debate options, with some seeking better relations with the United States as a useful way to counter the newly apparent Soviet threat.

BREZHNEV, LEONID ILYICH (1906–1982). As Soviet Communist Party leader from 1964–1982, Brezhnev rarely deviated from a tough line against China and often sought to pressure Chinese leaders with military deployments and strategic alignments around China's periphery. The rapid rise of Soviet military power and expanding Soviet international influence during his rule alarmed both Chinese and US leaders, providing common ground between China and the United States in opposition to Soviet **"hegemonism."** *See also* BREZHNEV DOCTRINE.

BRIDGES, STYLES (1898–1961). A US senator in the late 1940s and early 1950s, Bridges often spoke out against the actions of **Mao Zedong** and the **Communist Party** regime, while supporting **Chiang Kai-shek** and his **Nationalist Party** regime.

BRIDGMAN, ELIJAH C. (1801–1861) An American Protestant missionary sent to China in 1830, Bridgman was a leader in the small US community of **missionaries** and others in China for decades. In 1838 he published in Chinese a book about the United States that proved to be an important source at the time for Chinese officials and other readers seeking understanding of the United States.

BRITISH AMERICAN TOBACCO. This firm, with American tobacco interests holding the majority of stock, set up operations in China and by 1916 was producing annually 12 billon cigarettes for the Chinese market.

BROWN, HAROLD (1927–). As secretary of defense during the **Jimmy Carter** administration, Brown traveled to China in 1980, in the aftermath of the Soviet invasion of **Afghanistan**, and informed Chinese leaders of a US decision to sell China "non-lethal" defense equipment including air defense radar, computers, communication equipment, and transportation helicopters.

BROWN, RONALD (1941–1996). Secretary of commerce in the first term of the **William Clinton** administration, Brown advised the president in early 1994 against continuing a policy supported by the State Department that linked the US's granting **most-favored-nation tariff status** to China with Chinese government improvements in **human rights** policy and practice. The president decided to abandon the policy in May 1994.

BRUCE, DAVID (1998–1977). An experienced diplomat, Bruce served from 1973–1974 as the first head of the American **liaison office** in China.

BRYAN, WILLIAM JENNINGS (1860–1925). Appointed to the post of secretary of state in 1913 by President **Woodrow Wilson**, Bryan served until 1915. In 1913, reflecting new policy direction of the Wilson administration, Bryan supported the decision for the United States to withdraw from a consortium of foreign banks that were planning and carrying out loans to the Chinese government. He felt the consortium process made China a virtual vassal state under the powers controlling the loans. Bryan also supported China in 1915, when he spoke out against Japanese demands levied against China. The **Twenty-One Demands** were modified as a result of US and other foreign pressure, though the weak Chinese government was compelled to accept most of the Japanese conditions, which Bryan said for the record that the United States would not recognize. *See also* NON-RECOGNITION DOCTRINE.

BRZEZINSKI, ZBIGNIEW (1928–). President **Jimmy Carter**'s National Security Adviser Brzezinski was in the lead in seeking an agreement with China normalizing US–China relations in 1978, and in subsequent steps to advance US–China relations as a means to counter Soviet power and expansion. Carter followed Brzezinski's advice against that of Secretary of State **Cyrus Vance** who gave a higher priority to US–Soviet arms control agreements. Carter and Brzezinski followed the path of secret diplomacy used successfully by President **Richard Nixon** and National Security Adviser **Henry Kissinger** in early interaction with China, but they were less successful as Congress resisted the president's initiatives and passed laws tying the hands of the administration on Taiwan and other issues. *See also* CHINA CARD; TAIWAN RELATIONS ACT; UNITED STATES–CHINA COMMUNIQUE OF 1978.

BUCHANAN, PATRICK (1938–). A conservative commentator known for isolationist views in foreign affairs who periodically ran for the US presidency in the 1990s, Buchanan was a constant critic of Chinese government political, economic, and security policies after the **Tiananmen crackdown** of 1989.

BUCK, PEARL (1892–1973). Pearl Buck was the daughter of American **missionaries** who spent most of her childhood in China. She wrote a novel in 1931 on Chinese life called *The Good Earth*, which won the Pulitzer Prize. The book and a subsequent movie in 1937 added to the period's growing American sympathy for China.

BULLITT, WILLIAM (1891–1967). Having served earlier as US Ambassador to Russia, Bullitt came to prominence with charges he made in 1947 that the **Franklin D. Roosevelt** and **Harry Truman** administrations were selling out China. Bullitt judged that China must be kept from falling under the control of the Soviet Union. He argued that $1 billion of American aid for **Chiang Kai-shek** and his **Nationalist Party** forces was needed urgently. In his view, the fall of China to the Soviet Union would lead to the fall of the United States.

BURLINGAME, ANSON (1820–1870). Anson Burlingame served as minister to China from 1861–1867. He tended to support US cooperation with the Chinese government. After leaving his position as minister, he accepted a Chinese offer to head a delegation to observe and have talks with the West. The trip was moderately successful, meeting acceptance notably in America and England. *See also* BURLINGAME TREATY.

BURLINGAME TREATY. This treaty was signed by Chinese and US representatives during the visit of a Chinese delegation led by **Anson**

Burlingame to the United States in 1868. Among other provisions in the treaty, the United States said it would not interfere in the internal development of China, China recognized the right of its people to emigrate, and the United States gave Chinese immigrants the right to enter the United States. The latter pledge would soon be challenged by anti-Chinese **immigration** advocates in the United States. *See also* EXCLUSION MOVEMENT.

BURMA ROAD. This route connected the interior of China, where **Chiang Kai-shek** and his **Nationalist Party** government had their wartime capital, with Burma and the sea. It was closed to the Allies as a result of Japanese military advances in 1942 and was not re-opened until the latter stage of World War II. As a result, it was difficult for the United States to supply Chiang Kai-shek's armies.

BURTON, DAN (1938–). This Republican congressman from Indiana in the late 1990s used his committee chairmanship to investigate **William Clinton** administration fund-raising that allegedly involved illegal contributions from Chinese backers in return for the administration's turning a blind eye to Chinese illegal trading practices and Chinese espionage activities in the United States.

BUSH, GEORGE H. W. (1924–). As US representative to the United Nations, Bush led the vain US effort to preserve a seat for Taiwan as the United Nations voted to admit China in 1971. He served as the head of the US **liaison office** in China in the mid-1970s. As **Ronald Reagan**'s vice presidential running mate, he traveled to China in mid-1980 to explain Reagan's China policy to skeptical Chinese leaders. Bush took the lead in his own administration, 1989–1993, in dealing with severe problems in China–US relations caused by the **Tiananmen crackdown** and the decline in US strategic interest in China as a result of the collapse of the Soviet Bloc. He resorted to secret diplomacy to achieve constructive understandings with senior Chinese leaders, but the latter remained fairly rigid and were unable to make many gestures to help Bush to justify a continued moderate US stance toward China amid wide-ranging US skepticism and hostility in the Congress, media, and interest groups. Bush upgraded US interchange with Taiwan by sending a cabinet-level official, US Special Trade Representative **Carla Hills**, to Taiwan in 1992. He also seemed to abandon the limits on US arms sales set in accord with the **17 August 1982 communiqué** between the United States and China by agreeing in 1992 to a sale of 150 advanced F-16 jet fighters to Taiwan worth over $5 billion.

BUSH, GEORGE W. (1946–). The son of George H. W. Bush, George W. Bush became president in 2001 with a tougher policy toward China than the policy of his predecessor, **William Clinton**. Seeking to sustain economic relations with China, the new president was wary of China's strategic intentions and took steps to deter China from using military force against Taiwan. Relations deteriorated when a US reconnaissance aircraft, the EP-3, crashed with a Chinese jet fighter on 1 April 2001, but both governments worked to resolve the issue and establish a businesslike relationship that emphasized positive aspects and played down differences. The terrorist attack on America on 11 September 2001 diverted US attention from China as a potential strategic threat. Preoccupied with leadership transition and other issues in China, Chinese leaders moderated previous harsh rhetoric and pressure tactics in order to consolidate relations with the United States. The two powers found new common ground in dealing with the crisis caused by **North Korea's nuclear weapons program** beginning in 2002, and the Chinese appreciated Bush's warning in December 2003 to Taiwan's leader **Chen Shui-bian** to avoid steps toward independence for Taiwan that would lead to conflict in the **Taiwan Strait**. *See also* EP-3 INCIDENT.

BUTCHERS OF BEIJING. This term was used for many years by US media and other critics of the Chinese government's killing of unarmed demonstrators during the **Tiananmen crackdown** of June 1989 to refer to senior Chinese leaders responsible for the crackdown. The negative US publicity associated with such Chinese leaders, notably Premier **Li Peng**, complicated US leaders' meetings with these Chinese officials.

BUTTERWORTH, W. WALTON (1903–1975). Serving as head of the State Department's Bureau of Far Eastern Affairs in the late 1940s, Butterworth believed that the United States should practice restraint in the case of China's civil war. He felt, like many fellow advisors in the **Harry Truman** administration, that more money than was acceptable would be needed to win the war against the **Communist Party** forces.

– C –

CC CLIQUE. This term refers to a conservative faction of the **Nationalist Party** that was powerful both before and after the Nationalist regime moved to Taiwan in 1949. CC refers to the main leaders, Chen Kuo-fu and Chen Li-fu, who were brothers and close advisors to **Chiang Kai-shek**. They tended to resist US and other pressures for reform in the Nationalist regime.

CAIRO DECLARATION. This proclamation was issued following the Cairo Conference in 1943 of President **Franklin D. Roosevelt**, British Prime Minister **Winston Churchill**, and Chinese President **Chiang Kai-shek**. The declaration said that "territories Japan has stolen . . . such as Manchuria, **Formosa**, and the **Pescadores**," would be returned to China.

CAMBODIA. The **Richard Nixon** administration in 1970 launched a US-led military assault against Communist forces in Cambodia that saw China react with strong anti-US statements and suspension of **ambassadorial talks** with the United States. Opposition to the invasion and occupation of Cambodia by **Vietnam** in 1978 provided common ground between Beijing and Washington at the time of normalization of US–China diplomatic relations and Chinese leader **Deng Xiaoping**'s visit to the United States in January 1979. Though US policy opposed the odious Chinese-backed **Khmer Rouge** regime toppled by the Vietnamese, the United States and China worked pragmatically to shore up resistance against the Vietnamese occupiers and their Soviet supporters. China launched a military assault to destroy some Vietnamese border regions in 1979 and subsequently shelled and harassed Vietnamese defenders along the border. It continued support for Khmer Rouge guerrillas. US backing focused on non-Communist Cambodian resistance and shored up resolve by neighboring states to work against the Vietnamese occupation. As the Soviet Union declined in the 1980s, it scaled back support for Vietnam, which in turn decided to withdraw from Cambodia. The United States worked with other powers in reaching a peace agreement on Cambodia in 1991, made possible after China ended support for the Khmer Rouge, compelling it to come to terms with other Cambodian factions.

CANTON SYSTEM. When American traders went to China prior to the **Opium War** of 1839–1842, Chinese regulations under the **Tribute System** in foreign affairs confined them, along with most other foreign maritime traders, to Canton. There, local officials supervised and taxed foreign **trade**, foreigners were required to live and work in a designated area of Canton during the trading season, and foreign interaction with Chinese was kept to a minimum. Certain Chinese merchants were designated to deal with foreign merchants. This arrangement was known as the Canton system.

CARTER, JIMMY (1924–). Desiring to complete the normalization of US–China relations begun by **Richard Nixon**, Carter waited until after his success in spring 1978 in gaining Senate passage of a controversial treaty transferring control of the **Panama Canal** to Panama. Carter's senior advisers were divided over China policy. National Security Adviser **Zbigniew Brzezinski** was in the lead in seeking rapid progress in normalizing US–China relations in 1978, and in subsequent steps to advance US–China relations as a means to counter Soviet power and expansion. Carter followed Brzezinski's advice against that of Secretary of State **Cyrus Vance** who gave a higher priority to US–Soviet arms control agreements. Following the Soviet invasion of **Afghanistan** in late 1979, Carter sent Defense Secretary **Harold Brown** to China to improve US–China strategic cooperation and to inform the Chinese leadership of a US decision to sell non-lethal military equipment to China. In pursuing normalization of relations with China, Carter followed the pattern of secret diplomacy used successfully by President Nixon and National Security Adviser **Henry Kissinger** in early interaction with China, but he was less successful as Congress resisted President Carter's initiatives and passed laws, notably the **Taiwan Relations Act**, that tied the hands of the administration on Taiwan and other issues.

CARLSON, EVANS (1896–1947). In 1937–1938, Carlson was a US military attaché in China, where he assessed the **Communist Party** military forces. He was impressed with the Communist army and political structure. He resigned from the US military and pursued enthusiastic writings on the Chinese Communist forces and related subjects.

CASS, LEWIS (1782–1866). As secretary of state under President James Buchanan from 1857–1860, Cass followed a policy of avoiding direct US use of force in China, but he supported British and French efforts, backed by their military forces, to seek greater **trade**, opportunities for **missionaries**, and more equal diplomatic interchanges and access to the Chinese government under terms of new treaties with China. Cass instructed American minister to China **William Reed** to inform China that the United States had no imperial aspirations towards China but supported the actions of Britain and France. Cass also instructed Reed to offer the services of the United States as a mediator between China and the two European powers.

CASSIDY AND ASSOCIATES. This public relations firm in Washington, D.C. was already working for Taiwan clients when news reports in 1994 said it received $2.5 million from supporters of Taiwan President **Lee Teng-hui** with the goal to change US government policy so that Lee could obtain a visa to return to his alma mater, Cornell University. Lee received a visa in 1995.

CENTRAL INTELLIGENCE AGENCY (CIA). Created at the outset of the Cold War, this US government agency was able to carry out operations and initiatives, and to share intelligence, hidden from public view. These attributes proved useful to various US administrations. The agency was deeply involved with US support for **Chiang Kai-shek** and the **Nationalist Party** regime on Taiwan after the start of the **Korean War**. Some CIA operatives were captured by the Chinese **Communist Party** regime as they worked with Chinese Nationalist forces infiltrating mainland China. The agency supported Tibetan resistance to Chinese rule at the time of the uprising there in 1959. The US normalization with China saw a cutback in CIA support for operations against China, though close CIA ties with Taiwan persisted. President **Jimmy Carter** authorized the CIA to work closely with Chinese counterparts in providing clandestine support to the anti-Soviet resistance in **Afghanistan**, and there were reports of CIA involvement in working with China to monitor Soviet missile tests from sites in China and in cooperating to support resistance to the occupation of **Cambodia** by **Vietnam**.

CHAN, CHARLIE. Though US popular culture at the time tended to ignore the realities of China and Chinese people at home and abroad, several dozen films over the course of four decades in the middle of the 20th century featured this Chinese–American character, a Honolulu-based detective, highlighting positively his wisdom and resourcefulness. An equally prominent Chinese character in US movies in the mid-20th century was the bloodthirsty Dr. **Fu Manchu**, who tortured victims in pursuit of lust and power.

CHANG CHIH-TUNG (ZHANG ZHIDONG) (1837–1909). A powerful Chinese official, well entrenched as governor-general in the provinces, Chang endeavored in the period after Japan's defeat of China in 1895 and subsequent European powers' extortion of concessions, to cooperate with the United States as a power opposing seizure of Chinese territory. Though he supported China's reliance on Russia after the defeat by Japan in 1895, he came by 1898 to seek the support of Britain and the United States, viewing them as commercial powers with substantial interests in blocking seizures of Chinese territory by Japan, Russia, and others. That year, he entrusted an American consortium to build the **Hankow–Canton railway**. He made initiatives to the United States during and after the **Boxer uprising**, seeking US mediation with the foreign powers and US assistance in moderating the foreign reaction to the crisis. Chang sought without much success US help in limiting the size of the foreign indemnity and in dealing with Russian military occupation of Manchuria after the Boxer uprising. He became disillusioned with the American consortium for the Hankow–Canton railroad and sought and ultimately accomplished China's buying back the concession. Chang intervened at several points with the Chinese central government and the US government, emphasizing strong antipathy among Chinese patriots over the US exclusion of Chinese in the late 19th century and the early 20th century. During the **anti-American boycott** of 1905, prompted heavily by Chinese resentment over US restrictions on Chinese immigration, Chang privately advised President **Theodore Roosevelt** to ease the US restrictions. *See also* AMERICAN CHINA DEVELOPMENT COMPANY; EXCLUSION MOVEMENT.

CHANG YIN-HUAN (ZHANG YINHUAN) (1837–1900). As Chinese minister in Washington in 1885–1889, Chang followed and implemented a policy developed by his predecessor as minister, **Cheng Tsao-ju**. The policy sought to deal with rising friction in US–China relations over American discrimination and violence against Chinese in the United States, by reaching an agreement that would include American protection of Chinese and US indemnities for losses of Chinese suffering violence in the United States, in return for Chinese restrictions on emigration to the United States. A treaty was reached in 1888, but met with resistance in China and the United States, as the Chinese government withheld formal approval of the agreement. *See also* BAYARD, THOMAS; EXCLUSION MOVEMENT; IMMIGRATION.

CHEMICAL WEAPONS CONVENTION. As part of Chinese efforts to abide by international norms regarding the proliferation of weapons of mass destruction, China in 1993 signed this convention regulating the sale of dangerous compounds and ingredients used to manufacture chemical and biological weapons. The step helped to improve Sino–American relations during a difficult period.

CHENEY, RICHARD (1941–). A Republican congressman who later served as White House chief-of-staff for President **Gerald Ford**, and as secretary of defense for President **George H. W. Bush**, Cheney occasionally influenced China policy. In 1992, he strongly supported the sale of F-16 fighters to Taiwan. His more important role in US–China policy came as he served as vice president in the **George W. Bush** administration. Cheney appointed to his influential staff officials wary of China and supportive of Taiwan. Cheney in 2002 hosted visiting Chinese Vice President and soon-to-be party leader and President **Hu Jintao**, strengthening frank and businesslike relations between the two governments. His visit to China in 2004 deepened common ground between the two administrations.

CHENG TSAO-JU (ZHENG ZAORU). As Chinese minister in Washington in 1881–1885, Cheng formulated a policy developed by his successor as minister, **Chang Yin-huan**, in 1885–1889. The policy sought to deal with rising friction in US–China relations over American discrimination and violence against Chinese in the United States, by reaching an agreement that would include American protection of Chinese and US indemnities for losses of Chinese suffering violence in the United States, in return for Chinese restrictions on emigration to the United States. A treaty was reached in 1888, but met with resistance in China and the United States, as the Chinese government withheld formal approval of the agreement. *See also* BAYARD,THOMAS; EXCLUSION MOVEMENT; IMMIGRATION.

CHEN SHUI-BIAN (1950–). Chen was the first president of Taiwan who was not a member of the **Nationalist Party**. His election in 2000 and his reelection in 2004 showed that one-party rule was finished in Taiwan and that Chen's **Democratic Progressive Party (DPP)** was emerging as the dominant political party on the island. US policy welcomed the evidence of deepening democracy in Taiwan but feared that Chen would be inclined to pursue DPP goals asserting Taiwan's separate status and independence from China. Chinese officials distrusted Chen, warned of military attack if Taiwan moved toward independence, and supported Chen's political opponents whose views of Taiwan's status were more compatible with China's. In this context, US policy supported Taiwan militarily in order to deter attack from the Chinese mainland, while it pressured Chen to curb moves toward greater independence that might provoke a Chinese attack.

CHEN YI (1901–1972). This respected military leader served as Chinese foreign minister in the 1950s and 1960s. He duly followed the leadership's generally tough line toward the United States during this period.

CH'EN YI (CHEN YI) (1883–1950). The first governor of Taiwan after World War II, Chen was responsible for misrule that contributed to the mass uprising on the island in February 1947 and a bloody crackdown, strengthening US official views of the corruption and brutality of the **Nationalist Party** regime. *See also* FEBRUARY 28 UPRISING.

CHENNAULT, CLAIRE (1890–1958). Chennault was a US military pilot who, after his retirement, became an adviser to **Chiang Kai-shek** in 1937. In 1940, Chennault returned to the United States to request planes for a joint US–China force to fight against the Japanese. Subsequently, the **American Volunteer Group** was formed to train Chinese pilots and to fly fighter planes in defense of China. The group became known as the **"Flying Tigers"** and was involved in combat with Japanese forces. In 1942, Chennault became embroiled in an argument with the commanding US general in China, **Joseph Stilwell**, regarding the viability of using Chinese air bases to strike at Japanese shipping and home islands. Chennault argued that air attacks from China on Japan and Japanese forces would be an effective strategy to help defeat Japan. He lobbied President **Franklin D. Roosevelt** and White House aides. This strategy was opposed by Stilwell, but was supported by Chiang Kai-shek. It was approved by Roosevelt, though it subsequently failed as strong Japanese ground attacks destroyed US air bases in China.

CHI HAOTIAN (1929–). Chinese Defense Minister Chi delayed a scheduled visit to the United States in 1995 at first because of Chinese objections to the visit of Taiwan leader **Lee Teng-hui** to the United States, and later because of US objections to China's provocative military posture in the **Taiwan Strait**. The visit took place in December 1996, signaling a revival of high-level Sino–US military dialogue amid continuing differences over Taiwan, the **Tiananmen crackdown**, and other issues.

CHIANG CHING-KUO (JIANG QINGGUO) (1910–1988). As a close advisor to his father, President **Chiang Kai-shek**, Chiang played a key role in security and intelligence issues as the **Nationalist Party** regime rebuilt with US support following its retreat to Taiwan. He became premier in 1972 and president in 1978. He witnessed the steady erosion of US official ties with Taiwan, culminating with the break in all official ties, including the US defense treaty with Taiwan, in 1979. Chiang reacted pragmatically, endeavoring to develop substantive relations with the United States under the rubric of ostensibly unofficial ties, while pursuing reforms that opened Taiwan to democracy—a step welcomed in the United States.

CHIANG KAI-SHEK (JIANG JIESHI) (1887–1975). A revolutionary and military leader, Chiang assumed a leadership position in the **Nationalist Party** following the death of **Sun Yat-sen** in 1925. Launching a military expedition from southern China in 1926, he strengthened a still-tenuous position as China's dominant leader by 1928. Over the next decade, Chiang endeavored to consolidate his leadership position and pursue nation building while facing strong resistance from Japan and seeking to destroy **Communist Party** insurgents. Forced to come to terms with the Chinese Communists in late 1936, Chiang and his armies by 1937 were compelled to retreat into the interior of China as Japanese forces launched all-out war in 1937 and occupied much of eastern China. Chiang sought US support with only modest success until the Japanese attack on **Pearl Harbor** brought the United States into World War II. Chiang was dissatisfied with the relatively low priority the United States attached to the China theater during the war, the low level of US assistance able to reach China because of Japan's control of most supply routes, and US demands that China do more to confront the Japanese.

Chiang maneuvered with some success against US pressures for greater war efforts against Japan, internal reforms, and more cooperation with Chinese Communist forces resisting Japan. The end of World War II in China saw US policy side strongly with Chiang against the Chinese Communists, although there were active US mediation efforts to avoid a Chinese civil war. The **Harry Truman** administration eventually cut support for Chiang amid strong criticism from Chiang's supporters in the US Congress and media, but the policy was reversed after North Korea attacked South Korea in June 1950 and started the **Korean War**. During the 1950s and 1960s, the United States supported Taiwan as an important bulwark against the spread of hostile Communist expansion in Asia. Chiang was unable to halt the shift in US policy as President **Richard Nixon** by 1969 sought improved relations with China and cut back ties with Taiwan as a means to extricate the United States from its debilitating involvement in **Vietnam**, seek greater leverage against the Soviet Union, and create a new order in Asia less dependent on US military forces in the region. *See also* SOONG MAYLING.

CHIANG KAI-SHEK, MADAME. *See* SOONG MAYLING.

CHINA AID ACT. The **Harry Truman** administration in 1948 supported this allocation of $125 million for the failing **Nationalist Party** government in China in part in order to avoid resistance from pro-**Chiang Kai-shek** congressional members regarding the administration's requests for funding the Marshall Plan for Europe and Japan.

CHINA–BURMA–INDIA THEATER. This area of the US war effort after US entry into World War II received low priority. **Chiang Kai-shek** complained about inadequate US supplies while the American commander in China, General **Joseph Stilwell**, complained about Chiang's unwillingness to initiate a campaign to reopen the **Burma Road**, aggressively fight the Japanese, or enact military reforms.

CHINA "CARD." Considering reasons for the United States to pursue improved relations with China in the 1970s and 1980s, proponents of the United States "playing the China card" argued that improved US relations with China would cause the main US adversary, the Soviet Union, to react with alarm at a growing US–China united front and to seek accommodation with the United States in arms control agreements and other matters advantageous to the United States.

CHINA COMMITTEE, COORDINATING COMMITTEE OF EXPORTS TO COMMUNIST AREAS (COCOM). During the Cold War, this US-dominated group set guidelines for which manufactured products the European Allies and Japan could sell to China, and worked to restrict Chinese access to credit. Pressured by Washington, the committee imposed far stricter **trade** barriers on China than those applied to the Soviet Bloc, leading to the so-called **China "differential."**

CHINA DEFENSE SUPPLIES. This is the name of a company, successor to **Universal Trading Corporation**, which received US credits to support **Chiang Kai-shek's Nationalist Party** government against Japanese aggression in the years prior to the Japanese attack on **Pearl Harbor.**

CHINA "DIFFERENTIAL." US demands in the 1950s that Allied exports to China be more restrictive than Allied exports to the Soviet Bloc infuriated the Allies and received ambiguous backing from President **Dwight Eisenhower**. After 1957, the so-called China differential was abandoned. The Allies were permitted to sell to China the same goods they sold to the Soviet Union. For its part, the United States maintained a nearly total **trade** embargo on China until 1971. *See* CHINA COMMITTEE, COORDINATING COMMITTEE OF EXPORT TO COMMUNIST AREAS (COCOM).

CHINA FOUNDATION FOR THE PROMOTION OF EDUCATION AND CULTURE. Established in 1924, this body used funds from the US share of the **Boxer indemnity** that were returned for use in China to foster **education** and academic pursuits in China.

CHINA INLAND MISSION. Established in 1866, this evangelical agency grew to be the largest of all Protestant mission agencies in China, recruiting British, American, and other Western **missionaries** for work throughout China.

CHINA INTERNATIONAL FAMINE RELIEF COMMISSION. Responding to famine in China, many **missionaries** from the United States and elsewhere participated in this organization that by 1936 had used $50 million in foreign contributions for rural improvements in famine areas in China.

CHINA–JAPAN PEACE AND FRIENDSHIP TREATY. Signed in 1978, this agreement ended the state of war between China and Japan dating back to World War II, and underlined the two sides' opposition to **"hegemonism,"** China's codeword for Soviet expansionism and encirclement of China. It coincided with Beijing's normalization of relations with Washington on an implicitly anti-Soviet basis, and

Moscow's alignment with **Vietnam** as it prepared to topple the Chinese-backed **Khmer Rouge** regime in **Cambodia**.

CHINA LOBBY. With roots going back to Chinese **Nationalist Party** efforts, before the Japanese attack on **Pearl Harbor**, to foster a group of Americans to promote US support for China in the war against Japan, these American supporters of **Chiang Kai-shek** strongly backed the Chinese Nationalists and opposed the Chinese **Communist Party** leaders and policies before and after Chiang Kai-shek's retreat to Taiwan in 1949. Their influence on US policy appeared to wane as President **Richard Nixon** moved to improve relations with China in the 1970s.

CHINA POLICY ACT, 1995. Developed by Congressman **Douglas Bereuter** with the encouragement of the **William Clinton** administration, this legislation contained a long list of complaints about Chinese government policies and practices. Strongly supporting this legislation allowed congress to vent its anger at the Chinese government while simultaneously voting separately to sustain **most-favored-nation tariff status** for China for another year.

CHINA "WHITE PAPER." This lengthy (over 1,000 pages) document was issued by the US Department of State in August 1949. It was critical of **Chiang Kai-shek** and the **Nationalist Party** regime for corruption and other failures as they lost the **Chinese Civil War** with the Chinese **Communist Party** forces. The report served to support **Harry Truman** administration efforts to cut US support for Chiang's Nationalists. It was attacked by Chinese Nationalists, Chinese Communists, and many US supporters of Chiang Kai-shek.

CHINA'S DESTINY. Written by **Chiang Kai-shek** and published in 1943, this book reflected Chiang's conservative nationalism and strong anti-imperialism. He blamed China's ills on the **unequal treaties** and the foreign powers that benefited from them, including the United States.

CHINCHOW–AIGUN RAILROAD. Former American consul general in Mukden, Manchuria, **Willard Straight** signed an agreement with Chinese authorities in Manchuria in October 1909 to have an American banking group finance a railroad between these two cities. Before moving forward with the deal, the Chinese authorities in Peking awaited US efforts to deal with expected Japanese and Russian anger over this challenge to their spheres of influence in Manchuria. In response, Secretary of State **Philander Knox** proposed a bold scheme to internationalize all railroads in Manchuria. Japan and Russia rejected his plan and warned against the Chinchow–Aigun railroad, which also failed to get Chinese government approval. *See also* DOLLAR DIPLOMACY.

CHINESE CHARACTERISTCS. **Arthur Smith**, an influential spokesperson for **missionaries** in China, was pessimistic about China's future amid the anti-missionary violence and chaos leading to the **Boxer uprising** of 1899–1900. His book, *Chinese Characteristics,* published in the 1890s, was widely read by US officials and other Americans interested in China. It portrayed Chinese society negatively, with backward-looking, morally deficient people.

CHINESE CIVIL WAR. Though there were periodic truces and peace talks, this war between the Chinese **Nationalist Party** forces and the Chinese **Communist Party** forces was seen to have begun with Japan's defeat in 1945 and to have lasted on the Chinese mainland until 1949. *See also* MARSHALL, GEORGE.

CHINESE EXCLUSION ACT, 1882. Following earlier US legislative and diplomatic efforts to limit sharply Chinese entry into the United States, this act suspended immigration by all Chinese to the United States for 10 years. *See also* EXCLUSION MOVEMENT.

CHINESE IMPERIAL MARITIME CUSTOMS SERVICE. The opening of China under the terms of the treaties signed with foreign powers in the mid-19th century saw the evolution of this foreign-managed customs service. It provided a reliable source of revenue that at times was used by the Chinese government to pay compensation and indemnities to the United States and other foreign powers. The Chinese government achieved control over the Maritime Customs Service in the 1930s. *See also* HART, ROBERT.

CHINESE REPOSITORY. American Protestant **missionaries** founded this monthly journal in Canton in 1831. For over 20 years, it provided insights about China for missionaries, diplomats, and others concerned with China.

CHINESE STUDENT IMMIGRATION BILL. President **George H. W. Bush** vetoed this legislation in November 1989, arguing that he would implement the bill's provisions, extending the visas of Chinese students and scholars in the United States following the **Tiananmen crackdown**, through administrative means. There followed an acrimonious veto override effort in the Congress, where the president's action was sustained by the Senate.

CHINESE "VOLUNTEERS" IN THE KOREAN WAR. Chinese pronouncements throughout the **Korean War** maintained that Chinese soldiers fighting Americans, South Koreans, and their allies were "volunteers" assisting North Korea in the face of Allied "aggression."

CH'I-YING (QI YING) (1786–1858). Ch'i-ying was the governor-general of Guangxi and Guangdong provinces and served as the chief negotiator for the Chinese government during the negotiations with the British, Americans, and French between 1842 and 1844. He tended to follow a policy designed to accommodate and appease foreign demands. Like other Chinese officials of his time, Ch'i-ying underestimated the value of the treaties' concessions and minimized their long-term importance to the survival of the **Qing dynasty**. *See also* TREATY OF NANKING; WANG-HSIA TREATY.

CHRISTOPHER, WARREN (1925–). Christopher served as secretary of state in President **William Clinton**'s first term. He supported the administration's desire to move China towards democracy through economic development. When Christopher visited Beijing in March 1994, he became embroiled in a standoff between China and the United States regarding the Clinton administration's linkage of granting China **most-favored-nation (MFN) tariff status** and China's **human rights** abuses. Christopher and the administration eventually capitulated under economic pressures, as President Clinton agreed to maintain China's MFN status despite Beijing's continuing poor human rights record. In 1979, Christopher was deputy secretary of state and led a delegation to Taipei to deal with administrative matters following the US decision to break official ties with Taiwan and establish official ties with China. His motorcade was stoned and attacked by a mob on arrival, but the mission went ahead as planned.

CH'UN, TSAI-FENG (CHUN ZAIFENG), PRINCE (1882–1951). Regent for the boy emperor in the last years of the **Qing dynasty**, Ch'un by 1910 came to support a policy of seeking greater American investment in Manchuria and other support to offset Japanese and Russian expansion. The **William H. Taft** administration led by Secretary of State **Philander Knox** initially used proposed US investments in Manchurian railroads as a means to assert US **Open Door Policy** against Russian and Japanese expansion. After the failure of such efforts in the face of Russian and Japanese resistance, the US administration adopted by 1910 a more cooperative policy, working in consortiums with European powers and avoiding direct confrontation with Moscow and Tokyo in Manchuria. Ironically, Prince Ch'un and his Peking colleagues chose this time to try to consolidate ties with the United States and seek greater US support against Russia and Japan in Manchuria, but Chinese government emissaries found the Taft administration now maintaining a low profile regarding Manchuria. *See also* DOLLAR DIPLOMACY.

CHU, TEH (ZHU DE) (1886–1976). Chu was the Chinese **Communist Party**'s military leader for much of the 20th century. When the **People's Liberation Army** was founded in 1929, General Chu Teh was selected to serve as the commander. He interacted with American military and other visitors to the Communist headquarters in **Yenan** during World War II, and with US mediators during the **Chinese Civil War**, and he helped to plan and execute Chinese military operations directed against American forces in the **Korean War** and elsewhere around China's periphery in the first two decades of the Cold War.

CHUNG, JOHNNY (1954–). A businessman and Democratic Party fund-raiser from California, Chung was accused and eventually pled guilty to charges of illegally raising funds for the **Democratic National Committee (DNC)** in 1994. The donations he collected and the donations of some other Asian Americans led to official investigations of the DNC and various criminal investigations and prosecutions. There were repeated charges that some of these donations were linked to alleged Chinese government efforts to influence US policy, but the charges proved to be hard to verify.

CHUNGKING (CHONGQING). This city was the capital of **Chiang Kai-shek's Nationalist Party** regime following its retreat to the Chinese interior in the face of Japanese invasion in 1937–1938.

CHURCHILL, WINSTON (1874–1965). In deliberations about China's role in World War II and the postwar situation, this British prime minister often had reservations about President **Franklin D. Roosevelt**'s determination that China under **Chiang Kai-shek** be treated as one of the great powers. *See also* CAIRO CONFERENCE.

CLEVELAND, GROVER (1837–1908). Facing a close election in 1888, this president switched from his administration's previous efforts to deal with Chinese **immigration** though a treaty with China, and endorsed tougher restrictions on Chinese immigration seen in the Scott Act of 1888. *See also* BAYNARD, THOMAS; EXCLUSION MOVEMENT.

CLINE, RAY (1918–1996). Cline had a lengthy career in the **Central Intelligence Agency**, and developed a close relationship with Chiang Kai-shek and his son **Chiang Ching-kuo**. He wrote extensively on security issues, and also directed the State Department Bureau for Intelligence and Research. During the 1980s, Cline was an advisor to **Ronald Reagan**, and encouraged Reagan in his support of Taiwan. Throughout his career, Cline worked and spoke out against Communist governments.

CLINTON, HILLARY (1947–). Clinton's role in the **United Nations Fourth World Conference on Women** held in Beijing in September 1995 saw the **William Clinton** administration delay the final decision on her visit until Chinese authorities released and expelled **hu-**

man rights activist **Harry Wu,** then in their custody. Consistent with her strong positions on human rights issues, Clinton gave a speech at the conference underlining opposition to the human rights practices of China and other authoritarian governments.

CLINTON, WILLIAM (1946–). Presidential candidate Clinton used sharp attacks against Chinese government behavior, notably the **Tiananmen crackdown**, and President **George H. W. Bush**'s moderate approach to China to win support in the 1992 election. Reflecting the Clinton administration's tougher approach to China, the new US government proceeded to link US annual renewal of **most-favored-nation (MFN) tariff status** with Chinese government behavior regarding **human rights** and other issues. Meeting strong resistance from many American business and other interests that would suffer if the burgeoning Chinese economy were denied MFN tariff treatment, Clinton reversed policy in May 1994, ending efforts to link **trade** and human rights concerns. Facing an upsurge in 1995 in congressional, media, and other support for a US decision to allow Taiwan's president to visit his alma mater Cornell University, Clinton reversed policy in May 1995, allowing Taiwan President **Lee Teng-hui** to visit Cornell in June 1995. The Chinese government responded over the next nine months with varied retaliatory actions, notably a series of provocative military exercises in the **Taiwan Strait** area, including ballistic missile tests and live-fire exercises, which by March 1996 prompted the Clinton administration to dispatch two aircraft carrier battle groups to Taiwan in order to calm the situation.

The president and his senior White House aides subsequently took a much more direct role in US–China policymaking and gave higher priority to American–Chinese relations. They emphasized a moderate **engagement policy**, seeking change in offensive Chinese government practices through a gradual process involving closer Chinese integration with the world economic and political order. The US–China relationship improved but also encountered significant setbacks and resistance. The president's more activist and positive policy of engagement with China saw such high points as the China–US summits in 1997 and 1998, the Sino–US agreement on China's entry into the **World Trade Organization** in 1999, and passage of US legislation in 2000 granting China **permanent normal trade relations**. Low points in the relationship during this time included strong congressional opposition to the president's stance against Taiwan independence (the **three nos**) in 1998; the May 1999 bombing of the Chinese Embassy in **Belgrade**; Chinese demonstrators trashing US diplomatic properties in China; strident congressional criticism in the **Cox Committee** report of May 1999 charging administration officials with gross malfeasance in guarding US secrets and weaponry from Chinese spies; and partisan congressional investigations of Clinton administration political fund-raising that highlighted some illegal contributions from sources connected to the Chinese regime, and the alleged impact they had on the administration's more moderate approach to China.

CLINTON–HASHIMOTO DECLARATION. Formally known as the US–Japan Joint Declaration on the Alliance for the 21st Century, the document was the result of strong efforts by the US and Japanese governments in the previous two years to strengthen the bilateral alliance and to deal with possible contingencies, notably regarding North Korea. It was released during President **William Clinton**'s summit meeting in Japan with Prime Minister **Ryutaro Hashimoto** in April 1996. Coming one month after the first face-off of US and Chinese forces in the **Taiwan Strait** since the depths of the Cold War, the strengthened US–Japan alignment also was seen to have potent implications for US and Japanese relations with China and for possible US–Japan military cooperation in a Taiwan contingency.

CLUBB, O. EDMUND (1901–1989). Clubb served as a US Foreign Service Officer specializing in Chinese affairs from 1931–1951. In late 1951, he was a target of Senator **Joseph McCarthy** and congressional anti-Communist investigations, and was pressured to resign from his post due to his past work on China, which was deemed not suitably anti-Communist. Clubb became a writer and a teacher and published several books on Asian affairs.

COMING CONFLICT WITH CHINA. Written by Richard Bernstein and Ross Munro, prominent journalists with extensive experience with China, this book was in the lead among sometimes sensational

US assessments in the late 1990s depicting a rising threat posed by expanding Chinese economic and military power and calling for US actions to address it.

COMINTERN. Formally known as the Communist International, this Communist organization backed by the Soviet Union worked against US and Western interests in China. In the 1920s, it developed close relations with Chinese **Nationalist Party** leaders while working to establish the Chinese **Communist Party**. Its influence in China waned after **Chiang Kai-shek** consolidated his power and forced foreign Communists to flee as he carried out a violent purge of Communists and their sympathizers in 1927. The Comintern remained connected with the struggling Communist Party of China. *See also* WHITE TERROR.

COMMITTEE OF ONE MILLION. US congressional representatives were in the lead in this organization. The group was prominent during the 1950s and 1960s, supported Taiwan, and opposed China's entry into the United Nations.

COMMUNIST PARTY. Established in 1921, the Chinese Communist Party (CCP) at times was aligned with the Chinese **Nationalist Party** and at other times was in armed struggle with the Nationalists. The CCP remained little known by the United States until US involvement in China deepened during World War II, and American officials were able to visit and reside in CCP headquarters at **Yenan** in 1944. After Japan's defeat, the Communist–Nationalist rivalry overwhelmed US mediation efforts and led to the **Chinese Civil War** on the Chinese mainland from 1945–1949. The Communists won despite US backing for the Nationalists and established the **People's Republic of China** in 1949.

Mao Zedong emerged as the leading figure in the party in the 1930s and remained the dominant leader of the party, the most important leadership organization in China, until his death in 1976. **Deng Xiaoping** became defacto party leader until the mid-1990s though he allowed younger officials to hold the leading party positions. **Jiang Zemin** was the party leader and the most prominent among a collective leadership group managing Chinese affairs after

Deng's health faded in the mid-1990s. Jiang was succeeded as party leader by **Hu Jintao** in 2002.

After the establishment of the PRC in 1949, the Communists continued in a state of war with the Nationalists; tensions and military confrontations in the **Taiwan Strait** continued for over a decade following the Nationalists' retreat to Taiwan. The tensions subsided as the PRC emphasized a peaceful approach to Taiwan following the thaw in US–China relations in the 1970s, but tensions resumed as Taiwan moved toward greater independence from China beginning in the 1990s.

COMPRADORS. This name was given to Chinese merchants who represented American and other foreign firms engaged in **trade** in the Chinese **treaty ports** of the 19th and early 20th centuries.

COMPREHENSIVE NUCLEAR TEST BAN TREATY. China's signing this treaty in 1996 and concurrent halt of Chinese nuclear weapons tests were viewed as significant progress in US-backed efforts to curb China's proliferation of weapons of mass destruction.

CONABLE, BARBER B. JR. (1922–2003). Conable served as a congressman from New York from 1965 to 1985. He was appointed president of the **World Bank** in 1986, serving until 1991. The World Bank during this period was very active in aiding Chinese development and Conable considered China to be financially responsible. Conable finished his career serving as the chairman of the **National Committee on US–China Relations**, a leading American group focused on improving relations with China.

CONCESSIONS. In many of the **treaty ports** open to foreign residence in the mid-1800s, foreign governments leased in perpetuity tracts of land known as concessions. In Shanghai, the biggest treaty port, British and American areas coalesced in 1863 to form the Shanghai International Settlement. This term also was used to refer to special rights foreigners received to build, own, and operate railways and other properties, and for other purposes, in various parts of China in the 19th and early 20th centuries.

CONGER, EDWIN H. (1843–1907). Conger served as the American minister in China from 1898–1905. In this period of rebellion, antiforeign massacres, and foreign encroachment, Conger often advocated a tough approach, and at one point sought a US sphere of influence in China.

CONSTRUCTIVE STRATEGIC PARTNERSHIP. As a result of the **William Clinton** administration's new emphasis on a positive **engagement policy** with China following the **Taiwan Strait crisis** of 1995–1996, the US and Chinese governments reached a general understanding underlined in summit meetings in 1997 and 1998 that they were working toward establishing a "constructive strategic partnership" in the 21st century.

CONTAINMENT. This strategy of using American economic, military, and political strength to build allied relationships and counter the expanding Soviet Union in the wake of the World War II was applied vigorously to China after the Chinese intervention in the **Korean War**. A strict US economic and political embargo against China, large US force deployments, massive foreign aid allocations to US Asian allies and supporters, and a ring of US defense alliances around China were used to block Chinese expansion and to drive a wedge between China and its Soviet ally. The **Nixon Doctrine** of 1969 and the subsequent US opening to China ended this approach to China as the United States withdrew over 600,000 troops from the region and pulled back forces from its forward base against China, Taiwan. Nevertheless, Chinese officials continued to view US policy, even in periods of positive US–China relations, as also reflecting a sometimes hidden, sometimes overt, US effort to "contain" and hold back China's rising power and influence in Asian and world affairs.

CONTAINMENT WITHOUT ISOLATION. American foreign policy moderates in the late 1950s and early 1960s argued for this policy approach involving greater US contact and easing of tensions with China while remaining firm against Chinese aggression and expansion. *See also* CONTAINMENT.

CONVENTION AGAINST TORTURE AND OTHER CRUEL, IN-HUMAN OR DEGRADING TREATMENT OR PUNISHMENT. China was a signatory of this international agreement in 1988. US pressure on China to faithfully implement the standards of the accord rose after the **Tiananmen crackdown** and remained a feature of US government and non-government organization pressure on China into the 21st century.

COORDINATING COMMITTEE FOR EXPORT TO COMMUNIST AREAS (COCOM). *See* CHINA COMMITTEE, COORDINATING COMMITTEE FOR EXPORT TO COMMUNIST AREAS (COCOM).

COORDINATION COUNCIL FOR NORTH AMERICAN AFFAIRS (CCNAA). This ostensibly unofficial organization represented the Republic of China in the United States in lieu of an embassy and consulates, following the break in official US–Taiwan relations in 1979. The organization changed its name to **Taipei Economic and Cultural Representational Office (TECRO)** in 1994. The organization maintained offices in Washington and over a dozen US cities where Taiwan maintained consulates in 1979. The large office in Washington had divisions dealing with government relations with the US administration, liaison with Congress, economic and trade issues, military relations, cultural affairs, science and technology, press and public relations, and other issues previously handled by the Republic of China embassy. It was staffed by Taiwan Foreign Ministry and other officials from the Taiwan government. The counterpart to CCNAA/TECRO was the **American Institute in Taiwan (AIT)**.

CORCORAN, THOMAS G. (1900–1981). Corcoran was an adviser to President **Franklin D. Roosevelt** and was a prominent author of many New Deal laws. After leaving the administration, he was hired by the **Nationalist Party** to lobby for support for the Chinese Nationalist government.

COX, CHRISTOPHER (1952–). Cox served as a U.S. congressman from California after 1988. In 1997, he spearheaded the Laogai Slave

Labor Products Act which provided for additional US customs officers to investigate Chinese goods made with forced labor coming to the United States. As head of the House Policy Committee, a Republican group in the US House of Representatives, Cox also introduced various initiatives on U.S. policy regarding East Asia that tended to be critical of Chinese government policies and practices. Cox also chaired the **Cox Committee**, which was formed in 1998 to investigate technology transfers between the United States and China, and released a report giving an alarming view of Chinese threats to US national security interests.

COX COMMITTEE. Formally known as the Select Committee on US National Security and Military/Commercial Concerns with the People's Republic of China and named for its chairman, Republican Congressman **Christopher Cox**, the committee released in May 1999 an 800-page unclassified version of a larger classified report. It depicted longstanding and widespread Chinese espionage efforts against American nuclear weapons facilities that allowed China to build American advanced nuclear warheads for use on Chinese missiles that were made more accurate and reliable with the assistance of US companies. It portrayed the **William Clinton** administration as grossly negligent in protecting US national security secrets. The report added substantially to congressional, media, and other concerns that the United States faced a rising security threat posed by China's rapidly expanding economic and military power.

CULTURAL IMPERIALISM. This term was used by Chinese patriots and polemicists, especially after the founding of the People's Republic of China, to condemn US and other foreign efforts to influence religious, educational, and other cultural practices in China.

CULTURAL REVOLUTION. Beginning in 1966 and lasting until **Mao Zedong**'s death and the arrest of his radical followers in 1976, this period of leadership struggle, mass movements, and widespread urban violence in China at first saw the Chinese government cut off conventional diplomatic interaction. Faced with a massive threat from the Soviet Union, China by the late 1960s resumed more normal diplomacy and welcomed concurrent US moves to improve relations with China, though Chinese leadership struggles continued to complicate China's policy toward the United States.

CURRIE, LAUCHLIN (1902–1993). An economist and close advisor of President **Franklin D. Roosevelt**, Currie was called upon to travel to China and to determine appropriate US policy. A staunch supporter of **Chiang Kai-shek** and the **Nationalist Party** government led by Chiang, Currie influenced US–China policy, encouraging Nationalist government reform as well as US economic and military support, which included sending American advisers to back Chiang Kai-shek's government.

CUSHING, CALEB (1800–1879). Cushing was named commissioner to China and negotiated the **Wang-hsia Treaty** with Chinese government negotiator **Ch'i-ying** in 1844. The treaty said that Chinese concessions made to other nations would apply to the United States as well. It also opened the **treaty ports** to Americans and guaranteed **extraterritoriality** for Americans.

– D –

DAI LI (TAI LI) (1896–1946). Dai Li was selected by **Chiang Kai-shek** in 1934 to lead a fascist-style police force within the **Nationalist Party**, known as the **Blue Shirts**. The group modeled itself on the private party armies created by Adolf Hitler and Benito Mussolini to suppress dissent. In 1942, a small **US Naval Group China**, under the leadership of Navy Commander **Milton Miles**, worked with General Dai to establish the **Sino–American Cooperation Organization**. It funneled military aid to the Nationalist Party government with little oversight by senior US officers, assisting General Dai in fighting **Communist Party** opponents of the Nationalist regime.

DAI QING (1941–). This popular journalist was outspoken on several important issues in China at the end of the 20th century. Dai spoke out in particular about the negative environmental impact of the **Three Gorges Dam** project; she also was an ardent opponent of restrictive elements of China's Communist system. Her views and writings led various organizations to oppose the building of the Three Gorges Dam and her investigatory journalism was supported by many US and other international non-government organizations.

DALAI LAMA (1935–). This leader of **Tibet** fled to India amid a Tibetan uprising and Chinese crackdown in 1959. Backing the Dalai Lama's cause, the US government clandestinely supported armed resistance to Chinese rule in Tibet during the 1960s. US interest in supporting his cause declined with the US reconciliation with China in the 1970s and 1980s, but revived with the upsurge in US criticism of Chinese **human rights** practices in Tibet and other areas following the **Tiananmen crackdown** of 1989. That year, the Dalai Lama, admired around the world as the spiritual leader of Tibet, was awarded the Nobel Peace Prize. US presidents and senior officials met regularly with the Dalai Lama, Congress passed legislation recognizing Tibet as an independent country and condemning Chinese policies and practices in Tibet, and the State Department, with strong congressional prodding, established a special office to deal with Tibet. In the 1990s, US movies and movie stars brought the plight of Tibetans to a wider US public and reinforced pro-Tibet sentiment in the Congress. *See also* PANCHEN LAMA.

DALEY, WILLIAM M. (1948–) Daley served as secretary of commerce from 1997–2000. He strongly defended the **William Clinton** administration's **engagement policy** involving closer economic relations with China, despite often strident congressional, media, and other criticisms that the policy was accelerating China's ability to pose a threat to the United States.

DAVIES, JOHN P. (1908–1999). Davies was a Foreign Service officer from 1932–1954 who worked for General **Joseph Stilwell** during his tenure in China in the 1940s. Like Stilwell, Davies was critical of **Chiang Kai-shek**'s **Nationalist Party** regime and supportive of closer US ties with the Chinese **Communist Party** leaders. His record in China was used against him during congressional hearings and investigations spearheaded by Senator **Joseph McCarthy** in the early 1950s. In this atmosphere, Davies was pressured to leave the State Department.

DEMOCRATIC NATIONAL COMMITTEE (DNC). During the **William Clinton** administration, this organization of the US Democratic Party received controversial donations of campaign funds from foreign and other donors with an interest in promoting improved US relations with China. Congressional, media, and other investigations criticized the donations and some were returned.

DEMOCRACY WALL MOVEMENT. Coincident with **Deng Xiaoping**'s consolidation of power against Maoist leaders and the Chinese normalization of relations with the United States, **Wei Jingsheng** and other Chinese dissidents and reformers were allowed to post proreform tracts on a wall in Beijing beginning in December 1978. US and other Western media hailed this flowering of free political expression in China after so many years of repression. When the posters by March 1979 began to challenge **Communist Party** rule, they were torn down by the authorities, and activists, including Wei Jingsheng, were arrested and given long prison sentences. *See also* HUMAN RIGHTS.

DEMOCRATIC PARTY (HONG KONG). During the period after the **Tiananmen crackdown**, which seriously alarmed opinion in **Hong Kong**, and prior to Hong Kong's handover to Chinese sovereignty in 1997, this party and its leader **Martin Lee** — frequent critics of China — were active in seeking to guide US congressional actions and other US policy toward Hong Kong. On the one hand, they favored strong US expressions of concern to preserve freedoms in Hong Kong; on the other hand, they opposed US efforts to block US **most-favored-nation (MFN) tariff status** for China's trade, arguing that ending MFN treatment would seriously damage Hong Kong.

DEMOCRATIC PROGRESSIVE PARTY (DPP). Formed illegally in Taiwan in 1986 by groups of opponents of **Nationalist Party** rule in Taiwan, the DPP was soon accepted by the liberalizing Nationalist rulers and became the main opposition party. It grew in strength emphasizing issues including advocacy of greater Taiwan independence from China. The party candidate, **Chen Shui-bian**, won the presidency in 2000, and Chen was reelected in 2004. Chen and his party's advocacy of Taiwan sovereignty and independence from China antagonized Chinese leaders and complicated US efforts to maintain equilibrium in China–Taiwan relations based on a US **one China policy**.

DENBY, CHARLES SR. (1830–1904). Denby served as the American minister to China from 1885–1898. A loyal Democrat appointed by the first **Grover Cleveland** administration, Denby stayed as US minister through the end of the second Cleveland administration. Initially favoring a temperate position of seeking cooperation with Chinese officials seen as moving toward reform, Denby came later to the view that Chinese government incompetence and weakness endangered American and other **missionaries** and opened China to unchecked ambitions by outside powers. He saw little alternative to the United States' joining coercive foreign powers in order to protect US interests.

DENG XIAOPING (1904–1997). Given the authoritarian power structure of the Chinese **Communist Party** and the People's Republic of China, where the top leader dominated decisions on key foreign policy issues, Deng's position as paramount Chinese leader from the late 1970s until the mid-1990s made him the key Chinese decision maker concerning major turning points in US–China relations. They included the **US–China communiqué of 1978** establishing formal diplomatic relations; Sino–American cooperation against the invasion of **Cambodia** by Soviet-backed **Vietnam** in 1978 and the Soviet invasion of **Afghanistan** in 1979; Chinese pressure on the **Ronald Reagan** administration, leading to the **17 August 1982 US–China communiqué** limiting US arms sales to Taiwan; Chinese reversion to moderation toward Reagan, seen in positive treatment of the US president's 1984 visit to China; and China's firm stance against US pressure in the wake of the 1989 **Tiananmen crackdown**. Deng saw the importance of constructive relations with the United States and worked to see them grow, but he remained steadfast in resisting US actions that would compromise core Chinese interests regarding continued Communist Party rule and reunification with Taiwan.

DETENTE. Chinese leaders complained with varying degrees of intensity about the negative consequences for Chinese interests as a result of the improved US–Soviet relations, known as détente, which took place in the 1970s. Chinese officials sometimes warned that the United States might lower its guard against Soviet power, allowing Moscow to redeploy forces from its western flank in order to strike at China in the east. Chinese leaders at times showed interest in their own détente with Moscow, but usually reverted to a tough stance demanding an end to the Soviet military pressure along China's periphery, conditions that were not met until the end of the Cold War when **Mikhail Gorbachev** prepared to meet with **Deng Xiaoping** in Beijing in May 1989.

DEWEY, JOHN (1859–1952). This leading American philosopher responded with great enthusiasm to the nationalistic and cultural transformation seen in China as a result of the **May Fourth Movement** begun in 1919. Dewey supported democracy for China and engaged in a series of lectures in Peking in 1919 to further this goal. Dewey believed problems for the Chinese included such extremes as entrenched traditionalism and rapidly rising Bolshevism. After his return to the United States, Dewey continued in his interest in China, and was upset by such acts as the passage of US anti-immigration laws directed at Chinese. *See also* EXCLUSION MOVEMENT; IMMIGRATION.

DEWEY, THOMAS E. (1902–1971). Dewey was elected to a second term as New York's governor in 1946, and it was during this time that he spoke out against the China policy of President **Harry Truman** and in support of more aid for **Chiang Kai–shek** and the Chinese **Nationalist Party** government. He received the Republican presidential nomination in 1948 and attacked the Truman administration's record on China during the campaign. While he lost his bid for the presidency, his attacks pressured Truman to increase aid to Chiang.

DIAOYUTAI ISLANDS. Also known as *Tiaoyu t'ai* and *Senkaku Islands*, this small group of rocky islets became a focus of controversy after the United States returned Okinawa and these islets to Japanese rule in 1972. Both China and Taiwan claimed the islets, which reportedly had oil deposits, but Japan maintained control. The United States government at times endeavored to avoid taking a position on the territorial dispute or the implications of US commitments under terms of the **US–Japan Security Treaty** should Japan be attacked as it protected its claim. At other times, US policymakers said that US commitments under the security treaty would apply if Japan were attacked while protecting its territorial claim.

DIEN BIEN PHU. China backed the Communist Viet Minh victors with supplies and advisers, while the United States provided supplies to the French forces that ultimately were defeated at this Indochina stronghold on 7 May 1954. France sought peace at the Geneva Conference, 1954, while the United States deepened involvement in **Vietnam** and elsewhere in Southeast Asia to check Chinese-backed Communist expansion in Southeast Asia. *See also* GENEVA ACCORDS.

DIXIE MISSION. *See* AMERICAN MILITARY OBSERVER GROUP (YENAN).

DOLE, ROBERT (1923–). A Republican senator from Kansas, Dole was a strong supporter of Taiwan while he sought opportunities to sell Kansas grain to China. In 1978 he sponsored an amendment that passed into law requiring the president to notify the congress before ending a defense treaty. President **Jimmy Carter** ignored the provision when he agreed later that year to end the **US–Republic of China defense treaty** as part of the agreement normalizing US relations with China. As the Republican candidate for president against President **William Clinton** in 1996, Dole complained about the president's China policy and lack of sufficient support for Taiwan.

DOLLAR DIPLOMACY. During the **William H. Taft** administration, 1909–1913, the president and Secretary of State **Philander Knox** used schemes involving US investment to promote US influence in China and particularly to prevent Russia and Japan from dominating Manchuria. They tried to encourage major American investments in railroads as a means to counterbalance Japanese and Russian spheres of influence centered on Manchurian railroads, and they called for a plan to neutralize or internationalize all railway projects in Manchuria. As Japan and Russia objected and US investors showed little enthusiasm, this dollar diplomacy failed. The administration subsequently adopted a more moderate stance emphasizing cooperation with some European powers, and ultimately Russia and Japan, in an international consortium dealing with loans to China. *See also* CHINCHOW–AIGUN RAIL-ROAD; HUKUANG RAILWAY.

DULLES, JOHN FOSTER (1888–1959). As secretary of state in the **Dwight Eisenhower** administration until his death late in the president's second term, Dulles pursued the administration's stated **containment** policy against China. It involved an economic embargo, political isolation, subversion, and the strong support of US defense allies and friends around China's periphery; it was backed by large-scale US military deployments in Asia. Dulles privately had a skeptical view of **Chiang Kai-shek** and was vigilant against being led by the Chinese **Nationalist Party** leader into a war against the Chinese **Communist Party** regime. Dulles was wary of ultimately successful Nationalist Chinese efforts to sign a **US–Republic of China defense treaty** in December 1954. He maneuvered to sustain US political isolation of China even when compelled by circumstances to carry out **ambassadorial talks** with the Chinese Communists beginning in 1955. Dulles and other like-minded officials in the administration favored a tougher US policy toward China than toward the Soviet Union, forcing Beijing to rely on Moscow for economic and other needs the Soviet Union could not meet. In this and other ways, he hoped to divide China and the Soviet Union. At the outset of his tenure as secretary of state, Dulles endeavored to insulate himself from the attacks of stridently anti-Communist and pro-Chiang Kai-shek congressional lawmakers. He appointed an aide of Senator **Joseph McCarthy** to root out State Department personnel of perceived dubious loyalty and he fired **John Carter Vincent**, one of the few senior China experts remaining in the department. *See also* WEDGE STRATEGY.

– E –

EAGLEBURGER, LAWRENCE (1930–). As deputy secretary of state, Eagleburger played a key role in US relations with China when he visited China twice on secret missions with US National Security

Adviser **Brent Scowcroft** after the **Tiananmen crackdown** of 1989. The missions were designed by President **George H. W. Bush** to establish a foundation for continued US–China ties after the disastrous impact of the Tiananmen crackdown. Once they became known in late 1989, the secret missions were strongly criticized in the Congress and the media. This criticism made it difficult for the Bush administration to sustain constructive relations with China.

EDUCATION. American **missionaries** promoted educational endeavors in China beginning in the 19th century. At times, American foundations and US government officials supported these efforts and educational exchanges between the two countries. Highlights of US support for education in China included the **Hartford Education Mission** in the 1870s, the **Peking Union Medical College** begun in 1915, and the **China Foundation for the Promotion of Education and Culture** begun in 1924. The People's Republic of China forced US educational efforts to close and there was little contact between the United States and China for over 20 years. Educational efforts and exchanges blossomed again with the establishment of US–China diplomatic relations in 1979, as tens of thousands of Chinese students traveled to the United States each year for formal training and many thousands of Americans sought training and worked in educational institutions in China. The exchanges were supported by a wide range of arrangements between and among American and Chinese non-government educational institutions and organizations that had the support of the two governments.

EICHELBERGER, CLARK MELL (1896–1980). Eichelberger served as the head of the League of Nations Association from 1934–1945 and continued as head when the name was changed to the American Association for the United Nations until 1964. Eichelberger also headed the group Defend America by Aiding the Allies, which was among those groups prior to US entry into World War II that supported giving aid to China to help suppress the Axis powers.

EIGHT POINTS. Chinese **Communist Party** leader **Jiang Zemin** issued these points regarding Taiwan policy in January 1995. From Beijing's point of view, they were a moderate call for China and Taiwan to work toward formal cessation of hostilities on the basis of the concept of **one China**. They came as **trade** and economic relations between Taiwan and China were growing and they followed talks in 1993 in Singapore between senior unofficial envoys of each side. Taiwan's President **Lee Teng-hui** responded by demanding a precondition that Beijing drop its threat to use force against Taiwan—an unacceptable condition for China. Relations soon deteriorated sharply as Lee succeeded in efforts to get the **William Clinton** administration to reverse policy and allow him to visit Cornell University, which he did in June 1995, prompting major military operations by China in the **Taiwan Strait** over the following nine months. *See also* TAIWAN STRAIT CRISES.

EIGHTH ROUTE ARMY. This was the name given to **Communist Party** armed forces ostensibly under the command of the **Nationalist Party** government under terms of the united front agreement reached in 1937. The united front frayed and collapsed, but US officials and other observers continued to refer to the Communist forces with this name, comparing their morale and abilities favorably with those of Nationalist Chinese forces.

EISENHOWER, DWIGHT D. (1890–1969). As US president, Eisenhower pursued with less enthusiasm than others in his administration the US government's stated **containment** policy against China. It involved an economic embargo, political isolation, subversion, and the strong support of US defense allies and friends around China's periphery; it was backed by large-scale US military deployments in Asia. Eisenhower was wary of **Chiang Kai-shek**, seeing the **Nationalist Party** leader endeavoring to promote conflict with the Chinese **Communist Party** regime that would drag in the United States. He was more open than Secretary of State **John Foster Dulles** and others to applying flexibility regarding **trade** with China, and was sympathetic to British and Japanese complaints about US-imposed restrictions on their trade with China. Some scholars contrasted Eisenhower with Dulles, asserting that the president was prepared to use "soft" tactics in order to woo China to the US side and away from the Soviet Union, while Dulles favored using "hard" tactics against China, forcing it to make demands that Moscow could not meet and thereby splintering the **Sino–Soviet alliance**. *See also* WEDGE STRATEGY.

EMERGENCY COMMITTEE FOR AMERICAN TRADE. Founded in 1967, this group representing US manufacturing, banking, merchandising and publishing firms was of key importance in lobbying in the decade after the **Tiananmen crackdown** for unconditional annual renewal of US **most-favored-nation (MFN) tariff status** for China's **trade** with the United States. The group and its members strongly favored China's entry into the **World Trade Organization** and the US provision of **permanent normal trade relations** status for China. Some scholars saw their effective lobbying as far superior to efforts by labor, **human rights**, and other groups to impose conditions on the annual renewal of MFN status for China.

EMIGRATION. Under terms of the **Jackson–Vanik Amendment**, free emigration from China was a consideration in the annual US government determination granting **most-favored-nation (MFN) tariff status** to China. This became a serious issue after the **Tiananmen crackdown,** and free emigration was an explicit condition the Chinese government had to meet in order to qualify for MFN renewal under conditions set forth by the **William Clinton** administration in 1993. President Clinton abandoned those conditions in 1994. *See also* EXECUTIVE ORDER 128590.

EMPRESS DOWAGER TZ'U-HSI (CIXI) (1835–1908). A concubine who bore the emperor an heir and remained the most powerful Manchu in China for the last 50 years of the **Qing dynasty**, Tz'u-hsi was an expert at court intrigue but had little grasp of China's problems of modernization. Devoted to the Manchu dynasty and her own narrow interests, she maintained equilibrium between traditional central power and new regional interests that grew in suppressing mid-century rebellions. Her conservatism led her to suppress radical reformers who briefly won over the emperor and instituted a series of reforms in 1898 following China's defeat by Japan in 1895 and subsequent foreign demands for large territorial concessions. She sided with the xenophobic **Boxer uprising**, which saw the murders of many Christian **missionaries,** the siege of foreign legations in Peking, and the dispatch of multinational expeditionary forces, including US troops to put down the uprising and punish the culprits. The United States and other foreign powers demanded stiff punishments and large indemnities, but the Empress Dowager survived, continuing her leading court position until her death in 1908.

EMPRESS OF CHINA. Freed from British restrictions on trading with China following the victory in the American Revolution, US merchants sent this ship from New York to Canton in 1784, the first American commercial vessel to engage directly in the China trade.

ENGAGEMENT POLICY. This term was used by officials in the **George H. W. Bush** administration to describe US interaction with China, but officials in the **William Clinton** administration emphasized this term repeatedly in describing US policy toward China. A policy of engagement focused on the United States' interacting pragmatically and constructively with China in ways that supported the social, economic and structural changes underway in China in order gradually to bring Chinese administration policies and practices into accord with international norms supported by the United States. After a few years in office, the Clinton administration increasingly stressed the approach of engagement and deemphasized its initial emphasis on demanding that the Chinese administration conform to international norms or face sanctions and other punishments from the United States. The shift to a policy of engagement was controversial in the Congress, media, and among interest groups in the United States, and added to the active US debate over policy toward China in the 1990s.

ENLARGEMENT. Chinese officials and commentators strongly disagreed with a September 1993 foreign policy speech by National Security Adviser **Anthony Lake** emphasizing the **William Clinton** administration's interest at that time in pursuing the "enlargement" of democracy and free enterprise against reactionary "backlash" states. Lake included China, as well as Iran and Iraq, among the latter. The Chinese critics viewed the US policy of enlargement as part of broad US efforts to undermine the Chinese regime and thwart the rise of Chinese power and influence in Asian and world affairs.

EP-3 INCIDENT. On 1 April 2001, a Chinese jet fighter crashed with a US reconnaissance plane, the EP-3, in international waters off the China coast. The jet was destroyed and the pilot killed. The EP-3 was seriously damaged but managed to make an emergency landing on China's Hainan Island. The incident caused the first major US–Chinese crisis in the **George W. Bush** administration. The US crew was held for 11 days and the US plane much longer by Chinese authorities. Negotiations produced compromises that allowed the crew and eventually the plane to return to the United States, but neither side accepted responsibility for the incident.

"EVER-VICTORIOUS ARMY." This small mercenary army defended Shanghai during the **Taiping Rebellion**. Initially led by American commanders, it was later incorporated into Chinese government forces. *See also* WARD, FREDERICK TOWNSEND.

EXCLUSION MOVEMENT. Though earlier US governments had encouraged Chinese laborers to come to the United States and promised free **immigration** in the **Burlingame Treaty** of 1868, there emerged in the 1870s this broad US movement based on prejudice and fear of Chinese workers amid sometimes difficult economic times in the United States. Americans took legal and illegal actions, including riots and murder of Chinese, to stop Chinese immigration to the United States. The state governments and the national government passed an array of laws and the US courts made a variety of decisions that singled out Chinese immigrants for negative treatment and curbed the legal rights of Chinese residents and Chinese citizens of the United States. The movement soon broadened to include all Asians. The **National Origins Act of 1924** barred all new Asian immigration. US mistreatment of Chinese people in the United States became a major issue for the Chinese government, which complained repeatedly about unjust US actions, but with little effect. It was the target of a Chinese **anti-American boycott** in 1905. The US government in the 1940s and 1950s passed laws ending the exclusions but allowed little new immigration from China and other Asian countries until the **Immigration Reform Act of 1965** ended prejudice against Asians in US immigration procedures.

EXECUTIVE ORDER 128590. This legally binding **William Clinton** administration executive order of 28 May 1993 established seven **human rights**–related factors as the conditions for extension of US **most-favored-nation (MFN) tariff status** for China beyond 3 July 1994. Failure to meet two of the conditions (regarding free **emigration** and **prison labor** exports) required the secretary of state to recommend to the president not to continue MFN treatment. This action was the focus of US–Chinese wrangling over the next year. President Clinton abandoned it and "delinked" MFN and Chinese human rights conditions on 26 May 1994.

EXPORT–IMPORT BANK. After the normalization of US relations with the **People's Republic of China**, this US government bank provided loan guarantees for US firms doing business in China. As a result of the **Tiananmen crackdown** in 1989, Congress mandated a ban on the bank's loans to firms in business in the PRC, but President **George H. W. Bush** waived the ban in December 1989. In a separate episode, the State Department in April 1996 got the bank to delay loan guarantees for China for a few days in an apparent effort to pressure the Chinese government to curb sales of nuclear weapons technology to Pakistan. Amid strong opposition in the United States to the environmental consequences of China's **Three Gorges Dam** project, the board of directors of the bank said on 30 May 1996 that the bank would not be involved in financing the project.

EXTRATERRITORIALITY. This legal system allowed foreigners and their activities in China to remain governed by their own law and not Chinese law. The Chinese government granted this right to British citizens in an agreement reached in 1843 after the Sino–British **Treaty of Nanking** of 1842 ended three years of Sino–British warfare in China in the **Opium War**. In 1844 in the **Treaty of Wang-hsia**, the Americans reached their own agreement with China that provided extraterritoriality for US citizens and other benefits. Chinese patriots viewed the system as a key feature of foreign imposed **unequal treaties** that humiliated China for 100 years. A US–China agreement of January 1943 ended extraterritoriality for Americans in China, though US military personnel—the largest contingent of Americans in the country—remained free from Chinese legal jurisdiction as a result of a separate agreement signed in 1943.

– F –

FAIRBANK, JOHN K. (1907–1991). A Harvard University history professor who worked for the US embassy in China during World War II, Fairbank became the leading American historian on modern China and a strong advocate for greater US–China understanding and moderation in US policy toward China during the Cold War. His academic leadership saw the training of hundreds of China specialists and an array of publications and academic enterprises improving American knowledge of China and China–US relations.

FALUN GONG. The Chinese government's harsh crackdown against this religious movement in China began in 1999 and added to the array of negative features of Chinese government **human rights** practices as seen by US government officials and opinion leaders. The movement's leader, **Li Hongzhi**, resided in the United States, and its followers actively lobbied US government officials for support against the Chinese government's sometimes brutal suppression.

FANG LIZHI (1936–). A prominent Chinese astrophysicist, university president, and crusader for democratic reform, Fang was invited to attend a dinner hosted by visiting President **George H. W. Bush** in Beijing in February 1989 but was barred from attending by Chinese security forces. The incident embarrassed President Bush and his senior staff, who blamed US Ambassador **Winston Lord** for the incident. During the **Tiananmen crackdown** in June, Fang and his wife sought and were given refuge in the US embassy. Their presence was the subject of repeated high-level talks between the United States and China until a deal was reached on 25 June 1990 allowing them to leave the embassy for the United States.

FAR EASTERN AGREEMENT. In this secret agreement signed by the United States, the Soviet Union, and Great Britain at the **Yalta Conference** on 11 February 1945, the powers agreed that the Soviet

Union would enter the war against Japan two or three months after Germany's surrender, Russian territory taken by Japan would be restored, Russian interests in Manchuria, including a naval base, would be restored, and Outer Mongolia would remain independent. President **Franklin D. Roosevelt** promised to obtain the concurrence of China's **Kuomintang** government to provisions regarding Manchuria and Mongolia, which were claimed by China. The Soviet Union expressed willingness to negotiate a friendship and alliance treaty with China's government. The Far Eastern Agreement had negative implications for the Chinese Kuomintang government, which was not consulted on the territorial concessions to the Soviet Union, and for the Chinese **Communist Party** leaders, who appeared to be isolated from the Soviet Union as its leader, **Joseph Stalin**, pursued Soviet national interests in beneficial arrangements with the West and with the Chinese Kuomintang government.

FEBRUARY 28 UPRISING. After over a year of misrule by **Nationalist Party** forces that saw the collapse of economic and social order in Taiwan, police killing a woman illegally selling cigarettes prompted riots and violent protests beginning 28 February 1947, that eventually were put down by Nationalist reinforcements from mainland China. Many thousands were killed; Taiwan leaders were imprisoned, executed, or forced to flee Taiwan. The events deepened negative US official views of the Nationalist regime.

FEINSTEIN, DIANNE (1933–). As mayor of San Francisco in the 1970s and 1980s, Feinstein developed close relations with Shanghai leaders **Wang Daohan**, **Jiang Zemin**, and **Zhu Rongji**. As senator from California, Feinstein was active after the Tiananmen crackdown of June 1989 in trying to preserve **most-favored-nation tariff status** and other key elements of US relations with China while strongly condemning Chinese government actions offensive to the United States. Through many meetings with Jiang Zemin as leader of Shanghai and after his surprise elevation to Communist Party leader in 1989, Feinstein was the US official with the most experience in dealing with this Chinese leader.

FENG YU-HSIANG (1882–1948). Feng was a notable military leader in northern China during the 1920s. He was known as the "Christian general" because he converted to Methodism and encouraged his troops to adopt Christianity. His comparatively good reputation with US **missionaries** and other foreign observers during this chaotic time in China also had to do with his progressive campaigns against such practices as foot binding. He reversed decisions to support **Chiang Kai-shek** several times, and was crushed by Chiang when he rebelled in 1930.

FERGUSON, JOHN C. (1865–1945). Ferguson went to China in 1887, joining US **missionaries** there and opening two universities: Nanking University in 1888 and Chiaotung University in 1897. He also founded a newspaper. Despite these accomplishments, Ferguson was best known in his role as an aficionado of Chinese art. He wrote several books and was responsible for much of the New York Metropolitan Museum's acquisition of Chinese art.

FIVE POINT AGREEMENT. This agreement was reached as a result of US Ambassador to China **Patrick Hurley**'s negotiations with **Mao Zedong** and Chinese **Communist Party** leaders in **Yenan** in November 1944. Among other things, the agreement summarized Hurley's promises of equal treatment and US aid to the Communists in a coalition with the **Nationalist Party.** The deal soon collapsed in the face of Chinese Nationalists' opposition and Hurley's strong support for Nationalist leader **Chiang Kai-shek** in disputes with the Communists.

FLYING TIGERS. *See* AMERICAN VOLUNTEER GROUP.

FLEXIBLE DIPLOMACY. Beginning in the late 1980s, Taiwan President **Lee Teng-hui** and senior Taiwan government officials traveled to countries and met leaders of governments that did not officially recognize Taiwan, or they hosted such leaders in Taiwan. The practice also was known as "pragmatic diplomacy," and notably "vacation diplomacy," as the Taiwan president and senior leaders sometimes would portray their excursions as vacation trips where they would play golf with the leaders of foreign states visited. The Taiwan leaders used such contacts to confer the appearance of official status and international standing for Taiwan in the face of

China's strong efforts to prevent international recognition of the Taiwan government. The highlight of this effort was President Lee's June 1995 reunion visit to Cornell University in the United States, which precipitated a major crisis in China–US relations over Taiwan. *See also* TAIWAN STRAIT CRISES.

FOORD, JOHN (1842–1922). A contributing editor to the New York *Journal of Commerce,* Foord held a leading position in the **American Asiatic Association** that was organized in 1898 to protect US **trade** interests in China endangered by growing foreign spheres of influence and **concessions**. He pursued efforts to secure US access to the China market. He opposed the US **exclusion movement** against Chinese **immigration** and he opposed strong US retaliation against Chinese attacks on US missionaries in China.

FORD, GERALD (1913–). Succeeding **Richard Nixon** after Nixon resigned in August 1974, Ford dispatched Secretary of State **Henry Kissinger** to China to reaffirm Nixon's pledge to shift diplomatic recognition from Taiwan to China. But he soon backtracked in the face of US domestic opposition and other circumstances. Ford's pardon of Nixon was controversial, he faced strong congressional and media opposition to his policies toward the Soviet Union, and conservative Republicans headed by California Governor **Ronald Reagan** were strong supporters of Taiwan and were preparing to challenge Ford for the Republican nomination for the presidency in 1976. In this context, the collapse of US-backed regimes in **Cambodia** and South **Vietnam** in 1975 added to reasons to go slow in breaking US ties with Taiwan. When **Chiang Kai-shek** died in April 1975, Ford initially sought to send the agriculture secretary to the funeral but reconsidered under domestic US pressure and sent the vice president. Ford traveled to China in December 1975 where little progress on US–China normalization of relations was noted although the United States agreed to the transfer to China of jet engines and computers with military potential.

FOREIGN AFFAIRS LEADING SMALL GROUP. Following the passing of senior **Communist Party** leaders **Mao Zedong** and **Deng Xiaoping**, who dominated Chinese foreign policy decision making,

Chinese foreign policy, including policy toward the United States, was made more collectively. This senior Communist Party coordinating group, representing different bureaucratic and leadership interests, including the foreign ministry and the military, played a key foreign policy-making role in the post–Cold War period. The Communist Party general secretary often led and influenced the decisions on policy, but did not dominate them as had been the case under Mao Zedong, and to a somewhat lesser degree under Deng Xiaoping.

FORMOSA. This term was sometimes used by Americans and other Westerners to refer to the island of Taiwan.

FORMOSA RESOLUTION. Passed by the US Congress in January 1955 amid military tensions in the **Taiwan Strait** and after the December 1954 signing of the **United States–Republic of China Mutual defense treaty**, the resolution authorized the US president to "employ the armed forces of the United States as he deems necessary for the specific purpose of securing and protecting **Formosa** and the **Pescadores** against armed attack . . . to include related positions . . ." This extended the authority of the president to take action to help Taiwan defend its heavily fortified outposts along the China coast, notably **Quemoy** and **Matsu**, which came under threat of Chinese attack. Congress repealed the Formosa Resolution in 1974. *See also* TAIWAN STRAIT CRISES.

FORMOSAN ASSOCIATION FOR PUBLIC AFFAIRS. Taiwanese who were citizens and residents in the United States organized this group in 1982. The group worked to influence the US government and world opinion to support democracy, self-determination, and human rights in Taiwan. Based in Washington, D.C., it succeeded in promoting the passage of numerous congressional resolutions supporting Taiwan interests at odds with the Chinese government's position on Taiwan.

FORRESTAL, JAMES V. (1892–1949). Forrestal served as secretary of the navy from 1944 to 1947, and then became the first US secretary of defense. During this time, Forrestal differed with Secretary of State **Dean Acheson** and other **Harry Truman** administration officials, as he argued in favor of continuing US aid to **Chiang Kai-shek**.

FOSTER, JOHN W. (1836–1917) An international lawyer who briefly served as secretary of state, Foster was hired by **Qing dynasty** leader **Li Hung-chang** to accompany China's second peace mission to Japan after the Chinese defeat in the **Sino–Japanese War** of 1894–1895. Foster played an active role in the Sino–Japanese negotiations leading to the peace agreement, though US officials made known that he was not representing US government interests.

FOUR POLICEMEN. This was an idea of President **Franklin D. Roosevelt** regarding the post–World War II order, which he judged would be governed by four powers—the United States, Great Britain, the Soviet Union, and China. Their differences would be contained and mitigated by wartime cooperation, **trade**, and security pacts. China under a leadership friendly to the United States would become the leading policeman in Asia and support American interests in the region. The weakness and corruption of **Chiang Kai-shek**'s **Nationalist Party** government complicated the US president's plan, but he was reluctant to break with Chiang and continued to treat the Chinese Nationalists as one of the great allied powers.

14TH AIR FORCE. US General **Claire Chennault**'s wartime command in China after **Pearl Harbor**, this force launched attacks from bases in China against Japanese targets in 1943–1944. In response, Japanese forces launched ground attacks and overran the weakly defended US air bases and large parts of China that had resisted Japanese conquest since 1937, causing a major crisis in China. Reacting to the crisis, the United States at first insisted on enhancing the power of US General **Joseph Stilwell** to command Chinese troops, but backed down in the face of **Chiang Kai-shek**'s resistance and the recommendations of a senior US envoy, **Patrick Hurley**, who supported Chiang and called for Stilwell's recall.

FREEMAN, CHARLES (1943–). A prominent Chinese language officer and Chinese affairs specialist in the US Foreign Service during the period of US reconciliation with China, Freeman worked from posts in Washington and Asia to improve US–China relations and to defend the relationship in times of difficulties caused by bilateral differences or circumstances in the United States and China. Policy debates in the

United States sometimes pitted Freeman and like-minded officials against those who were more critical of China or less convinced that US accommodation with China on Taiwan and other issues served US interests. Some scholars claim that Freeman and others were removed from China-related positions following a shift in China policy in the middle of the **Ronald Reagan** administration toward a less solicitous US stance regarding China on issues like Taiwan. Freeman returned to prominence regarding China when as assistant secretary of defense, he led in 1993 the first senior US military delegation to China since the **Tiananmen crackdown**, resuming senior-level US–China military dialogue that had been suspended since 1989.

FREER, CHARLES L. (1856–1919). Freer was a railroad car manufacturer who imported art from China in the early 1900s. He was deeply interested in Chinese art and helped to increase its prestige in America through donating much of his collection to museums. The Freer Gallery of Art, an Asian art museum he supported, was opened in Washington, D.C. in May 1923.

FULBRIGHT, J. WILLIAM (1905–1995). As chairman of the Senate Foreign Relations Committee, Fulbright held hearings in 1964 and 1966 that provided a prominent public forum for Americans with moderate views on the People's Republic of China and US policy toward China. Their arguments in favor of less isolation and greater US engagement with China added to calls from various US groups for a reassessment of US **containment** policy, prompting the US State Department to modify slightly strict restrictions on exchanges of specialists and some other interaction with China.

FU MANCHU. This fictional Chinese character created by writer **Sax Rohmer** was featured in thirteen novels, numerous films, and other media for over 50 years beginning in 1913. A bloodthirsty and insidious schemer, Dr. Fu Manchu routinely tortured victims in pursuit of lust and power. He was one of the most notorious villains in American popular culture.

FX AIRCRAFT. This term was used to refer to two fighter aircraft—the F-16/J79 and the F-5G—which were proposed for sale to Taiwan in the late 1970s amid strenuous objections from China. The **Ronald Reagan** administration in December 1981 decided against the sale of either plane, but continued US co-production in Taiwan of a less advanced US aircraft, the F-5E.

– G –

GANG OF FOUR. These four radical Chinese **Communist Party** leaders rose to prominent positions as members of the party's Politburo during the **Cultural Revolution** (1966–1976). They were Jiang Qing, the wife of **Mao Zedong**, Zhang Chunqiao, a Shanghai political leader, Wang Hongwen, an industrial worker promoted to prominence by Mao Zedong, and Yao Wenyuan, a polemical literary critic who was close to Jiang Qing. The four radicals resisted moderation in Chinese policy toward the United States during early efforts at Chinese–US reconciliation. Chinese leaders with direct responsibility for managing relations with the United States during this period, notably **Zhou Enlai** and **Deng Xiaoping**, had to take the resistance of these leaders into account in making policy toward the United States, especially as the radicals frequently found Party Chairman **Mao Zedong** sympathetic to their views. The four leaders were removed from power and arrested soon after Mao's death in September 1976.

GAUSS, CLARENCE (1887–1960). Gauss became the US ambassador to China in 1941. He encouraged cooperation between **Nationalist Party** forces and **Communist Party** forces to resist Japan. Gauss had an uneasy relationship with **Chiang Kai-shek** due to the US ambassador's wariness regarding the Chinese Nationalist government's integrity, his advice against several large loans requested by Chiang, and his continuous suggestions of Nationalist–Communist cooperation. In 1944, Gauss was removed from his position amid changes in US representation in China including the recall of General **Joseph Stilwell** who had conflicts with Chiang Kai-shek regarding the leadership of the Nationalist military. Gauss shared Stilwell's views of Chiang. He was replaced by **Patrick Hurley**, who was more supportive of Chiang.

GEARY ACT. Named for a Democratic congressman from California, this legislation passed in 1892. It extended the restrictive anti-Chinese legislation of the previous decade, stripped Chinese in the United States, whether citizens or not, of substantial legal rights, and required all Chinese in the United States to obtain and carry at all times a certificate showing their right to reside in the United States. Without such proof, the punishment was hard labor and deportation. *See also* EXCLUSION MOVEMENT; IMMIGRATION.

GENERAL AGREEMENT ON TARIFFS AND TRADE (GATT). The most influential international organization dealing with world **trade** and predecessor to the **World Trade Organization** (created 1 January 1995), GATT granted China permanent observer status in 1984. In 1986, China applied for full membership in the organization. Chinese officials initially thought that China's rapidly growing economy, dynamic economic reforms, and burgeoning foreign trade would assure quick acceptance, but the **Tiananmen crackdown** added to serious economic issues to slow the process. The United States took the lead among the organization's members in protracted negotiations (1986–1999) to reach agreements with China on a variety of trade-related questions before Chinese accession could move forward.

GENERAL ORDER #1. Issued by President **Harry Truman** upon announcing Japan's surrender on 15 August 1945, this order commanded among other things that Japanese-controlled forces in China surrender their positions and arms to **Chiang Kai-shek**'s representatives, not to **Communist Party** forces in the field. The Japanese-controlled forces were ordered to hold and defend their positions against the Communists until properly relieved. The Chinese Communists denounced the US action as a betrayal of wartime cooperation and declared Communist commanders would move to disarm Japanese-controlled forces on their own.

GENEVA ACCORDS. These agreements dealing with issues in Indochina reached at the Geneva Conference, 1954, were not signed by the United States though the United States promised not to disturb the accords. The United States participated in the conference as an observer; China, France, Great Britain, and the Soviet Union formally participated. After the conference, US policy worked to support a non-Communist regime in South **Vietnam**, backing the regime when it resisted steps toward reunification set forth in the Geneva accords. The United States also deepened and broadened defense and other links with powers in Southeast Asia in order to check Chinese-backed Communist expansion in the region.

GENEVA AMBASSADORIAL TALKS. *See* AMBASSADORIAL TALKS.

GENEVA CONFERENCE ON LAOS, 1961–1962. This meeting attended by US and Chinese officials eventually reached an understanding on the Communist vs. non-Communist armed struggle in Laos. The understanding temporarily defused this flashpoint of US–Chinese conflicting interests, although the United States and China subsequently deepened military involvement in the country, as did the Chinese-backed forces from North **Vietnam**.

GEPHARDT, RICHARD (1941–). As leader of Democrats in the US House of Representatives in the period after the **Tiananmen crackdown**, and as a presidential candidate in 2000 and 2004, Gephardt took a tough stance toward China, particularly on **trade** and **human rights** issues. He favored strict conditions on the US's granting **most-favored-nation tariff status** to China and favored US trade restrictions and other measures to counter what he viewed as widespread unfair Chinese trading practices.

"GERM" WARFARE. As part of Chinese efforts to mobilize domestic and international support and undermine America's stature in China and abroad, Chinese officials and propagandists made repeated charges accusing the United States of engaging in the illegal use of biological weapons, "germ" warfare, against Chinese forces during the **Korean War**. The charges were not independently verified.

GIBBONS, SAMUEL (1920–). A strong believer in free **trade**, Congressman Gibbons, a Democrat, served as chairman of a congressional subcommittee that dealt with trade issues in the period after the **Tiananmen crackdown**. He supported US business interests seeking to preserve continued **most-favored-nation tariff status** for China, free of onerous conditions.

GILMAN, BENJAMIN (1922–). This Republican congressman took the helm of the US House of Representatives International Relations Committee when Republicans won control of the House of Representatives in 1995. Unlike his more moderate predecessor, Representative **Lee Hamilton**, Gilman advocated a tough US stance toward China on **human rights**, economic and security issues, strict conditions on the US's granting **most-favored-nation tariff status** to China, and strong support for Taiwan and for the **Dalai Lama**'s cause in **Tibet**.

GINGRICH, NEWT (1943–). As speaker of the US House of Representatives after Republicans in 1995 took control of the legislative body for the first time in decades, Gingrich pursued a tough policy toward China and pushed support of Taiwan at odds with the Democratic **William Clinton** administration. Though a supporter of free **trade**, he favored new US conditions on **most-favored-nation tariff status** for China, supported Taiwan President **Lee Teng-hui**'s visit to the United States in 1995, and bluntly warned leaders in Beijing in 1997 that the United States would defend Taiwan against Chinese attack. He backed subsequent congressional investigations attempting to link the Clinton administration with illegal Chinese campaign contributions, and the 1999 **Cox Commission** report that charged the Clinton administration with gross negligence in protecting vital US national security secrets from perceived widespread threats from Chinese spies.

GLENN, JOHN (1921–). Enjoying broad national recognition as the first US astronaut to enter space, Democratic Senator Glenn, as the chairman of the Senate Foreign Relations Committee's subcommittee on East Asia, was a critic of the **Jimmy Carter** administration's abrupt break in relations with Taiwan, and pressed to strengthen the administration's subsequent cautious support for Taiwan. He later worked against **Ronald Reagan** administration efforts to conclude a nuclear cooperation agreement with China at a time when China was engaging in nuclear proliferation activities with Pakistan and other countries.

GOLDWATER, BARRY (1909–1998). US senator from Arizona from 1953–1965 and 1969–1987, Goldwater was a strong anti-Communist who had a close relationship with Taiwan. He was an outspoken critic of President **Jimmy Carter**'s decision in 1978 to cut US relations and end the US defense treaty with Taiwan, and took the administration to court in a vain effort to reverse the decision.

GOODNOW, FRANK (1859–1939). A political scientist, Goodnow was a professor and served as president of Johns Hopkins University. In 1913, Goodnow traveled to China to serve as an advisor to **Yuan Shi-kai**. He advised Yuan to form a monarchy, which Yuan did in 1916.

GORBACHEV, MIKHAIL (1931–). Taking power as leader of the Soviet Union in 1985, Gorbachev initiated sweeping policy changes that saw major cutbacks in Soviet military spending and development, Soviet military withdrawal from **Afghanistan**, and large cutbacks in Soviet support for client and allied states abroad, leading to major breakthroughs in relations with the United States under President **Ronald Reagan**. Soviet relations with China also improved but at a slower pace. The Sino–Soviet improvement culminated with a summit in Beijing in May 1989 that was overshadowed by popular demonstrations leading to the **Tiananmen crackdown** in China and by the crumbling of Communist rule in the Soviet Bloc. The rapid decline in US perceptions of the Soviet threat during Gorbachev's rule plus the strongly negative US reaction to the Chinese government's crackdown on the Tiananmen demonstrators in June 1989 undermined strategic and ideological justifications for US efforts to improve relations with China.

GORE, ALBERT (1948–). Vice President Gore was a strong supporter of and active participant in the **William Clinton** administration's **engagement policy** toward China following the face-off of US and Chinese forces amid the **Taiwan Strait Crisis** of 1996. He traveled to China in March 1997 for talks with Chinese leaders as a prelude to the US–China summits of 1997 and 1998. Though Gore sought to direct attention to environmental, business, and other issues of substance, US media remained focused on the vice president's role in administration campaign fundraising involving large donations from sources said to be close to the Chinese government. Witnessing a signing of US–China trade deals during the visit, the vice president also was photographed with champagne glass in hand toasting his host, Premier **Li Peng**, widely reviled by the US media as one of the **"butchers of Beijing"** during the **Tiananmen crackdown**. Such reflections of continued sour American attitudes toward China meant that Gore was reluctant to highlight the achievements of the Clinton administration's engagement policy with China when he ran for president in the 2000 presidential campaign. The Republican candidate in the race, **George W. Bush**, staked out a tougher stance toward China.

GRAND ALLIANCE. This term was used to refer to the allied powers in World War II, and it notably included the Chinese **Nationalist Party** government of **Chiang Kai-shek** despite that government's faltering contribution to the war effort. President **Franklin D. Roosevelt** strongly supported Chiang's role, while British Prime Minister **Winston Churchill** had serious reservations about Chiang and his government.

GRANT, ULYSSES S. (1822–1885). President Grant favored a cooperative US policy toward China and was a personal friend of **Anson Burlingame**, a prominent proponent of cooperative China–US relations. After leaving office, Grant traveled to Asia in 1879 where he was encouraged by Chinese leader **Li Hung-chang** to intercede with Japan on China's behalf regarding a dispute over the **Liu-ch'iu (Ryukyu) Islands**. Grant also received at this time a promise from the Chinese government to negotiate treaty restrictions on Chinese **immigration** into the United States.

GREAT LEAP FORWARD. This utopian mass campaign vainly promoted rapid economic modernization in China in the late 1950s. It was accompanied by hardening Chinese policy toward the United States over Taiwan, contributing to the **Taiwan Strait Crisis** of 1958, and toward the Soviet Union, contributing to a public **Sino–Soviet split** by 1960.

GREENBERG, MAURICE R. "HANK" (1925–). Greenberg was the leader of **American International Group (AIG)**, an insurance corporation, and chairman of the **U.S.–China Business Council** at the end of the 20th century. Under his leadership, AIG in 1992 was the first foreign company to be allowed to sell insurance in the People's Republic of China. Greenberg helped to introduce China to practices of international business, was a lobbyist in the area of Sino–American relations, and served as an adviser to leaders on both sides. He also was influential in Sino–American relations through his **trade** policy advising and through his work with the **Starr Foundation**, an organization that promoted training of Chinese area specialists in US universities, Sino–US exchanges, and research to deepen Sino–US understanding.

GREENE, ROGER (1881–1947). Prior to US direct involvement in World War II, Greene was chairman of the Committee for Non-Participation in Japanese Aggression, which advocated giving US aid to China. He also was associate director of the Committee to Defend America by Aiding the Allies. Through both these organizations, Greene worked to increase US aid to the Chinese **Nationalist Party** government then resisting Japan.

GUAM. Guam is a Pacific island and a US territory close to China and East Asia. With extensive military bases, it figured prominently in US policy toward China during and after the Cold War. It was a forward base for US long-range nuclear-capable aircraft for use in the western Pacific and adjoining areas during much of the Cold War and thus played an important role in the military **containment** of China. President **Richard Nixon** announced his new strategy for Asia during a 1969 stop in Guam. His **Nixon Doctrine** was sometimes referred to as the Guam Doctrine. With the end of the Cold War and the decline in the danger posed by Soviet forces in the Pacific theater, US forces on the island declined markedly. The **George W. Bush** administration began increasing submarine, long-range bombers, and other forces in Guam that would be useful in contingencies like a **Taiwan Strait** crisis that could involve Chinese forces.

GULF WAR. *See* PERSIAN GULF WAR.

GUNBOAT DIPLOMACY. Following mid-19th-century treaties between China and foreign powers, foreign powers deployed naval forces in China's rivers and used them to support diplomatic and other demands to the Chinese government while trying to protect the lives and properties of their nationals in China. For much of the next 100 years, the US Navy deployed armed vessels in China's rivers.

– H –

HAASS, RICHARD (1951–). As the State Department's director of policy planning in the early years of the **George W. Bush** administration, Haass took an interest in building closer relations with China and in publicizing and explaining US policy toward China. He traveled to China for meetings with Chinese officials and made speeches detailing the administration's approach to China.

HAIG, ALEXANDER (1924–). As deputy to National Security Adviser **Henry Kissinger**, General Haig played an important role in planning and executing early US–China leadership exchanges and President **Richard Nixon**'s February 1972 visit to China. After retirement from the US Army, Haig returned to prominence in US–China relations as President **Ronald Reagan**'s first secretary of state. Haig sought to deepen strategic cooperation with China, including sales of US weapons, as a means to counter Soviet international expansion. He was prepared to give ground to Chinese demands for an end to US arms sales to Taiwan in order to preserve US–China cooperation. He participated actively in US deliberations dealing with strenuous pressure from China to halt plans for sales of a more advanced US jet fighter to Taiwan, and in negotiations leading to the US–China **17 August 1982 communiqué** that limited US arms sales to Taiwan. Haig resigned in June 1982.

HANKOW–CANTON RAILWAY. *See* AMERICAN CHINA DEVELOPMENT COMPANY.

HARDING, HARRY (1946–). This internationally recognized political scientist and international relations specialist was prominent in American academic and public policy groups dealing with China from the 1970s into the 21st century. Harding advocated in numerous writings, commentaries, and congressional testimonies an overall positive

US approach to China that also reflected firm defense of US interests in disputes with China.

HARRIMAN, AVERELL (1891–1986). This leading US political figure in the mid-20th century occasionally played an important role in US relations with China. As US ambassador to Moscow at the end of World War II, he influenced President **Harry Truman** to continue support for **Chiang Kai-shek**'s **Nationalist Party** government and to avoid US steps that he judged would allow Soviet leader **Joseph Stalin** to control China. As President **John F. Kennedy**'s assistant secretary of state for East Asian affairs, Harriman was sent to Taiwan to squelch Chiang Kai-shek's plans to invade the Chinese mainland at the time of the economic collapse in the Chinese mainland in 1962. He also contributed to the limited reassessments of China policy taking place within the Kennedy administration, which was generally unwilling to make dramatic changes in US policy toward China.

HARRIMAN, EDWARD H. (1848–1909). This American railway magnate looked for investment and other economic opportunities in China in the first decade of the 20th century, getting involved with the **Hankow–Canton Railway** concession and proposed rail lines in Manchuria. Chinese officials vainly sought his backing as a means to offset Japanese and Russian control in Manchuria.

HARRISON, BENJAMIN (1833–1901). Harrison campaigned and won the presidency in 1888 advocating exclusion of Chinese **immigration**. His secretary of state, James Blaine, was a longstanding foe of Chinese immigration. A highlight of the anti-Chinese legislation at this time was the **Geary Act** of 1892. Chinese government protests had little effect on the growing political support in the United States to stop Chinese immigration and to pressure Chinese in the United States to leave. *See also* EXCLUSION MOVEMENT.

HART, ROBERT (1835–1911). As the inspector general of the **Chinese Imperial Maritime Customs Service**, Hart advocated equal commercial opportunity in China. His aide **Alfred Hippisley** worked closely with State Department China expert **William Rockhill** to produce a statement that in its essentials became the policy expressed by Secretary of State **John Hay** in his **Open Door Notes** of 1899.

HARTFORD EDUCATION MISSION. Marking the first such educational exchange between China and the United States, 120 Chinese students were sent to the United States in 1872 to study Western learning while they also were prepared by Chinese scholars for the traditional Chinese government examinations. The program lasted until 1881. *See also* EDUCATION.

HASHIMOTO, RYUTARO (1937–). As prime minister of Japan, Hashimoto signed along with President **William Clinton** in April 1996 the US–Japan Joint Declaration on the Alliance for the Twenty-first Century, also known as the **Clinton–Hashimoto Declaration**. The document was the result of strong efforts by the US and Japanese governments in the previous two years to strengthen the alliance and to deal with possible military contingencies, notably regarding North Korea. Coming one month after the first face-off of US and Chinese forces in the **Taiwan Strait** since the depths of the Cold War, the strengthened US–Japan alignment also was seen to have potent implications for US and Japanese relations with China and for possible US–Japan military cooperation in a Taiwan military contingency.

HAY, JOHN (1838–1905). Secretary of state under President **William McKinley**, and after his assassination in 1901, President **Theodore Roosevelt**, Hay strove to preserve US commercial access to China and other interests amid widespread foreign encroachment on the weakened **Qing dynasty**. Responding to the unexpected Japanese defeat of China in 1895, and European powers' extortion of leaseholds and **concessions** in the following three years, Hay used the work of State Department China expert **William Rockhill** and his British colleague from the **Chinese Imperial Maritime Customs Service**, **Alfred Hippisley**, as the basis for official US messages sent to all foreign powers concerned with China in September 1899. The notes sought the powers' agreement that even if they established special spheres in China, they would not discriminate against foreign **trade** or interfere with customs collection. Though generally unenthusiastic about the US initiative, most concerned powers offered evasive and qualified responses but all in effect endorsed the principles in the so-called **Open Door Notes**.

As the United States and other foreign powers dispatched troops to crush the **Boxer uprising** and lift the siege of foreign legations in Peking, Hay in July 1900 sent a second round of Open Door Notes in which he expressed concern for preserving Chinese sovereignty. He depicted local Chinese authorities as responsible for law and order and the safety of foreigners in China. This helped the United States and other powers continue to work constructively with regional Chinese leaders in central and southern China who were maintaining law and order, and focus their anti-Boxer suppression more narrowly, in northern China. The foreign powers went along with Hay's notes.

Though Hay tried to reduce the large size of the foreign indemnity demanded of China, the United States took its $25 million share of the $333 million indemnity China was required to pay the foreign powers under terms of the **Boxer Protocol** signed in September 1901, and it stationed troops along with other powers in northern China. Though continuing to work in support of China's territorial integrity and equal commercial access to China, Hay responded to US pressures to obtain a coaling station in China by making a perfunctory and ultimately vain effort in December 1900 to acquire such a station on the China coast.

Meanwhile, as Russia endeavored to consolidate its hold in Manchuria, and Japan and Great Britain worked together against it and ultimately formed an alliance in 1902, Hay endeavored to secure US interests with a new Sino–American trade treaty and a request for opening two new **treaty ports** in Russian-dominated areas of Manchuria. Russia at first resisted Chinese acceptance of the US request but decided to withdraw its opposition when it was clear to them that Americans or other foreigners, notably Japanese, would not settle in the ports.

HAYES, RUTHERFORD (1822–1893). As US president, Hayes in 1879 was presented with a bill severely limiting Chinese **immigration**. Due to existing US treaty commitments with China, he vetoed the bill, but US pressures to exclude Chinese immigration continued to grow. *See also* EXCLUSION MOVEMENT.

HEARD AND COMPANY. Founded in 1840, this trading company generally ran second to **Russell and Company** among American firms in China until its demise in 1875 amid the decline of US–China **trade** during and after the US Civil War.

"HEGEMONISM." Chinese officials often used this term and the term *hegemony* in the 1970s to refer to Soviet expansionism and encirclement of China. The term *hegemony* appeared in such documents as the **Shanghai Communiqué**, the **United States–China communiqué of 1978** establishing official US–China diplomatic relations, and the **China–Japan Peace and Friendship Treaty** of 1978. With the collapse of the Soviet Union and the rise of US pressure on China after the **Tiananmen crackdown**, Chinese officials tended to refer to the United States and its policy toward China and others as hegemonism.

HELMS, JESSE (1921–). A strong anti-Communist and supporter of Taiwan, this Republican senator from North Carolina served from the 1980s until the early 2000s as the chairman or ranking member of the US Senate Foreign Relations Committee. An expert on legislative maneuver and congressional prerogatives, Helms used these skills for decades to slow the pace of improving US relations with the **People's Republic of China**, to sharply criticize China's practices regarding **human rights, trade**, proliferation of weapons of mass destruction, and other questions, and to shore up US support for Taiwan and **Tibet**.

HILLS, CARLA (1934–). As the US special **trade** representative in the **George H. W. Bush** administration, Hills oversaw difficult negotiations with Chinese officials over **intellectual property rights** in 1991–1992. She became the first US cabinet-level official to visit Taiwan following the break in US official relations with Taiwan in 1979 when she was sent to Taiwan in December 1992.

HILSMAN, ROGER (1919–). Assistant secretary of state for Far Eastern affairs during the **Lyndon B. Johnson** administration, Hilsman in December 1963 publicly advocated significant changes in US policy toward China that involved the possibility of American coexistence with **Mao Zedong**'s government while maintaining US ties with **Chiang Kai-shek**.

HIPPISLEY, ALFRED E. (1848–1949). A British commissioner of the **Chinese Imperial Maritime Customs Service**, Hippisley worked with State Department China expert **William Rockhill** to draft language that became the basis for official messages known later as the **Open Door Notes**, sent by US Secretary of State **John Hay** to all foreign powers concerned with China in September 1899. The notes sought the powers' agreement that even if they established special spheres in China, they would not discriminate against foreign **trade** or interfere with customs collection.

HOLBROOKE, RICHARD (1941–). Holbrooke was the assistant secretary of state for East Asian and Pacific affairs at the time of President **Jimmy Carter**'s decision in December 1978 to break relations with Taiwan and establish relations with China. He was a strong advocate of the decision and defended it and the administration's subsequent efforts to strengthen ties with China in the face of considerable resistance from Congress, the media, and US interest groups.

HOLDRIDGE, JOHN (1924–2001). A National Security Council staff member who accompanied **Henry Kissinger** on his first trip to China in 1971, Holdridge served in the US **liaison office** in Beijing and later reached public prominence as assistant secretary of state for East Asian affairs in the first two years of the **Ronald Reagan** administration. He strongly defended the pro-China policies of Secretary of State **Alexander Haig** against opponents in the administration and the Congress who particularly questioned Haig's willingness to cut back US military support for Taiwan in the face of Chinese demands. He duly defended the **17 August 1982 US–China communiqué** limiting US arms sales to Taiwan. After Haig's resignation in 1982, Holdridge was replaced as assistant secretary by **Paul Wolfowitz**, a strong supporter of Taiwan who gave less emphasis to close US relations with China.

HONG KONG. Hong Kong long served as a base of US commercial and government activities dealing with China. Though US **trade** with

China was cut off during the first two decades of the Cold War, American trade and investment in Hong Kong grew. As the Chinese government opened to foreign economic exchange in the 1970s, American businesses used Hong Kong as a base of operations to take advantage of China's opening. The US government adopted a low posture and seemed quietly supportive of Britain's efforts regarding Sino–British negotiations in 1982–1984, leading to the **Joint Declaration**, an agreement in 1984 calling for the British colony to return to Chinese sovereignty in 1997. The **Tiananmen crackdown** and large-scale demonstrations in Hong Kong in 1989 prompted greater British and US interest in securing guarantees for democracy and stability in the territory. Subsequent US legislation conditioning the annual US renewal of **most-favored-nation tariff status** for China routinely had provisions dealing with China's policy toward Hong Kong. The last British governor of Hong Kong, **Christopher Patten**, and leading Hong Kong **Democratic Party** leader **Martin Lee** made annual visits to the United States seeking support while urging continued open US trade with China, an essential element in Hong Kong's economy. At congressional initiative, the United States passed the **Hong Kong Policy Act** in 1992, laying out US concerns about Hong Kong's future and calling for regular US reports monitoring China's treatment of the territory. The US media, Congress, and the State Department remained attentive into the 21st century to oppose perceived Chinese efforts to curb those in Hong Kong seeking greater democracy for the people of Hong Kong. *See also* LEGISLATIVE COUNCIL (LEGCO).

HONG KONG POLICY ACT. Amid growing US concerns about US interests in **Hong Kong** following the **Tiananmen crackdown**, and as the territory prepared to return to Chinese sovereignty in 1997, congressional initiatives with the support of the US administration led to legislation that became the US Hong Kong Policy Act of 1992. The law laid out US concerns about Hong Kong's future and called for regular US reports monitoring China's treatment of the territory.

HONG MERCHANTS. Designated by **Qing dynasty** authorities to manage **trade** with foreigners, these Canton-based merchants dominated Sino–Western trade until the **Opium War** of 1839–1842, and the establishment of the first **treaty ports** in the 1840s.

HOOVER, HERBERT (1874–1964). Dealing with the disastrous consequences of the Great Depression, this US president was reluctant to respond forcefully to Japan's aggression in Manchuria and its breach of US-backed security arrangements in the **Nine Power Treaty** of 1922 and the **Kellogg–Briand Pact** of 1928. With his Secretary of State **Henry Stimson** in the lead, Hoover favored a moral stance of non-recognition of the changes brought by Japan's aggression. This **Hoover–Stimson Doctrine** failed in 1932 as Japanese forces expanded their military aggression in China to include attacks on Chinese forces in Shanghai. The Hoover administration formally protested, sent additional forces to China, and appealed to the world not to recognize the Japanese aggression. The Japanese halted the assault on Shanghai, the **League of Nations** adopted a resolution of non-recognition, but Japan created a puppet state of **Manchukuo** and withdrew from the League of Nations when it approved a report critical of Japan's actions. *See also* LYTTON COMMISSION; NON-RECOGNITION DOCTRINE.

HOOVER–STIMSON DOCTRINE. In response to Japan's aggression in Manchuria in 1931 and 1932, President **Herbert Hoover** and Secretary of State **Henry Stimson** proposed a stance of non-recognition of the Japanese gains. This Hoover-Stimson Doctrine failed in 1932 as Japanese forces expanded their military aggression in China to include attacks on Chinese forces in Shanghai. Among other things, the Hoover administration appealed to the world not to recognize the Japanese aggression. The **League of Nations** adopted a resolution of non-recognition, but Japan withdrew from the League of Nations when it approved a report critical of Japan's actions. *See also* LYTTON COMMISSION; NON-RECOGNITION DOCTRINE.

HOPKINS, HARRY (1890–1946). Hopkins was a close adviser to President **Franklin D. Roosevelt** who was sympathetic to China's cause and provided a channel of communication between **Chiang Kai-shek**'s administration and the US president.

HORNBECK, STANLEY (1883–1966). A senior State Department specialist on China, Hornbeck played important roles in advising and implementing US policy toward China, especially in the period of

Japanese aggression in China in the 1930s. A strong supporter of China, he tended to be realistic about Chinese weaknesses and capabilities in the face of Japanese power, and was involved in various efforts to provide US support for the Chinese **Nationalist Party** government and to resist Japanese aggression without directly confronting Japan.

HSI-LIANG (XI LIANG) (1853–1917). Appointed governor-general in Manchuria in the last years of the **Qing dynasty**, this Chinese government official encouraged the United States to become more deeply involved in railway and development schemes as a means to counter Japanese and Russian encroachment in Manchuria. He concluded a railroad deal with Americans regarding a proposed **Chinchow–Aigun Railroad** that in the face of Japanese and Russian disapproval failed to get Chinese government approval. The **William H. Taft** administration and its Secretary of State **Philander Knox** initially used the railroad plan as a means to assert US **Open Door Policy** against Russian and Japanese expansion. After this failed in the face of Russian–Japanese resistance, the US government leaders adopted in 1910 a more cooperative policy, working in concert with European powers and avoiding direct confrontation with Moscow and Tokyo in Manchuria. Ironically, Hsi-liang and his Qing dynasty colleagues chose this time to consolidate ties with the United States and seek greater US support against Russia and Japan in Manchuria, but Chinese government emissaries found the Taft administration now maintaining a low profile regarding Manchuria.

HSU CHI-YU (XU JIYU) (1795–1873). An important Chinese scholar of foreign relations in the period after the **Opium War**, Hsu conveyed a positive view of the United States as a country at odds with Great Britain and the center of new world power. His writings, along with those of **Wei Yuan** and others, supported the belief among Chinese officials in the 19th century that the Chinese could use relations with the United States as a means to offset the demands of Great Britain and other powers.

HSU SHIH-CH'ANG (XU SHICHANG) (1855–1939). As governor-general in Manchuria, Hsu endeavored in 1906–1908 to interest **E.H.**

Harriman and other Americans to invest in Manchurian railroads as a means to offset Japanese and Russian control there. He rose to greater prominence as head of the cabinet and president of the Republic of China, and was known for his pro-American viewpoint.

HUA GUOFENG (1920–). Succeeding **Mao Zedong** for a few years as leader of the Chinese **Communist Party** following Mao's death in 1976, Hua dealt with intense leadership struggle and notably carried out the arrest of the radical **Gang of Four** soon after Mao's death. A Mao loyalist who rose to power in the **Cultural Revolution**, Hua was wary of the implications of the return to power of senior leaders purged during the Cultural Revolution, notably **Deng Xiaoping**. He supported Deng's negotiations leading to the **United States–China communiqué of 1978** normalizing China's diplomatic relations with the United States.

HUAI-HAI. This months-long battle between **Nationalist Party** and **Communist Party** forces north of Nanking in 1948–1949 saw the loss of half a million Chinese Nationalist forces and signaled to American observers that the Nationalist regime was finished on mainland China.

HUANG CHEN (1909–1989). As Chinese ambassador in Paris, Huang was involved in the secret negotiations leading to **Henry Kissinger**'s secret visit to China in 1971. He was the first head of the Chinese **liaison office** established in Washington in 1973.

HUANG HUA (1913–). Huang spent his career as a Chinese **Communist Party** foreign policy specialist who dealt repeatedly with US issues. A former student of US Ambassador **John Leighton Stuart**, he was sent by the Communist leaders to investigate US intentions as Stuart sought to approach the Communist leaders as they were defeating **Chiang Kai-shek**'s **Nationalist Party** forces on the Chinese mainland in 1949. He was involved in supporting **Zhou Enlai** in early interaction with the **Richard Nixon** administration, and was appointed China's ambassador to the United Nations in 1971 where he dealt extensively with American leaders. As foreign minister, he took a tough line on US arms sales to Taiwan and other bilateral disputes during the early years of the **Ronald Reagan** administration.

HUGHES, CHARLES EVANS (1862–1948). Secretary of state during the Warren Harding administration, Hughes took the lead in calling a major conference of powers with interests in the western Pacific, including China but not the Soviet Union, to deal with relevant security issues. The result was the **Washington Conference** of 1921–1922 that saw passage of the **Nine Power Treaty** supporting non-interference in Chinese internal affairs. The treaty disappointed Chinese patriots as it had no enforcement mechanisms and did nothing to retrieve the rights of sovereignty China had been forced to give up over the previous 80 years. Other agreements at the conference included one concerning Japan's withdrawal from China's Shantung province, a goal of Chinese patriots. *See also* SHANTUNG LEASEHOLD.

HUGHES ELECTRONIC CORPORATION. This American company built telecommunications satellites worth hundreds of millions of dollars and launched them via Chinese rockets in the 1990s. Such launches were curbed as part of US sanctions after the **Tiananmen crackdown**, but presidential waivers permitting launches were allowed, and both President **George H. W. Bush** and President **William Clinton** provided waivers allowing launches. In 1992 and 1995 Hughes satellites were destroyed, and in 1996 a satellite built by another US firm, **Loral Space Systems**, was destroyed, when Chinese launch-rockets exploded. Without proper US government authorization, an independent review commission composed of engineers from the US firms found flaws in the Chinese launch rockets and recommended corrections. The commission sent its report to the Chinese company without required US government clearance. Many strong critics in Congress, the media, and elsewhere of the Clinton administration's **engagement policy** to China connected these illegal acts with the large campaign contributions both satellite company directors had made to the Democratic Party. Extreme charges alleged that these US companies were helping to increase the accuracy of Chinese nuclear missiles targeted at the United States and that the Clinton administration was cooperating with them in order to gain campaign contributions. Conclusive proof of such allegations was lacking, though they represented an important element in the vituperative US debate over China policy in the late 1990s.

HU JINTAO (1942–). As vice president of China, Hu visited the United States in 2002 and held meetings with President **George W. Bush** and Vice President **Richard Cheney** that added to positive momentum in US–China relations at that time. Becoming leader of the Chinese party and president in 2002–2003, Hu interacted regularly with senior US leaders and followed the existing Chinese approach seeking to improve relations with the United States while remaining vigilant in defense of important Chinese interests, especially regarding Taiwan.

HUKUANG RAILWAY. The **William H. Taft** administration insisted on and gained a share in the international consortium financing this proposed railway between Hankow and Canton, with a link to Szechuan. International cooperation in this project saw the Taft administration alter its previous efforts to confront foreign powers in demanding equal economic access to commercial opportunities in China, and adopt a more accommodating stance that led by 1911 and 1912 to US willingness to work cooperatively with powers wishing to be part of an international financial consortium regarding loans to China.

In 1982, a federal district court in Alabama ruled that the People's Republic of China was responsible for redeeming bonds issued by the **Qing dynasty** to finance the construction of the Hukuang Railway. Chinese officials protested strongly to the American government. They eventually fought the case in court and had the 1982 decision reversed.

HULL, CORDELL (1871–1955). As secretary of state in the **Franklin D. Roosevelt** administration in the years prior to World War II, Hull shied away from support of China, then at war with Japan. He sought to avoid US involvement in an Asian war at a time of heightened tensions and war in Europe. Hull disapproved a plan supported by Treasury Secretary **Henry Morgenthau** to provide China $25 million in credits to purchase supplies in the United States, but President Roosevelt approved the plan while Hull was out of the country in December 1938. Hull resisted efforts to impose sanctions on Japan, but eventually the State Department in January 1940 announced that the United States would not renew a 1911 commercial treaty with Japan. This step allowed the United States subsequently to impose selective embargoes on the sale of strategic materials to Japan, leading to a US oil embargo in 1941. Hull negotiated with Japanese envoys in the period before the surprise Japanese attack on **Pearl Harbor**, sticking to a hard line requiring Japanese withdrawal from China and Indochina before US oil sales would be resumed.

HUMAN RIGHTS. Though American officials, **missionaries**, and business people were careful to secure US rights in China beginning in the 19th century, the US government repeatedly failed in the late 19th and early 20th centuries to address often gross discrimination against Chinese and violations of Chinese rights in the United States as anti-Chinese **immigration** forces strove to restrict Chinese immigration and to press Chinese in the United States to leave. American critics of the Chinese **Communist Party** government highlighted human rights policies and practices of the People's Republic of China as an issue in US–China relations. American concern markedly broadened and deepened following the **Tiananmen crackdown** of 1989. This coincided with broad American satisfaction with improving human rights conditions in Taiwan as the government there moved from authoritarian rule to greater democracy. A wide range of human rights issues—suppression of democratic activists, prison conditions and prison labor, religious freedom, suppression of ethnic rights, coerced abortions, media control, and other questions—were part of the often vituperative US policy debate over China in the 1990s. They were featured in the annual congressional consideration of renewing China's **most-favored-nation tariff status** that tended to pit US business interests against human rights organizations and their supporters, notably in US organized labor. The US administration registered official concern in annual reports on human rights and religious freedom conditions in China, statements by US leaders interacting with China, and support for congressionally backed initiatives establishing independent radio service for Chinese audiences and a special US office for Tibet. US concern declined as the 11 September 2001 terrorist attack on America reduced negative US attention to China. *See also* AMNESTY INTERNATIONAL; HUMAN RIGHTS WATCH–ASIA; LINKAGE POLICY; RADIO FREE ASIA; TIBET.

HUMAN RIGHTS WATCH–ASIA. This **human rights** group was among the most active after the **Tiananmen crackdown** of 1989 in urging the Congress and the administration to impose conditions on the United States' granting **most-favored-nation trade status** to China, and on the United States' agreeing to China's membership in the **World Trade Organization**.

HUMP AIRLIFT. This term referred to US military planes being forced to fly over the Himalaya Mountains in order to provide supplies to **Chiang Kai-shek**'s **Nationalist Party** forces after the Japanese military cut off all land routes to the Nationalists in central China in the months after **Pearl Harbor**.

HUNDRED DAYS OF REFORM. Leaders of this failed reform movement in China in 1898, **Kang Yu-wei** and **Liang Ch'i-ch'ao**, fled abroad where they became active in the United States, organizing Chinese communities, gaining financial and other support, and lobbying against US exclusion of Chinese **immigration** and US economic expansion in China. The Chinese legation in the United States worked against these reformers and the more radical leader **Sun Yat-sen** who was also active in the United States.

HUNG HSIU-CH'UAN (HONG XIUQUAN) (1814–1864). Leader of the **Taiping Rebellion**, the visionary and charismatic Hung saw himself as the younger brother of Jesus Christ. He came to his own unique views of Christianity, though he had three months of study in 1837 with an American missionary in Canton, **Issachar Roberts**. Hung's movement tended to alienate Americans and other Westerners in China, who came to see their interests better served by siding with the **Qing dynasty** against the Taiping rebels.

HURLEY, PATRICK J. (1883–1963). A prominent Republican who served as President **Herbert Hoover**'s secretary of war, Hurley was a key figure in US policy toward the Chinese **Nationalist Party** and the Chinese **Communist Party** in 1944–1945. He was sent as a special envoy by President **Franklin D. Roosevelt** to China in September 1944. Dealing with major disputes then causing a crisis between **Chiang Kai-shek** and the US commander in China, General **Joseph Stilwell**, Hurley sided with Chiang. Roosevelt recalled Stilwell in October 1944, appointing General **Albert Wedemeyer** as his replacement. Hurley was appointed as ambassador to replace **Clarence Gauss**, who shared Stilwell's negative opinions about Chiang and the Nationalists.

In November 1944, Hurley traveled to **Yenan** and negotiated a **Five-Point Agreement** with **Mao Zedong** and his senior colleagues. Among other things, the agreement summarized Hurley's promises of equal treatment and US aid to the Communists in a coalition with the Nationalists. The deal soon collapsed in the face of Chinese Nationalist opposition and Hurley's strong support for Chiang Kai-shek in disputes with the Communists.

The US embassy staff in **Chungking** in February 1945 sent a message to the State Department warning against Hurley's one-sided support for the Nationalists and opposition to the Communists. Hurley subsequently responded to the charges and succeeded in persuading President Roosevelt to support him. At Nationalist–Communist peace talks in Chungking in September 1945, Chiang Kai-shek, backed by Hurley and the **Harry Truman** administration, demanded the Communists surrender their forces and territory as a precondition for joining a coalition. Fighting spread in China and the talks collapsed. Hurley was unsuccessful in urging a full US commitment to Chiang's cause. He abruptly resigned as ambassador in November 1945, blaming pro-Chinese Communists in the State Department for thwarting US policy. After the Communist victory in China and the Chinese intervention in the **Korean War**, Hurley's charges provided a leading wedge for congressional investigators seeking to purge alleged pro-Communists and other security risks from among the ranks of the Chinese affairs specialists in the State Department and other agencies.

HU SHIH (HU SHI) (1890–1962). A major intellectual leader of China in the first half of the 20th century, Hu participated actively in the **May Fourth Movement**. In contrast to more radical political advocates in China at this time, Hu promoted more gradual social and educational reforms, notably including the use of vernacular Chinese language instead of classical Chinese language in written media and other documents. Hu studied in the United States and became deeply influenced by the reformist ideas of philosopher **John Dewey**. Hu served as ambassador to the United States from 1938–1942.

HUTCHINSON WHAMPOA LIMITED. In the late 1990s, amid intense US debate over China policy and concern in some US quarters regarding the transfer of the **Panama Canal** to Panama, prominent members of Congress, including Senate Majority Leader Trent Lott, as well as some US media and interest groups, saw serious implications for US national security in the investments of this **Hong Kong**–based company to operate ports on either end of the canal. The company was headed by **Li Kashing**, who had close ties with Chinese leaders in pursuing a Hong Kong–based international enterprise, worth $25 billion, including port operations in Europe, Hong Kong, Shanghai, and the Caribbean. The charges that the Chinese Communist regime was using this means to take control of the Panama Canal were among the most extreme of the many unsubstantiated charges made during the US–China debate of the 1990s.

HU YAOBANG (1915–1989). A close ally of **Deng Xiaoping** as Deng pursued reforms in the post–**Mao Zedong** period, Hu served as general secretary of the **Communist Party** of China in the 1980s. Leaving key foreign policy issues like relations with the United States to Deng, Hu followed the party's foreign policy approach and pursued a reform agenda in both economic and political areas. His political reforms created strong opposition and eventually alienated Deng, who removed him from his leadership positions in 1987. Hu's death in April 1989 prompted an outpouring of public sympathy that grew to become the mass demonstrations urging reform at Tiananmen Square in Beijing and in other Chinese cities that captured the attention of US and world audiences and led to the **Tiananmen crackdown**.

– I –

IMMIGRATION. The US government in the 1860s encouraged Chinese laborers to come to the United States, notably promising free immigration in the **Burlingame Treaty** of 1868. However, in the 1870s a broad US **exclusion movement** emerged that was based on prejudice and fear of Chinese workers amid sometimes-difficult economic times in the United States. Americans took legal and illegal actions, including riots and murder of Chinese, to stop Chinese immigration to the United States. Various state governments and the national government passed an array of laws and the US courts made a variety of decisions that singled out Chinese immigrants for negative treatment and curbed the legal rights of Chinese residents and Chinese citizens of the United States. The exclusion movement broadened to include all Asians. The **National Origins Act of 1924** barred all new Asian immigration. US immigration policy and mistreatment of Chinese people in the United States was a major issue for the Chinese government, which complained repeatedly against unjust US actions, but with little effect. US policy in these areas was the target of an **anti-American boycott** in China in 1905.

The US government in the 1940s and 1950s passed laws ending formal restriction on Chinese immigration but allowed little immigration from China and other Asian countries until the **Immigration Reform Act** of 1965 ended prejudice against Asians in US immigration procedures. After the United States established diplomatic relations with the People's Republic of China in 1979, some Americans highlighted the Chinese government's restrictions on free immigration as a reason to deny **most-favored-nation (MFN) tariff status** to China under terms of the **Jackson–Vanik Amendment** of the Trade Act of 1974. Other Americans complained about Chinese workers entering the United States illegally.

IMMIGRATION REFORM ACT. Passed in 1965 at the urging of President **Lyndon Johnson**, this law ended the virtual ban on Chinese **immigration** to the United States in effect since the late 1800s.

INCHON. As **United Nations** Commander in the **Korean War**, General **Douglas MacArthur** oversaw an ambitious amphibious assault in Inchon in September 1950 that marked the beginning of the end of the North Korean forces and opened the way for the US-led United Nations forces to move into North Korea, seeking to reunify the country. Chinese forces soon intervened to drive back the US and other UN forces, and more than two years of intense but inconclusive warfare followed.

INDIGENOUS DEFENSE FIGHTER (IDF). Facing strong Chinese objections to more advanced US fighter-aircraft and other armaments sales to Taiwan, the **Ronald Reagan** administration cooperated with Taiwan in arranging for US companies to provide components and guidance as Taiwan produced its first fighter aircraft, the IDF. Beijing viewed the US arrangement with Taiwan as violating the terms of the **17 August 1982 communiqué** between the United States and China that limited US arms transfers to Taiwan, but the US administration argued that the arrangement with US private companies did not violate the communiqué.

INSTITUTE FOR PACIFIC RELATIONS. Looking for subversives and security risks, the US Senate Internal Security Subcommittee beginning in 1951 spent years investigating, among others, specialists affiliated with this non-governmental, international organization concerned with Chinese and Asian affairs

INTELLECTUAL PROPERTY RIGHTS (IPR). With the exception of the burgeoning US **trade** deficit with China, disputes over intellectual property rights represented the most contentious set of issues in Sino–US trade relations after the normalization of relations in the 1970s. US companies complained of massive losses, with the American computer software industries saying they lost $11 billion in sales in China in 1998. US companies also complained about the danger posed by poor Chinese copies of sensitive products like drugs, chemical agents, and other goods that directly affected the health and safety of consumers in China and, if exported, elsewhere in the world. The US government, armed with sanctions and other procedures provided by Congress backed by US industries, pressured the Chinese government to crack down on clearly evident and rampant intellectual piracy in China. It also worked to educate Chinese officials and businesses as to why adherence to internationally accepted intellectual property guidelines was in the best long-term interest of Chinese development, and helped China set up legal regimes with adequate enforcement to insure an appropriate intellectual property rights climate in China. Progress in this area was mixed and remained incomplete. Issues concerning Chinese intellectual piracy continued to prompt strong US complaints in the 21st century.

INTERNATIONAL ATOMIC ENERGY AGENCY (IAEA). This international organization was established in 1957 under **United Nations** auspices to promote peaceful uses of atomic energy. With the backing of the United States and broad international support, the agency has been authorized to facilitate and control the peaceful application of nuclear energy. As China moved slowly to bring its nuclear weapons development and nuclear exports into conformity with internationally accepted norms, the Chinese government agreed to participate with the IAEA in the 1980s. In 1997, China issued regulations regarding its nuclear exports that said the recipients would be subject to IAEA supervision. The latter step was particularly welcomed by the US government, which saw China's longstanding export of nuclear weapons technology abroad, notably to Pakistan, as a grave danger. At the same time, the US government continued periodic criticism of Chinese nuclear proliferation practices. *See also* ARMS CONTROL.

INTERNATIONAL CAMPAIGN FOR TIBET. This non-government organization was the most influential Tibetan advocacy group in the United States in the post–Cold War period. It was sharply critical of Chinese government policies in **Tibet**, and insured that issues related to Tibet were highlighted in US interaction with China.

INTERNATIONAL COVENANT ON ECONOMIC, SOCIAL, AND CULTURAL RIGHTS. Under strong pressure from the United States and others, the Chinese government signed this international **human rights** accord just before Chinese **Communist Party** leader **Jiang Zemin**'s summit **meeting** with President **William Clinton** in Washington in 1997.

INTERNATIONAL COVENANT ON CIVIL AND POLITICAL RIGHTS. Under strong pressure from the United States and others, Chinese leaders in March 1998, a few months before President **William Clinton**'s visit to China, said they would sign this international **human rights** accord, and did so in October that year.

INTERNATIONAL DEVELOPMENT ASSOCIATION (IDA). Despite various international sanctions after the **Tiananmen crackdown**

that had a temporary effect on China's relations with the **World Bank**, China in 1992 became the largest recipient of World Bank funds. By 1999, China's cumulative borrowings from the World Bank were about $33 billion, with about one-third of that coming from the International Development Association (IDA), the bank's concessional lending window. The US government was very supportive of closer China–World Bank relations after China decided to join the international financial institution in 1980. US policy was constrained to some degree by legislative and other sanctions imposed after the Tiananmen crackdown.

INTERNATIONAL MONETARY FUND (IMF). China's relations with this US-supported international financial institution and specialized agency of the **United Nations** grew after China joined the IMF in 1980. China benefited from advice and credits during periods of economic retrenchment, high inflation, and foreign exchange difficulty. China worked with the IMF and the United States in reacting to the **Asian economic crisis** of 1997–1998 that had a big impact on the Thai, South Korean, and Indonesian economies in particular. China pledged support for IMF loan packages for Thailand and Indonesia. It also cooperated with Asian governments dissatisfied with the IMF and US response to the Asian economic crisis and supported Asian-only cooperative means to deal with future economic shocks. *See also* WORLD BANK.

INTERPRETERS COLLEGE. Set up in Peking in 1862 and led for years by an American missionary, **W. A. P. Martin**, this institution taught foreign languages to young Manchu and Chinese students who would engage in diplomatic negotiation. At the end of the **Qing dynasty**, the college was incorporated into the Imperial University.

INVESTMENT. US investment in China was small through much of the 19th and early 20th centuries, though the **William H. Taft** administration endeavored to use proposed US investment in railways in China as a means to promote US interests through so-called **dollar diplomacy**. Subsequent conflict and revolution in China limited US investment, while a US economic embargo was imposed after the start of the **Korean War**. Following the breakthrough in US–China relations in the 1970s, growing US **trade** with China in the latter decades of the 20th century was accompanied by growing US investment, with the United States becoming one of the largest foreign investors in China in the early 21st century.

– J –

JACKAL DIPLOMACY. US treaties with China in the 19th century included a **most-favored-nation clause**, which assured that the United States would receive benefits given by China to any other nation. Thus, whenever Britain, France, or other powers extracted new privileges from China by force, intimidation, or other coercive means, the benefit passed automatically to the United States. In this context, Chinese patriots were not convinced of the American image of a moral policy toward China that left violence and intimidation more to others. Rather, they saw US behavior as "jackal diplomacy."

JACKSON–VANIK AMENDMENT. Under terms of this amendment of the Trade Act of 1974, each year the president had to inform Congress of the intention to extend **most-favored-nation (MFN) tariff status** to China in regard to China's **trade** with the United States. Congress had 90 days to reject the move by majority vote in both houses of Congress. The president could veto the congressional action and Congress had the option to override the veto by a two-thirds vote in both houses. This annual exercise became a focal point of US debate on China policy after the **Tiananmen crackdown**.

JAPANESE FORMULA. When Japan established diplomatic relations with China in 1972, it severed all official ties with Taiwan and placed responsibility for trade, travel, and other contact with Taiwan under the control of a private organization staffed by retired diplomats. When establishing unofficial relations with Taiwan in 1979, US officials followed this formula, also know as the Japanese model, with certain changes and variations, notably those set forth in the **Taiwan Relations Act**.

JIANG QING (1914–1991). Wife of **Mao Zedong** and a leading member of the radical **Gang of Four** that rose to power during the **Cultural**

Revolution, Jiang repeatedly raised objections to the more pragmatic policies toward the United States advocated by **Zhou Enlai** and **Deng Xiaoping**, slowing the pace of US–China reconciliation. She lost power when she and the other members of the Gang of Four were arrested soon after Mao's death in 1976.

JIANG ZEMIN (1926–). This Shanghai **Communist Party** leader was brought to Beijing and installed as general secretary of the Chinese Communist Party in 1989 by **Deng Xiaoping** and his backers. He replaced **Zhao Ziyang** who was removed from power following demonstrations in Beijing and other cities leading to the **Tiananmen crackdown**. Adhering to the leadership consensus led by Deng regarding policy toward the United States, Jiang adopted a higher profile on issues related to the United States, including Taiwan, as Deng's health faded in the mid-1990s. Jiang was criticized for failing to prevent Taiwan President **Lee Teng-hui**'s visit to the United States in 1995, and, in response, he supported the provocative Chinese military exercises of 1995–1996 in the Taiwan area, and increased Chinese military spending and preparations for a Taiwan contingency that continued into the 21st century.

Jiang sought to improve China's relations with major powers and neighboring countries, and gave top priority in foreign affairs to managing relations with the United States in ways that would avoid serious confrontation while maximizing Chinese benefits. Pleased with the US–China summits of 1997 and 1998, he nonetheless reacted strongly to perceived US international expansion and efforts to contain China. He and the Chinese administration reacted very strongly to the US bombing of the Chinese embassy in **Belgrade** in 1999, and with somewhat less vitriol to the **EP-3 incident** involving a collision between a Chinese jet fighter and a US reconnaissance plane in 2001.

Adjusting China's stance in the face of US power and international circumstances, Jiang significantly reduced China's confrontational public posture against the United States in 2001, and used the September 2001 terrorist attack on the United States as an opportunity to build bridges with the **George W. Bush** administration that was deeply suspicious of China's strategic intentions. Jiang capped his tenure as party general secretary and national president with a 2002 summit meeting with President Bush at his Texas ranch, one of the few world leaders to be received at the ranch. Jiang remained chairman of the party's central military commission after the party congress of 2002, staying in this post until 2004. He continued to play an important role in national security questions involving the United States.

JOHNSON, LYNDON B. (1908–1973). President Johnson's Asian policy was dominated by the escalating US military commitment and related difficulties in **Vietnam.** There was some movement within the US government for a more flexible approach to China, consistent with growing signs of congressional and interest group advocacy of a US policy of **containment without isolation** toward China. But they came to little as China experienced the violent and often xenophobic practices of the **Cultural Revolution**, and the American force buildup in Vietnam was confronted with deployments of Chinese antiaircraft, railway, construction, and support troops to Vietnam. Johnson was anxious to avoid prompting full-scale military involvement of China in the Vietnam conflict. US diplomats signaled these US intentions in the otherwise moribund US–China **ambassadorial talks** in Warsaw, and Chinese officials made it clear China would restrain its intervention accordingly.

JOHNSON, NELSON T. (1887–1954). As a senior State Department specialist on China, Johnson assisted Secretary of State **Frank Kellogg** in reacting with moderation and restraint to the violence and challenges to US and foreign rights in China at the time of the **Nationalist Party**–led revolution in the latter years of the 1920s. This US stance helped to facilitate US rapprochement with the Nationalist regime of **Chiang Kai-shek** once it consolidated power in 1928. Johnson served as US ambassador to China in the 1930s. Sympathetic to Chinese interests but realistic about US power and influence in the face of Japanese expansion, Johnson played an important role in US decisions dealing with Japanese expansion in Manchuria and support for the Chinese Nationalists after the start of the **Sino–Japanese War** in 1937.

JOINT COMMISSION ON RURAL RECONSTRUCTION (JCRR). Established under terms of the **China Aid Act** of 1948, this US–China body carried out agricultural reforms on the Chinese mainland before being compelled to move operations to Taiwan where it planned and to a large degree carried out the major land reform campaign on the island. In Taiwan, it also created farmers' associations and government programs to improve agriculture.

JOINT DECLARATION, 1984. Although the United States had strong and longstanding interests in **Hong Kong** as a base of US commercial and government activities, the US government adopted a low posture regarding Sino–British negotiations in 1982–1984, leading to this agreement calling for the British colony to return to Chinese sovereignty in 1997. The **Tiananmen crackdown** and large-scale demonstrations in Hong Kong in 1989 prompted greater British and US interest in securing more democracy for Hong Kong people and guarantees that provisions of the Joint Declaration would be carried out. US legislation conditioning the annual US renewal of **most-favored-nation tariff status** for China routinely had provisions dealing with China's adherence to the Joint Declaration and other aspects of policy toward Hong Kong. At congressional initiative, the United States passed the **Hong Kong Policy Act** in 1992 that laid out US concerns about Hong Kong's future and called for regular US reports monitoring China's treatment of the territory and implementation of the Joint Declaration.

JUDD, WALTER (1898–1994). A former medical missionary in China, this congressman was an important member of the group of US legislators urging strong US support for **Chiang Kai-shek** and his **Nationalist Party** government, and opposition to the Chinese **Communist Party** forces during the **Chinese Civil War** and the Cold War.

– K –

KANTOR, MICKEY (1939–). The US special trade representative in the first term of the **William Clinton** administration, Cantor carried out a tough US policy toward China on **trade** issues, especially regarding Chinese violations of **intellectual property rights**. Kantor signed an agreement with Chinese officials on this issue in 1995 and followed up with strong pressure when the Chinese side failed to implement the agreement.

KANG YU-WEI (KANG YOUWEI) (1858–1927). The top leader of the failed **hundred days of reform** in China in 1898, Kang fled abroad where he became active in the United States, organizing Chinese communities and gaining financial and other support. He lobbied strongly against US exclusion of Chinese **immigration** and other discrimination. His efforts were countered by the Chinese legation in the United States which worked against Chinese reformers and more radical Chinese leaders seeking support in the United States.

KAOHSIUNG INCIDENT. Violence during a major demonstration by political oppositionists in the southern Taiwan city of Kaohsiung in December 1979 prompted a government crackdown on political opposition leaders, resulting in arrests, reported torture, and long prison sentences for many key leaders. The events increased US administration and congressional concern with **human rights** conditions in Taiwan, adding to forces that encouraged Taiwan authorities to moderate their stance to the political opposition and move toward greater political liberalization and democracy over the next decade.

KELLOGG–BRIAND PACT. Signed in Paris in 1928 and bearing the name of US Secretary of State **Frank Kellogg**, this international agreement was seen to outlaw war. When Japan launched aggression against China and occupied Manchuria in 1931–1932, the United States government condemned the action as a violation of the pact.

KELLOGG, FRANK B. (1856–1937). Secretary of State Kellogg reacted with moderation and restraint to the violence and challenges to US and foreign rights in China at the time of the **Nationalist Party**–led revolution in the latter years of the 1920s. Notable among these challenges were the attacks on US diplomatic and other properties and the killing of Americans by Nationalist forces in the **Nanking incident** of March 1927. Kellogg's moderation and restraint helped to facilitate US rapprochement with the Nationalist regime of **Chiang Kai-shek** once it consolidated power in 1928.

KENNAN, GEORGE F. (1904–). This key State Department strategist at the start of the Cold War argued for priorities in US foreign policy that put US support for **Chiang Kai-shek** and the anti-Communist cause in China lower than support for the struggle against Soviet-backed communism in Europe and the need to provide US assistance for West European allies and Japan. He supported the **Harry Truman** administration decisions to curb aid to Chiang and he played down the negative implications for US interests of a victory by **Communist Party** forces in China.

KENNEDY, JOHN F. (1917–1963). Though several key advisers favored a less rigid US policy toward China, US domestic opposition and the administration's concerns over Chinese nuclear weapons development, aggression against India, and expansion into Southeast Asia were among factors that blocked meaningful US initiatives toward China during the administration of this president. During the presidential election campaign, Senator Kennedy criticized the "tired thinking" of the outgoing administration on issues regarding China, but said little about China once he assumed office. The administration took firm action in 1962 to block plans by **Chiang Kai-shek** to attack the mainland at a time of acute economic crisis in China, while it continued strong US backing of Chiang in the **United Nations**.

KERRY, JOHN (1943–). US Senator Kerry ran for president as the Democratic Party nominee in 2004, losing to President **George W. Bush**. US policy toward China was not a significant issue in the campaign, although Kerry complained that President Bush was not doing enough to protect US jobs and economic interests from unfair **trade** competition from China.

KHMER ROUGE. China strongly supported the victory of this radical and ruthless insurgency over the US-backed regime in **Cambodia** in 1975, and became the main foreign backer of the new regime. After **Vietnam**, backed by the Soviet Union, toppled the Khmer Rouge Cambodian regime in a military assault in late 1978, the Chinese and US governments worked together with Southeast Asian governments and others to resist and roll back the Vietnamese military occupation. China's efforts included strong support for the Khmer Rouge insurgents who represented the most potent of the guerrillas resisting the Vietnamese occupation. The resistance in Cambodia and cutbacks in Soviet support eventually prompted Vietnam to withdraw and seek an international settlement on Cambodia, which was reached in 1991 only after China adhered to US and other demands that it halt support to the Khmer Rouge and pressure them to come to terms in a Cambodian settlement. US officials subsequently sought to bring Khmer Rouge leaders before international tribunals on charges of crimes against humanity, but the Cambodian government, backed by China, temporized and resisted.

KHRUSHCHEV, NIKITA (1894–1971). This leader of the Soviet Union in the latter 1950s failed to meet Chinese demands for support, differed strongly with key Chinese domestic and foreign policies, and carried out pragmatic interchange with US leaders, resulting by 1960 in a **Sino–Soviet split**, an open break in Sino–Soviet relations that was long sought by US officials. The split resulted in little immediate change in US policy toward China, however.

KISSINGER, HENRY (1923–). As national security adviser, Kissinger along with President **Richard Nixon** planned and carried out the largely secret US moves in the initial US opening to China that led to Kissinger's clandestine trip to China in July 1971 and President Nixon's trip in 1972. His interaction with senior Chinese officials set the foundation of US–China understandings on key issues, notably Taiwan, leading to US moves to reduce commitments with an eye toward ending official relations with the Chinese **Nationalist Party** government. Kissinger endeavored to use the opening to China to increase US leverage in efforts to deal with the war in **Vietnam** and the expanding power and assertiveness of the Soviet Union.

As national security adviser and then secretary of state, Kissinger was the leading US official dealing with China as President Nixon became preoccupied with the **Watergate Scandal** and was forced to resign in 1974, and President **Gerald Ford** was inexperienced in Chinese affairs. Kissinger's trips to China and other interchange with Chinese leaders underlined the slow pace of US–China normalization on account of, among other things, domestic resistance in the United

States and China, and US focus on **arms control** and other arrangements with the Soviet Union in a period of **détente**.

After leaving government, Kissinger remained one of the most influential Americans concerned with US policy toward China into the 21st century. He advised senior officials in the United States and China, counseling moderation, restraint, and stronger efforts to build common ground. He was particularly active working against strong US efforts to sanction China after the **Tiananmen crackdown**, notably by withholding or applying strict conditions to US **most favored-nation tariff status** for Chinese **trade**. He judged such steps were contrary to long-term US national interests in maintaining and developing a cooperative relationship with China's government.

KIM IL SUNG (1912–1994). This North Korean leader received Chinese and Soviet backing for a military assault in June 1950 to destroy the South Korean regime and unify Korea. His attack started the **Korean War**. The unexpected US military intervention in Korea and the **Taiwan Strait**, and the subsequent Chinese military intervention in Korea resulted in over two years of Chinese–US combat, decades of strategic competition in Asian and world affairs, and continued strong differences over Korean issues and especially over Taiwan following the normalization of US–China relations in the 1970s.

Kim's determination to develop North Korean nuclear weapons after the Cold War saw **North Korea's nuclear weapons program** continue after his death in 1994. This prompted repeated crises with the United States and other concerned powers. Chinese officials differed with the United States on some issues regarding Korea, but generally endeavored to cooperate in efforts involving the United States that sought to deal with North Korean nuclear weapons development through diplomacy and negotiations.

KIM JONG IL (1942–). Son of **Kim Il Sung**, Kim succeeded his father as North Korean leader after his father's death in 1994. He notably continued **North Korea's nuclear weapons program** that prompted repeated crises with the United States and other concerned powers. Chinese officials differed with the United States on some issues regarding North Korea, notably urging the United States to adopt a more moderate and flexible stance toward North Korea. But

Chinese officials generally endeavored to cooperate in efforts involving the United States that sought to deal with North Korean nuclear weapons development through diplomacy and negotiations.

KNOWLAND, WILLIAM (1908–1974). A Republican senator from California, Knowland worked hard during and after the **Chinese civil war** to support **Chiang Kai-shek**'s **Nationalist Party** forces and to oppose the Chinese **Communist Party** forces.

KNOX, PHILANDER (1853–1921). Secretary of state during the **William H. Taft** administration, Knox tried to use schemes involving US investment to prevent Russia and Japan from dominating Manchuria. With the backing of President Taft, he tried to encourage major American investments in railroads as a means to counterbalance Japanese and Russian spheres of influence centered on Manchurian railroads. He also called for a plan to neutralize or internationalize all railway projects in Manchuria. As Japan and Russia objected and US investors showed little enthusiasm, Knox's so-called **dollar diplomacy** failed. He then led the administration to adopt a more moderate stance emphasizing cooperation with European powers, and ultimately Russia and Japan, in an international arrangement dealing with loans to China. *See also* CHINCHOW–AIGUN RAILROAD; HUKUANG RAILWAY.

KOO CHEN-FU (GU ZHENFU) (1917–2005). A prominent Taiwan business leader, Koo held two sets of talks with a senior Chinese counterpart, **Wang Daohan**, in the 1990s. Koo and Wang represented ostensibly unofficial bodies in Taiwan and China that were created to facilitate cross-strait issues and dialogue. US policy strongly supported such dialogue. *See also* ASSOCIATION FOR RELATIONS ACROSS THE TAIWAN STRAIT; STRAITS EXCHANGE FOUNDATION.

KOREAN WAR. North Korean leader **Kim Il Sung** received Chinese and Soviet backing for a military assault in June 1950 to destroy the South Korean regime and unify Korea. His assault started the Korean War. The United States surprised the Communist leaders by intervening promptly in Korea and in the **Taiwan Strait**. Defeating the

North Korean forces, US-led forces under the auspices of the **United Nations** moved into North Korea and attempted to reunify the country. This resulted in Chinese military intervention in Korea and over two years of Chinese–US combat. This experience laid the foundation for decades of US–China strategic competition in Asian and world affairs, and continued strong differences over Korean issues and especially Taiwan following the normalization of US–China relations in the 1970s.

KOSOVO. China supported the authoritarian Yugoslavia regime, and viewed Kosovo, officially part of Yugoslavia, as an internal affair of the Belgrade government. In October 1998, Serbian repression of ethnic Albanians, the majority of Kosovo's population, prompted NATO forces, including US forces, to begin an air war against the Belgrade regime. Chinese leaders protested strongly, viewing US-led military intervention on humanitarian grounds as an excuse to set a precedent to intervene in the internal affairs of other countries, including China. Chinese military planners saw the US air attacks and use of precision munitions as the kind of attack the United States might use against China in case of a conflict over Taiwan.

During US-led air attacks, two US planes on 7 May 1999 dropped guided gravity bombs on various targets in Belgrade. One target was misidentified by US forces and turned out to be the Chinese embassy in Belgrade. It was hit by three bombs, killing three, wounding 20, and causing great damage to the building. The reaction in China included mobs stoning the US embassy in Beijing and burning US diplomatic property in Chengtu. It was the most serious incident in US–China relations after the **Tiananmen crackdown**. *See also* BELGRADE, US BOMBING OF CHINESE EMBASSY.

KUNG, H.H. (1881–1967). A brother-in-law and trusted adviser of **Chiang Kai-shek**, Kung was responsible for various financial endeavors, currency reforms, and related policies of the **Nationalist Party** government in the 1930s, while remaining active in interacting with American officials, encouraging greater US support for the Nationalists as they faced Japanese expansion and aggression.

KUNG I-HSIN (GONG YIXIN) (1833–1898). Also known as Prince Kung, this key **Qing dynasty** leader from the late 1850s until the

1880s pushed foreign policy reforms, established Chinese foreign policy institutions, and emphasized cooperative engagement with foreign powers under terms of the treaties governing Sino–foreign interaction in China. His policies were welcomed by US and other officials in China. They helped to foster a period of generally cordial Sino–foreign relations which saw China reach out to the United States and other foreign powers through such means as the diplomatic mission in the late 1860s under **Anson Burlingame**, a former US minister in China. Kung also attempted to elicit former President **Ulysses Grant**'s assistance in resolving a Chinese dispute with Japan over the **Liu-ch'iu (Ryukyu) Islands** in 1879.

KUOMINTANG (GUOMINDANG) (KMT). *See* NATIONALIST PARTY.

KYOTO PROTOCOL. At the December 1997 Third Conference of the Parties to the **United Nations** Framework Convention on Climate Change in Kyoto, Japan, at which the Kyoto Protocol was drafted, China pressed to exempt developing countries from greenhouse gas reduction targets, thereby putting the burden for such reductions on the United States and other developed countries. Subsequently, the United States did not ratify the protocol partly for the same reason Beijing did not wish to be bound by greenhouse gas emission caps—both governments feared that doing so would retard domestic economic growth.

– L –

LAKE, ANTHONY (1939–). The national security adviser in the first term of the **William Clinton** administration, Lake was not in the lead in dealing with China policy for much of this period, though he agreed with the tough administration actions toward China and publicly identified the Chinese regime as a "backlash state" akin to Iraq and Iran. This situation changed markedly with the **Taiwan Strait crises** posed by prolonged and provocative Chinese military exercises in the months after Taiwan President **Lee Teng-hui**'s June 1995 visit to the United States. Lake led the US officials in negotiations with a senior Chinese envoy **Liu Huaqiu**, who met with him and the

US secretaries of state and defense in March 1996 as Chinese forces announced another series of provocative military exercises and US leaders considered sending aircraft carriers to the Taiwan area. After the face-off of US and Chinese forces in the Taiwan area later in March, Lake actively pursued the Clinton administration's new emphasis on an **engagement policy** with China and he traveled to Beijing in June 1996 for talks with senior leaders.

LAND REFORM. US officials encouraged land reform in China notably through the **Joint Commission on Rural Reconstruction (JCRR)** established under terms of the **China Aid Act** of 1948. This US–China body carried out agricultural reforms on the mainland before being compelled to move operations to Taiwan where it planned and to a large degree carried out the major land reform campaign on the island in the early 1950s.

LANSING, ROBERT (1864–1928). A counselor at the State Department during the **Woodrow Wilson** administration, Lansing argued against confrontation with Japan in defense of China's integrity at the time of Japan's **Twenty-One Demands** in 1915. As secretary of state in 1917, he negotiated and exchanged notes with Japanese envoy Ishii Kikujiro that acknowledged Japan's "special interests" in China, even though Japan privately agreed not to seek privileges at the expense of other friendly powers in China. The notes were used by Japan as evidence of tacit US support for Japanese expansion in China. Lansing opposed President Wilson's decision at the **Versailles Peace Conference** in 1919 to accept Japanese claim to the German **concessions** in China's Shantung province. *See also* SHANTUNG LEASEHOLD.

LANTOS, TOM (1928–). A senior Democratic congressman and member of the US House of Representatives committee dealing with foreign affairs, Lantos was a leading critic of China's **human rights** policies in the period after the **Tiananmen crackdown** and a strong supporter of closer US ties with Taiwan and the **Dalai Lama**.

LAOGAI RESEARCH FOUNDATION. This organization was linked with the **American Federation of Labor–Congress of In-**

dustrial **Organizations (AFL-CIO)** and led by prominent US activist **Harry Wu** who had spent many years in Chinese prisons. Wu achieved prominence in US–China relations following the **Tiananmen crackdown**. He worked from the United States using the Laogai Research Foundation and other means to expose and force change in Chinese prison and penal practices.

LATTIMORE, OWEN (1900–1989). This Johns Hopkins University Asian affairs expert worked briefly for **Chiang Kai-shek**, criticized the **Nationalist Party** regime, and predicted its defeat at the hands of the Chinese **Communist Party** forces that he had visited in the 1930s. Lattimore became a favorite target of Senator **Joseph McCarthy** in the congressional investigations in the early 1950s searching for spies and security risks that could explain the failure of US policy toward China. Lattimore was exonerated after enduring two trials in which he was accused of lying about harboring pro-Communist sentiment.

LEAGUE OF NATIONS. Although the League of Nations was originally founded at the suggestion of President **Woodrow Wilson**, the United States did not join this international body created after World War I. US policymakers worked in close consultations with the League in dealing with Japanese aggression in Manchuria and elsewhere in China in 1931–1932. Among the US steps in response to Japanese action was Secretary of State **Henry Stimson**'s repeated articulation of a **non-recognition doctrine**—the US government refused to recognize the Japanese gains. Stimson in 1932 appealed to the world to do the same. The Assembly of the League passed a resolution adopting the non-recognition policy. As the League-appointed **Lytton Commission** investigated and issued a report critical of Japan, Japan withdrew from the League in 1933. *See also* HOOVER–STIMSON DOCTRINE.

LEAN-TO-ONE-SIDE POLICY. Mao Zedong declared in mid-1949 that his **Communist Party**–led government would lean to the side of the Soviet Union and the socialist countries in the emerging Cold War and would lean against the United States and its allies and associates. Mao followed through after the establishment of the People's Republic of China on 1 October 1949 by traveling to Moscow in late 1949, seeking a **Sino–Soviet alliance**, which was signed in February 1950.

LEE, MARTIN (1938–). An opposition political leader and prominent advocate for greater democracy and **human rights** in **Hong Kong** following the **Tiananmen crackdown** of 1989, Lee was popular in the US Congress and with the US media, and he met regularly with senior US administration officials. Urging the United States to take concrete steps to press the Chinese government to improve human rights conditions in China and Hong Kong, Lee also warned against the United States' withholding **most-favored-nation tariff status** for US **trade** with China, a step that would devastate the Hong Kong economy and the well-being of its residents.

LEE TENG-HUI (1923–). Lee succeeded **Chiang Ching-kuo** as president of Taiwan and chairman of the **Nationalist Party** following Chiang's death in 1988. The first **Taiwanese** to hold these posts, Lee vigorously promoted greater democracy and self-determination in Taiwan, and asserted Taiwan's separate status abroad during his leadership of the government and the party until 2000 and as a leader of a separate political party after that. US opinion and official policy welcomed greater democracy in Taiwan and tended to support Lee.

Lee's efforts to assert Taiwan's separate international status strongly antagonized Chinese officials, who came to view him as pursuing Taiwan independence, an anathema to China. As support for Lee and for Taiwan in the US Congress and broader American opinion grew, President **William Clinton** was persuaded to reverse existing policy and granted Lee a visa to visit his alma mater Cornell University in 1995. China reacted harshly with months of provocative military exercises near Taiwan, and the United States eventually dispatched two aircraft carrier battle groups to the Taiwan area, causing the most serious US–China military crisis in the **Taiwan Strait** since the Cold War. Subsequently, the Clinton administration tried to assuage China and distance the US government from the Taiwan leader, though support for Taiwan and Lee's promotion of democracy continued to be strong in the Congress and US media. Lee renewed tension in the Taiwan Strait when he declared to Western media in 1999 that Taiwan's relations with mainland China were **"special state-to-**

state" relations. China sharply criticized this step as part of what it saw as Lee's further moves toward Taiwan independence. *See also* TAIWAN STRAIT CRISES.

LEE, WEN HO (1939–). In the context of the often bitter and partisan Chinese policy debate in the United States in the late 1990s, including charges of lax US government safeguards of US weapons secrets and related technology, and of Chinese government illegal campaign contributions, influence peddling, and spying, the *New York Times* in a front-page story on 6 March 1999 claimed that China had access to advanced US nuclear warhead designs. It said that the designs had been taken from one of the Department of Energy national nuclear laboratories, probably the one in Los Alamos, New Mexico. Suspecting espionage, the Federal Bureau of Investigation (FBI) detained and interrogated a Taiwan-born scientist at the lab, Wen Ho Lee, as a suspect in the case. Searching Lee's office, they found he had placed and then erased classified files containing nuclear test data on his unclassified office computer. Amid rushed US efforts to tighten security at the nuclear laboratories, Lee was quickly fired from his job. He was held in solitary confinement for one year and reportedly was threatened with execution unless he confessed. Investigators found no evidence of espionage. The case ended in a plea bargain where Lee admitted unauthorized copying of classified data, which Lee insisted was for his own use.

LEGISLATIVE COUNCIL (LEGCO). The democratically elected members of this **Hong Kong** legislative body were a minority in the body, but they had broad influence in the United States following the **Tiananmen crackdown** of 1989. Their leaders were received by leaders in the Congress and senior officials in the administration. Their advice was sought regarding Hong Kong provisions in US legislation.

LEND-LEASE AID. Early in 1941, President **Franklin D. Roosevelt** proposed and Congress approved a massive lend-lease foreign aid program designed to give the president freedom in assisting any nation whose defense he deemed vital to the United States. China became eligible to receive lend-lease aid on 6 May 1941. Lend-lease continued to the Chinese **Nationalist Party** forces during the 1940s.

LETTER TO TAIWAN COMPATRIOTS. On 1 January 1979, the date the United States formally broke official ties with Taiwan and established official ties with China, the Standing Committee of the National People's Congress of the People's Republic of China issued this letter to officials in Taiwan proposing the establishment of trade, travel, and communications links (the **three links**), while promising to "respect Taiwan's status quo" in seeking to reunify Taiwan with the Chinese mainland.

LIAISON OFFICES. Prior to the establishment of official diplomatic relations between the United States and the People's Republic of China in 1979, the two governments established official liaison offices, headed by senior diplomats, in their respective capitals in 1973.

LIANG CH'I-CH'AO (LIANG QICHAO) (1873–1929). The top aide to the leader of the failed **hundred days of reform** in China in 1898, **Kang Yu-wei**, Liang fled abroad during the crackdown on the reform movement and became the most important of Chinese reform intellectuals in the early 20th century. His views on the United States were influenced by a seven-month visit there in 1903, which hardened his opposition to US commercial expansion in China. He strongly warned against repeated **Qing dynasty** efforts to use American commercial involvement in Chinese railway and loan schemes as a means to balance the European powers and Japan.

LIANG TUN-YEN (LIANG DUNYAN) (1858–1924). Educated in the United States and a foreign affairs specialist, Liang worked with **Chang Chih-tung**, Prince **Ch'un Tsai-feng**, and **Yuan Shih-kai** in the waning years of the **Qing dynasty** and the early years of the **Republic of China**. Prince Ch'un, regent of the empire, sent him to the United States in 1910 in a vain search for strong US support for China in the face of foreign expansion in Manchuria. While in the United States in 1911, Liang concluded a $25 million deal with Bethlehem Steel to enhance China's shipbuilding and naval arsenals.

LI DAOYU (1932–). China's ambassador to the United States during much of the **William Clinton** administration, Li dealt with the wide swings in the relationship prompted notably by US administration actions. The Clinton White House first pressed for conditions on granting **most-favored-nation tariff status** to China, then reversed that policy. The US administration then reversed US policy by granting a visa to Taiwan President **Lee Teng-hui** to visit Cornell University (Ambassador Li was recalled to China as part of China's reaction to the Lee visit.). The Clinton administration then emphasized a positive **engagement policy** with China in President Clinton's second term, culminating with Chinese leader **Jiang Zemin**'s summit visit to Washington in 1997.

LIEBERTHAL, KENNETH (1943–). A prominent China scholar and academic leader based at the University of Michigan, Lieberthal was the senior National Security Council specialist with responsibility for China in the last years of the **William Clinton** administration. He played important roles in managing **Taiwan Strait** tensions caused by Taiwan President **Lee Teng-hui**'s assertion in 1999 that Taiwan and the mainland were two states, and in formulating administration strategy leading to US agreement on China's entry into the **World Trade Organization** and congressional approval of **permanent normal trade relations** for China.

LIEN CHAN (1936–). A **Nationalist Party** leader and vice president of Taiwan, Lien ran unsuccessfully for president in 2000 and 2004. His stance on Taiwan's status was more acceptable to China than that of the victorious **Democratic Progressive Party** candidate **Chen Shui-bian**. Chen's election victories added to frictions in cross-strait relations and difficulties for US policy seeking to balance interests in US relations with Taiwan and China.

LIEN-CHOU MASSACRE. This 1905 murder of five US **missionaries** in southern China was the most serious incident in US–China relations in the decade. It prompted President **Theodore Roosevelt**, already critical of the **anti-American boycott** underway in China at the time, to consider the use of force in Canton, and American forces began gathering in Canton harbor. Chinese authorities ultimately took steps to punish those responsible and to pay an indemnity.

LI HUNG-CHANG (LI HONGZHANG) (1823–1901). Dominating Chinese foreign policy in the last third of the 19th century, this senior regional and national leader and commissioner of trade in northern China made initiatives toward the United States for assistance in dealing with Chinese crises with other powers. The United States was seen as posing little threat to Chinese territories or tributary states, while its commitment to commerce provided common ground in US–China relations that could be used by Chinese officials to win American support. US **immigration** policy discriminating against Chinese, by contrast, was a growing source of friction between the two countries.

Li sought US assistance in dealing with difficulties with Japan over the **Liu-ch'iu (Ryukyu) Islands** in the 1870s and in providing US endorsement of Chinese claims in Korea in the 1880s. He sought US mediation in a growing dispute with France over **Vietnam** in the 1880s. These initiatives achieved little of benefit to China, and Li in July 1894 sought US good offices to avoid a war with Japan over Korea only after exhausting other options. Li endeavored to rely on Russia and other European powers to deal with Japanese demands after the Japanese defeated China in 1895, and unlike his colleague **Chang Chih-tung**, Li did not emphasize the option of tuning to the United States for meaningful assistance in the period before or after the **Boxer uprising**.

LI HONGZHI (1951–). Li was the leader of the **Falung Gong** movement that spread widely in China in the 1990s and prompted a crackdown by Chinese leaders. Declaring the movement illegal in 1999, Chinese officials sought to arrest Li, who had taken refuge in the United States while continuing to guide the movement via the internet and other means.

LI KASHING (1928–). *See* HUTCHINSON WHAMPOA LIMITED.

LILLEY, JAMES (1928–). A veteran **Central Intelligence Agency (CIA)** operator and China specialist, Lilley was among the initial group of US officials in the US **liaison office** in Beijing in 1973. He advised **Ronald Reagan** in the 1980 presidential campaign and traveled to China with vice presidential candidate **George H. W. Bush** to explain Reagan's China policy. Lilley served on Reagan's National Security Council staff before going to Taipei as the director of the US office there where he delivered to Taiwan leaders both the **17 August 1982 communiqué** limiting US arms sale to Taiwan and the **six assurances** of US support for Taiwan. He served President George H. W. Bush as an assistant secretary of defense with responsibility for Asia and was selected by the president as US ambassador to China, arriving on the eve of the **Tiananmen crackdown**. He dealt with the fallout of the crackdown, notably giving refuge to dissident **Fang Lizhi** who was eventually allowed to leave China.

LIMITED TEST BAN TREATY. As part of incremental Chinese efforts to adhere to international norms regarding **arms control** and proliferation, China agreed to this treaty regulating nuclear weapons testing in 1986, a step welcomed by the United States.

LIN BIAO (1907–1971). This Chinese defense minister rose to the top levels of power during the first years of the **Cultural Revolution**. He opposed China's opening to the United States, arguing for a tough Chinese approach toward both the Soviet Union and the United States that also was favored by radical Chinese leaders known as the **Gang of Four**. In the intense leadership struggle then prevailing in China, Lin split with **Mao Zedong** and reportedly died in 1971 in a plane crash allegedly as he was trying to escape to the Soviet Union after a failed coup attempt.

LINKAGE POLICY. This referred to the policy in the first two years of the **William Clinton** administration in which the annual renewal of US **most-favored-nation tariff status** for US **trade** with China was linked to China's human rights policies and practices. President Clinton ended this linkage policy in May 1994.

LI PENG (1928–). China's premier and a top foreign policy decision maker in much of the 1990s, Li adhered to a firm approach in response to US pressures following the **Tiananmen crackdown** of 1989, often seeking ways to reciprocate US demands with demands on China's part. Protocol required meetings with most high-level visiting US officials, some of whom were reluctant to be seen on friendly terms with one of the Chinese leaders most strongly identified with the **Tiananmen crackdown**. Unlike **Jiang Zemin** and Li's successor as premier, **Zhu Rongji**, Li was never invited to Washington after 1989. He did attend a summit of world leaders at the **United Nations** in New York in February 1992, and President **George H. W. Bush** agreed to a private meeting there that was recorded in an official photograph. Replaced as premier in 1998, Li gradually lost influence in China's foreign relations and Jiang Zemin became the preeminent Chinese leader dealing with the United States.

LI TSUNG-JEN (LI ZONGREN) (1890–1969). A leader in the **Nationalist Party**, Li was elected vice president of the Republic of China in 1947. He became president of the failing Nationalist regime on the Chinese mainland after **Chiang Kai-shek** resigned as president in 1949 and moved to consolidate his regime on Taiwan. Li fled the mainland in December 1949 and went to the United States where he endeavored in vain to win support from the **Harry Truman** administration and to protest Chiang Kai-shek's resumption of the presidency in Taiwan in March 1950.

LIU-CH'IU (RYUKYU) ISLANDS. After leaving office as US president, **Ulysses S. Grant** traveled to Asia in 1879 where he was encouraged by Chinese leaders, notably **Li Hung-chang**, to intercede with Japan on China's behalf regarding a dispute over the Liu-ch'iu (Ryukyu) Islands. The intervention was unsuccessful.

LIU HUAQIU (1939–). This vice foreign minister and director of the foreign affairs office of the Chinese government's State Council played a key role in coordinating, facilitating and implementing China's policy toward the United States in the years after the **Tiananmen crackdown**. He reached prominence when he met with the US National Security Adviser **Anthony Lake** and the US secretaries of state and defense in the Washington, D.C. area at the time of serious tensions in the **Taiwan Strait** caused by escalation in China's military exercises against Taiwan in March 1996. He conveyed a firm Chinese line to the Americans and they were explicit in return in warning of the consequences of Chinese military escalation. When Lake traveled to China in July 1996, endeavoring to develop the

William Clinton administration's **engagement policy** with China, he had extensive private talks with Liu. Liu also accompanied President **Jiang Zemin** on his trip to Washington in 1997.

LIU SHAOQI (1898–1969). This senior Chinese **Communist Party** leader, at times second only to **Mao Zedong**, played a supporting role in China's foreign relations, backing Mao's policies of leaning to the Soviet Union in the Cold War, breaking with Moscow in the early 1960s, and maintaining China's tough approach against US **containment** and isolation. During the early stages of the **Cultural Revolution**, he was removed from power before China considered the opening to the United States. He died under persecution.

LI ZHAOXING (1940–). Li played a prominent role in China–US relations as vice foreign minister in charge of relations with the United States and as ambassador to the United States during the last years of the **William Clinton** administration. He was outspoken in publicly condemning to US media the US bombing of the Chinese embassy in Belgrade in 1999. He was promoted to foreign minister and worked closely with senior Chinese leaders in guiding Chinese relations with the **George W. Bush** administration. *See also* BELGRADE, BOMBING OF CHINESE EMBASSY.

LORAL SPACE SYSTEMS. This American company and the **Hughes Electronic Corporation** built telecommunications satellites and launched them via Chinese rockets in the 1990s. US sanctions after the **Tiananmen crackdown** curbed the launches, but they were allowed with US presidential waivers. In 1996 a satellite built by Loral Space Systems was destroyed when the Chinese launch rocket exploded. Earlier Chinese rocket explosions destroyed satellites built by Hughes Electronic Corporation. A review commission headed by a Loral employee and including representatives from Hughes found flaws in the Chinese launch rockets and recommended corrections. It did so without proper US government authorization and review. As these events became known, they prompted strong US critics of the Clinton administration's **engagement policy** to China to connect these illegal acts with the large campaign contributions both satellite company directors had made to the Democratic Party. Extreme charges alleged that these US companies were helping to increase the accuracy of Chinese nuclear-weapons missiles targeted at the United States and that the Clinton administration was cooperating with them in order to gain campaign contributions. Conclusive proof of such allegations was lacking.

LORD, WINSTON (1937–). Lord served as an assistant to National Security Adviser **Henry Kissinger**. He accompanied him on his secret trip to Beijing in 1971 and was involved in other early steps in the US opening to China. As ambassador to China in the late 1980s, Lord fell out of favor with President **George H. W. Bush** by inviting prominent dissident **Fang Lizhi** to a banquet the president hosted while visiting China in February 1989. Lord left China just before the **Tiananmen crackdown**, which he strongly condemned.

He was selected as State Department assistant secretary for East Asia in 1993. He played a central role in working with congressional leaders and others to establish the **human rights** conditions the **William Clinton** administration would require before renewing **most-favored-nation (MFN) tariff status** for China. The terms he worked out were widely welcomed in the United States in 1993, but by the next year business and other interests were unwilling to see MFN stopped even though the Chinese government had not significantly improved human rights practices. President Clinton decided to reverse Lord's approach. Clinton also did a reversal of Lord's and State Department policy when in 1995 he agreed to give Taiwan President **Lee Teng-hui** a visa to visit Cornell University. The following military crisis in the **Taiwan Strait** saw the president and his White House advisers take more direct control of China policy, placing Lord and other China policymakers in the State Department in a less prominent position. *See also* LINKAGE POLICY; TAIWAN STRAIT CRISES.

LUCE, HENRY (1898–1967). The child of Christian **missionaries** in China, Luce created a powerful media enterprise in the United States centered on *Time* and *Life* magazines. He used his widely read publications to strongly support **Chiang Kai-shek** and his American-educated wife, **Soong Mayling,** hailing the nation-building struggles of the **Nationalist Party** government and its protracted resistance to Japanese aggression. These positive views of Chiang persisted despite growing reports of Chinese Nationalist corruption, malfeasance, and neglect coming from Americans in wartime China. Luce publications sided with Chiang in the **Chinese Civil War** and were strong advocates for the Nationalist leader after his retreat to Taiwan.

LYTTON COMMISION. US diplomats worked closely with the **League of Nations** (the United States was not a member of the League) to counter Japanese aggression in Manchuria in 1931–1932. A climax of sorts was reached when in 1933 the League adopted a report by this commission critical of Japan's actions in Manchuria, prompting Japan to withdraw from the League of Nations.

– M –

MACARTHUR, DOUGLAS (1880–1964). A veteran US general honored for leading victories in World War II and conducting the US military occupation of Japan, MacArthur showed brilliance in commanding the US-led counterattack against North Korea's aggression against South Korea at the start of the **Korean War** in 1950. But he miscalculated against China, which intervened in Korea in large numbers, driving back advancing US forces in late 1950. MacArthur remained hostile to China, calling for US military strikes against China and employing **Chiang Kai-shek**'s **Nationalist Party** forces against the Chinese **Communist Party** forces. Dismissed as US commander in April 1951, MacArthur denounced those who would appease China or accept a compromise peace in Korea.

MACMURRAY, JOHN (1881–1960). Counseling Secretary of State **Charles Evans Hughes** and the Warren Harding administration as a State Department adviser in Washington, MacMurray argued against giving in to Chinese demands for return of rights involving tariff autonomy and **extraterritoriality** until stable governance was restored in China. He stuck to this position when he was appointed US minister in Peking in 1925. The upsurge of often violent and anti-foreign nationalism that swept China after the **May 30th incident** in 1925 prompted the new secretary of state, **Frank Kellogg,** and his adviser, **Nelson Johnson,** to yield to the Chinese demands. However, the political turmoil in China delayed concrete action until 1928 when the United States signed a new tariff treaty with **Chiang Kai-shek**'s **Nationalist Party** government.

MAINLAND CHINESE. This term and the term mainlanders were used in Taiwan to describe those officials, soldiers, and others from the Chinese mainland that retreated to Taiwan with **Chiang Kai-shek**'s **Nationalist Party** regime after the victory of **Communist Party** forces in 1949. Representing about 15 percent of Taiwan's population, these people tended to dominate the government and related positions of power as the Nationalist regime consolidated and maintained its position in Taiwan. Demographic and democratic trends gradually reduced their power and a non-mainlander **Taiwanese, Lee Teng-hui**, was selected as president and chairman of the Nationalist Party in 1988. The decline in mainland Chinese and Nationalist Party influence that followed meant that support in Taiwan for a position that Taiwan was part of China declined while support for greater independence for Taiwan increased. This situation raised tensions with China and complicated US policy premised on the broad principle of **one China**.

MAJOR, JOHN (1943–). Traveling to Beijing in September 1991, this British prime minister became the first Western leader to visit China after the **Tiananmen crackdown**. He endeavored to use the visit to secure **Hong Kong**'s economic and political future. To counter opinion at home and abroad that he was appeasing the Chinese leaders, Major appointed a new governor for Hong Kong, **Christopher Patten**, who pursued a tougher and pro-democratic line in negotiations with Beijing that infuriated the Chinese but was warmly welcomed in the United States, especially in the Congress, the media, and among **human rights** groups.

MANCHUKUO. Japanese creation of this puppet state in Manchuria in 1932 followed Japanese military actions to drive out Chinese forces and intimidate foreign opposition. The United States joined others in condemning Japanese aggression but eschewed major sanctions or shows of force. *See also* HOOVER–STIMSON DOCTRINE; LYTTON COMMISSION; NON-RECOGNITION DOCTRINE.

MAO ZEDONG (1893–1976). This **Communist Party** activist and insurgent rose to become Chinese Communist leader in the mid-1930s and remained preeminent until his death in 1976. Impatient in pursuing development and revolutionary goals in China, Mao initiated the radical development programs of the Great Leap Forward in the late 1950s that resulted in economic collapse and 30 million deaths. Struggling for power and pursuing revolutionary ideals, Mao led the Cultural Revolution beginning in the mid-1960s that purged and persecuted hundreds of thousands of senior party and government officials and massively disrupted Chinese policy-making for 10 years. Mao's revolutionary outlook, often favoring violent struggle against enemies at home and abroad, placed him and his movement fundamentally at odds with the United States and its interests in Asian and world affairs. During the Cold War, he was prepared to take significant risks in confronting US military power, especially in the **Korean War**, in the **Taiwan Strait**, and along China's bordering regions in **Vietnam** and Laos. Nevertheless, when circumstances warranted, he was prepared to be pragmatic, moderating relations with the United States in order to pursue more important priorities. Most notably, Mao switched in the face of a burgeoning Soviet strategic threat to China in the late 1960s, from a stridently ideological and somewhat xenophobic stance against the United States to a stance welcoming President **Richard Nixon**'s visit to China and forward movement in US–China relations, partly on the basis of common US–China opposition to Soviet "**hegemonism**." Mao participated actively in meetings with Nixon, **Henry Kissinger**, and other US envoys as US–China reconciliation developed in the early 1970s.

MARSHALL, GEORGE (1880–1959). As army chief-of-staff during World War II, Marshall supported efforts in China of General **Joseph Stilwell**, a personal friend, who focused on building Chinese ground armies to deal with Japanese forces in and around China. He opposed competing plans of General **Claire Chennault** emphasizing using air power against the Japanese. He and Secretary of War **Henry Stimson**

proposed sending **Patrick Hurley** to China in 1944 to resolve issues between Stilwell and **Chiang Kai-shek.** Hurley did not support Stilwell, who was removed from China. When Hurley abruptly resigned after one year of erratic service in China, President **Harry Truman** sent Marshall to China in December 1945 to mediate between Chinese **Nationalist Party** forces and Chinese **Communist Party** forces and avoid a civil war. A few months of shaky peace were followed by frequent fighting in Manchuria as Nationalist and Communist forces vied to take control as Soviet occupiers retreated. US aid continued to go exclusively to Nationalist-held areas and increased markedly in mid-1946. On 1 July 1946, Chiang Kai-shck ordered a nationwide offensive against the Communists. Marshall intervened, got Truman to stop US arms aid to Chiang, and Chiang agreed to US–Nationalist–Communist truce teams to prevent fighting in northern China. But the fighting still spread and soon became a full-scale war. Peace talks and a Nationalist–Communist cease-fire collapsed in December 1946. In January 1947, President Truman called Marshall home to become secretary of state.

MARSHALL, HUMPHREY (1812–1872). The American commissioner in China, 1852–1854, Marshall advocated strong US support for the Chinese government in the face of the **Taiping Rebellion** and perceived sinister designs of Great Britain and Russia to divide China and exclude US interests. His sometimes bold proposals were rejected in Washington.

MARTIN, W. A. P. (1827–1916). This American went to China as a missionary but pursued a career of **education,** scholarship, and achievement in assisting China's learning of modern diplomacy. He advised US ministers in China and was notable for serving as director of the **Interpreters College** from 1869 to 1895. This Chinese institution prepared the bulk of Chinese diplomatic staff at this time. Among his scholarship and writings was a translation of Henry Wheaton's standard work, *Elements of International Law,* which provided Chinese officials in the 1860s with knowledge of international norms useful in the conduct of China's foreign relations.

MATSU. This group of small islands near the China coast remained under the control of **Nationalist Party** forces after 1949, were fortified by **Chiang Kai-shek**, and figured in Nationalist–Communist military confrontations in the **Taiwan Strait** during the 1950s. *See also* QUE-MOY; TAIWAN STRAIT CRISES.

MAY FOURTH MOVEMENT. Begun by thousands of students protesting on 4 May 1919 the decision by US and other peacemakers at the Versailles peace conference to leave in Japanese hands the former German **concessions** in China's Shantung province, the movement spread and deepened, promoting intellectual changes as well as radical political movements challenging US and other foreign rights and holdings in China. *See also* SHANTUNG LEASEHOLD; VERSAILLES, TREATY OF.

MA YING-JEOU (1950–). This **Nationalist Party** leader and government official defeated Taipei mayor **Chen Shui-bian** in elections in 1998. Chen went on to win the presidency in 2000 and reelection in 2004, while Ma won reelection in Taipei by a landslide in 2002. Ma's views on cross-strait relations were much more moderate than Chen's. Some Chinese and US officials concerned with Chen's tendency to provoke China by moving toward independence hoped that stability could be maintained until 2008, and that Ma or a like-minded candidate then would run and win the presidential election.

MAY 30TH INCIDENT. An incident in Shanghai on 30 May 1925, arising out of a strike against Japanese-owned textile mills, led to an outburst of anti-imperialist and anti-foreign sentiment that spread from Shanghai throughout China's cities and into the countryside. Against this background and after the start in 1926 of the **Nationalist Party** and **Communist Party**–led **Northern Expedition**, Nationalist and Communist leaders warned that China would unilaterally terminate the treaties giving foreign powers special rights in China. US officials, with considerable internal debate, agreed not to stand firm in defense of US legal rights but to grant China tariff autonomy and to negotiate the end of **extraterritoriality**. They had difficulty doing so given the turbulent political events in China and the lack of an effective national government.

MCCARRAN, PAT (1876–1954). A strong anti-Communist and ardent backer of **Chiang Kai-shek**, this US senator looked for subversives and security risks in directing the US Senate Internal Security Sub-committee. Beginning in 1951, he spent years investigating, among others, specialists involved with Chinese and Asian affairs.

MCCARTHY, JOSEPH (1908–1957). Beginning in early 1950, this US senator launched a series of attacks in the media and in investigative hearings in Congress on alleged subversives and Communists in the State Department and other government agencies. He focused special attention on Foreign Service officers and academic specialists who had contacts with the Chinese **Communist Party** officials and were critical of **Chiang Kai-shek**. Others in Congress followed his example. The **Harry Truman** and **Dwight Eisenhower** administrations carried out a series of security investigations that saw many State Department China experts unfairly dismissed or pressured to resign.

MCHUGH, JAMES. The US naval attaché in **Chungking** and a personal friend of **Chiang Kai-shek** and **Madame Chiang Kai-shek**, McHugh was asked by the Chiangs in 1939–1942 to pass messages for them to senior US Navy officials and President **Franklin D. Roosevelt**, indicating the need for greater US support for **Nationalist Party** government in China.

MCKINLEY, WILLIAM (1843–1901). President McKinley reacted with restraint to the major developments in China during his time in office at the turn of the 19th century. He supported the **Open Door Notes** of his secretary of state, **John Hay**, as a suitable means to register American concerns with foreign expansion in China without significant risks. The **Boxer uprising** and attacks on the foreign legations in Peking saw McKinley keep US forces in check. He focused their efforts on relief and rescue, moved to scale back the US contingent once the Boxers were suppressed, and avoided association with other foreign forces pursuing punitive expeditions.

M-11 MISSILES. Chinese shipments of these short-range ballistic missiles to Pakistan was reported by US intelligence agencies in 1992 and remained a source of controversy in US–Chinese leadership discussions throughout the 1990s. The shipments were viewed by the

Americans as signaling Chinese rejection of international norms governing international missile sales that Chinese officials had earlier said they would abide by. The **William Clinton** administration in 1993 imposed limited sanctions in response to the Chinese actions. Critics in Congress and the media argued for stronger sanctions. *See also* MISSILE TECHNOLOGY CONTROL REGIME.

MILES, MILTON (1900–1961). In 1942, a small **US Naval Group China**, under the leadership of Commander Milton Miles, worked with General **Dai Li**, head of **Chiang Kai-shek**'s secret police, to establish the **Sino–American Cooperation Organization**. It funneled military aid to the **Nationalist Party** regime with little oversight by senior US officers, assisting General Dai in fighting **Communist Party** forces in China.

MISSILE TECHNOLOGY CONTROL REGIME (MTCR). Under pressure from the United States, China agreed in 1992 and 1994 to abide by the guidelines of this international **arms control** group that endeavored to restrict the transfer of nuclear-capable missiles and related technology. However, Chinese transfers of **M-11 missiles** to Pakistan reported by US intelligence agencies in late 1992, and lesser transfers to Iran and other countries, seemed to contradict these agreements. They prompted US sanctions against China and repeated difficulties in negotiations between the two countries in the 1990s.

MISSIONARIES. Coming to China in small numbers in the 1830s, American Protestant missionaries expanded the size and scope of their evangelical, medical, **education**, and social welfare endeavors along with the forced opening of China to foreign contact in the 19th century. There were hundreds of US missionaries in China by the end of the century. They had a strong impact on US–China relations. Their writings and advice were important in determining how US and Chinese officials understood each other. Their demands for US and Chinese government support and protection for their work in China became a major issue in relations between the two countries in the latter 19th century as many in the Chinese elite resisted the missionaries and incited popular violence against them. The US missionaries tended to be more supportive of **Chiang Kai-shek** and the **Nationalist Party** government that emerged from the turmoil following the collapse of the **Qing dynasty** in the early 20th century, and they tended to be wary of the more radical Chinese **Communist Party** leaders.

MITCHELL, GEORGE (1933–). A sharp critic of the **George H. W. Bush** administration's policy toward China, Senate Majority Leader Mitchell worked closely with the incoming **William Clinton** administration's Assistant Secretary of State **Winston Lord** and Congresswoman **Nancy Pelosi** to establish the **human rights** conditions the Clinton administration would require before renewing **most-favored-nation (MFN) tariff status** for China. The terms worked out were widely welcomed in the United States in 1993, but by the next year business and other interests were unwilling to see MFN stopped even though the Chinese government had not significantly improved human rights practices. President Clinton decided to reverse the policy in May 1994. *See also* LINKAGE POLICY.

MORGAN, JOHN P. (1837–1914). This American financier was interested in **investment** in China and involved with Americans seeking the **concessions** to build the **Hankow–Canton Railway** at the beginning of the 20th century. With the urging of the **Theodore Roosevelt** administration, he worked to restore US financial control over the enterprise but ultimately the stockholders sold out when receiving an advantageous offer for the concessions from Chinese buyers in 1905. *See also* AMERICAN CHINA DEVELOPMENT COMPANY.

MORGENTHAU, HENRY (1891–1967). Secretary of the treasury in the **Franklin D. Roosevelt** administration, Morgenthau endeavored to support the struggling Chinese **Nationalist Party** government against Japanese aggression. In 1934, the US government inaugurated, primarily for domestic reasons, a silver purchase program which caused great turmoil in the Chinese economy as massive amounts of silver left China by 1935. In response, Morgenthau initiated a silver purchase program for Nationalist China, paying it hundreds of millions of dollars in gold or US dollars for 500 million ounces of silver. Morgenthau later worked with **Claire Chennault** and others to get President Roosevelt prior to **Pearl Harbor** to authorize the transfer of US fighters and pilots to create the **American**

Volunteer Group, later also known as the **"Flying Tigers,"** to defend Nationalist China against Japan. He subsequently became disillusioned with Chiang Kai-shek's Nationalist regime when audits turned up massive fraud by Nationalist officials regarding the use of US aid.

MOSCOW DECLARATION. China was excluded from the Allied high command of World War II at the British–American conference in Quebec in August 1943, but it was included along with the Soviet Union in the US-backed Moscow Declaration of great-power principles in October 1943. **Chiang Kai-shek** participated in a subsequent conference with President **Franklin D. Roosevelt** and Prime Minister **Winston Churchill** in Cairo in December 1943. *See also* CAIRO DECLARATION.

MOST-FAVORED-NATION PRINCIPLE. Language supporting this principle was used widely in the 19th-century foreign agreements with the Chinese government establishing **treaty ports** and the so-called **treaty system**. The language meant that all foreign powers, including the United States, shared in whatever privileges any of them could get from China through force, intimidation, or other means. *See also* MOST-FAVORED-NATION (MFN) TARIFF STATUS.

MOST-FAVORED-NATION (MFN) TARIFF STATUS. In the last half of the 20th century, the United States applied the low tariff rates mandated under this status to most countries. A few, mainly Communist, countries were exceptions and were subject to much higher tariff rates. Under US law, certain conditions had to be met for a country like China to receive MFN tariff treatment. After the conclusion of the US–China **trade** agreement in 1980, the main condition for MFN for China was seen in the **Jackson–Vanik Amendment** of the Trade Act of 1974. Under its terms, each year the president had to inform Congress of his intention to extend MFN tariff status to China; then Congress had 90 days to reject the move by majority vote in both houses of Congress. The president could veto the congressional action and Congress had the option to override the veto by a two-thirds vote in both houses.

There was not much controversy about the annual MFN extension until after the **Tiananmen crackdown** in 1989. The extension process then became an annual focal point of congressional-executive wrangling over China policy, with various interest groups, lobbyists, specialists, and others engaging in lively and sometimes bitter debates as they anticipated the president's waiver and the congressional reaction. US legislation later changed the name of MFN to **normal trade relations**. After the United States agreed in late 1999 to China's joining the **World Trade Organization**, US legislation passed granting China **permanent normal trade relations (PNTR)** in 2000. This ended the occasion for the annual congressional debate over China policy.

MOTOROLA. This large US company had strong and growing **trade** and **investment** interests in the China market (10 percent of the company's global sales were in China in 1998). It lobbied strongly in the US debates over China policy in the 1990s for continued **most-favored-nation tariff status** for China as well as expedited US government consideration of technology transfers to China.

– N –

NANKING INCIDENT. During the military advance of **Nationalist Party** forces in the **Northern Expedition**, some Nationalist forces attacked foreigners and foreign property in this city, including the American, British, and Japanese consulates in March 1927. Several foreigners including Americans were killed. Looting and threats against foreigners did not stop until British and US gunboats began to bombard the attackers. The Americans joined the other powers in demanding punishment, apology, and compensation from the Nationalist authorities. The Nationalist authorities at the time were in turmoil with a power struggle for leadership that saw **Chiang Kai-shek**'s forces kill several hundred **Communist Party** and labor leaders in Shanghai the day after the Nanking incident, foreshadowing the start of a broader and violent Nationalist campaign against Communists and other perceived enemies. Maneuvering within the Nationalist leadership resulted in Chiang Kai-shek's emergence as dominant leader in January 1928. In March 1928, Chiang's regime accepted American terms about the incident while the US expressed regret about the gunboat bombardment.

NANKING, TREATY OF. This Chinese–British agreement of 1842 ended the **Opium War** and was the first of many treaties and other agreements between foreign powers, including the United States, and the Chinese government that until well into the 20th century gave special rights for foreigners in a growing number of **treaty ports**, eventually broadening such rights to special **concessions** and to the country as a whole.

NATIONAL COMMITTEE ON US–CHINA RELATIONS. This group of US experts, specialists, and other professionals dealing with China promoted greater public understanding of China during and after the Cold War. Its leaders played an active role in the public China debates of the 1990s, arguing for continued **most-favored-nation tariff status** for China and a moderate US stance regarding Taiwan that would avoid seriously jeopardizing US relations with China.

NATIONAL ORIGINS ACT. Marking a high point capping over five decades of US efforts to exclude Chinese **immigration** into the United States that prompted repeated Chinese protests and friction in US–Chinese relations, this 1924 US law codified many of the statutes and other legal measures since the 1870s to produce a blanket ban against all new Asian immigrants. *See also* EXCLUSION MOVEMENT.

NATIONALIST PARTY. Also known as the **Kuomintang (KMT)**, the Nationalist Party traced its origins to revolutionary organizations led by **Sun Yat-sen**. **Chiang Kai-shek** emerged as party leader after a power struggle following Sun's death in 1925. He remained the dominant leader of the party as it fostered one-party authoritarian rule in China, and in Taiwan after Chiang and his followers retreated there in 1949. Amid growing political liberalization in Taiwan beginning in the 1980s, the party competed with a major opposition party, the **Democratic Progressive Party (DPP)**, losing control of the presidency to the DPP in 2000.

NAVAL GROUP CHINA. In 1942, a small US Naval Group China worked with **Chiang Kai-shek**'s secret police to establish the **Sino–American Cooperation Organization**. It funneled military aid to the **Nationalist Party** government with little oversight by senior US officers, assisting the Nationalist police in fighting **Communist Party** supporters in China.

NEUTRALITY LAWS. Reflecting the interests of a politically powerful peace movement in the United States in the 1930s, these US laws, passed in the mid-1930s, barred US government and private weapons sales and loans to warring nations. They and the political forces they represented were a major concern and impediment for the **Franklin D. Roosevelt** administration as it deliberated over possible ways to assist the Chinese **Nationalist Party** government and its forces facing Japanese aggression in the 1930s.

NINE POWER TREATY. The United States after World War I took the lead in calling a major conference to include powers with interests in the western Pacific, including China but not the Soviet Union, to deal with relevant security issues. The result was the **Washington Conference** of 1921–1922 that saw passage of a Nine Power Treaty supporting non-interference in Chinese internal affairs. The treaty disappointed Chinese patriots because it had no enforcement mechanisms and did nothing to retrieve the rights of sovereignty China had been forced to give up over the previous 80 years. The treaty was invoked repeatedly but without much effect in subsequent US efforts to support Chinese territorial integrity against Japanese expansion in the 1930s.

NIXON DOCTRINE. Speaking in **Guam** on 25 July 1969, President **Richard Nixon** announced his Nixon Doctrine, calling for reduced American military involvement in all of Asia. This doctrine revealed a significant downgrading of the China threat in the eyes of American leaders and implied an important reassessment of US **containment** policies in Asia. Under its heading, the Nixon administration carried out the withdrawal of over 600,000 US forces from Asia, the bulk from **Vietnam** but many from other points around China's periphery.

NIXON, RICHARD (1913–1994). As a US senator at the start of the Cold War, Nixon was a strong anti-Communist and sought to root out

Communists and other subversives allegedly influential in the US government. As President **Dwight Eisenhower**'s vice president, he was a strong supporter of the US military **containment** and diplomatic isolation of China and firmly supported **Chiang Kai-shek**'s **Nationalist Party** government on Taiwan. Returning to public life in 1968, Nixon won the presidential election in that tumultuous year of US divisions, demonstrations, riots, and assassinations of leaders Martin Luther King and Robert Kennedy. Working closely with National Security Adviser **Henry Kissinger**, he followed incremental steps, some overt but many secret, seeking an opening to China that would realign forces in Asian and world affairs to the benefit of the United States while implementing a US withdrawal from the **Vietnam** War and other strategic commitments in Asia.

The July 1971 announcement of Nixon's planned trip to China came as a surprise to most Americans, who supported the initiative. Americans watched with interest the president's February 1972 visit to China. Nixon privately indicated to Chinese leaders he would break US ties with Taiwan and establish diplomatic relations with China, and US–Chinese **liaison offices** were established in Beijing and Washington in 1973. But the US president became mired in the **Watergate Scandal** and was forced to resign in 1974. He remained active, encouraging constructive US–China relations and advising leaders on both sides, notably urging US and Chinese leaders to avoid extremes and seek mutual interests in the period after the **Tiananmen crackdown** of 1989.

NIXON–SATO COMMUNIQUE. This 1969 agreement between President **Richard Nixon** and the Japanese Prime Minister **Sato Eisaku** indicated US support for a greater Japanese role in Asian affairs and noted explicit Japanese security interests in Korea and Taiwan. Eliciting public statements of concern in Beijing, it strengthened Chinese strategic interest in seeking closer understanding with the United States over the future order in Asia.

NON-PROLIFERATION TREATY (NPT). China's decision in 1992 to join this international **arms control** regime, after decades of refusal, represented one of the few positive developments in this difficult year in US–China relations. The decision was part of incremental

Chinese efforts in the 1980s and 1990s to join arms control regimes or adhere to internationally accepted norms regarding control of the proliferation of weapons of mass destruction, their delivery systems, and related technologies.

NON-RECOGNITION DOCTRINE. US Secretary of State **William Jennings Bryan** announced in 1915, after China was forced to accept most of the Japanese **Twenty-One Demands** grossly infringing on Chinese territory and sovereign rights, that the United States would not recognize any agreement that infringed on American treaty rights, Chinese sovereignty, or the **Open Door Policy**. President **Herbert Hoover** and Secretary of State **Henry Stimson** resorted to a similar stance in the face of Japanese aggression and expansion in Manchuria in 1931–1932. *See also* HOOVER–STIMSON DOCTRINE.

NORMAL TRADE RELATIONS (NTR). Affecting the name of a major issue in US–China relations after the **Tiananmen crackdown**, US law in the late 1990s changed the name of **most-favored-nation tariff status** to normal trade relations. *See also* PERMANENT NORMAL TRADE RELATIONS; TRADE.

NORTHERN EXPEDITION. This military campaign was led by **Chiang Kai-shek** and was composed of aligned and **Comintern**-advised and supported **Nationalist Party** and **Communist Party** forces that moved from Canton into the Yangtze valley in 1926–1927. Major anti-foreign incidents occurred, notably the **Nanking incident** in March 1927. After the advance to the Yangtze, Chiang and conservative Nationalists split with and violently purged the Communists, unleashing a **White Terror** in 1927 that forced Comintern agents to flee. Chiang emerged from the power struggle as the predominant leader of China.

NORTH KOREA'S NUCLEAR WEAPONS PROGRAM. North Korean leader **Kim Il Sung** initiated an effort to develop nuclear weapons, and the program continued after his death in 1994 under the direction of his son **Kim Jong Il**. Beginning in the 1990s, the North Korean nuclear weapons efforts prompted repeated crises with the

United States and other concerned powers. Chinese officials differed with the United States on some issues, but generally endeavored to cooperate in efforts involving the United States that sought to deal with North Korean nuclear weapons development through diplomacy and negotiations

– O –

OIL FOR THE LAMPS OF CHINA. This 1937 American film was an example of the often exaggerated American views of the potential China market for American products, in this case US petroleum products.

OKSENBERG, MICHEL (1938–2001). A leading academic specialist on China, Oksenberg influenced US policy toward China as the senior China expert on the staff of National Security Adviser **Zbigniew Brzezinski** during the negotiations leading to the normalization of US–China relations in 1978 and subsequent steps advancing US–China ties during the **Jimmy Carter** administration. He returned to academic and research enterprises, leading and producing a wide range of studies on contemporary China and US–China relations.

OLNEY, RICHARD (1835–1917). Secretary of state in the second **Grover Cleveland** administration, Olney supported efforts by US legation minister **Charles Denby** to force the Chinese government to provide greater protection for US **missionaries** and to provide compensation for anti-missionary incidents.

OLYMPIC GAMES. In 1993, the US Congress, supported by many US media commentaries, went on record opposing Beijing's bid to host the 2000 Olympic Games. The Chinese leadership was working hard to win the bid, and when it was awarded to Sydney, Australia, they complained bitterly about American government schemes to thwart Chinese advances in international affairs.

ONE-CHILD POLICY. In the post–**Mao Zedong** period, Chinese leaders instituted a strict birth control policy whereby each couple generally was allowed to have only one child. The leaders judged that large-scale economic, health, and environmental problems caused by China's one billion people would be impossible to deal with if population growth were not severely cut. With the new American attention on **human rights** conditions in China after the **Tiananmen crackdown**, abuses associated with this strict birth control policy (e.g. coerced abortions, forced sterilizations, and female infanticide) received wide attention, especially in the US media, in the Congress, and among human rights groups. Such coverage swayed votes in the annual congressional debate on renewing **most-favored-nation tariff status** for China and had a strong negative impact on the prevailing atmosphere in US–China relations.

ONE CHINA. This term was used in discourse between officials from the People's Republic of China and officials from the Republic of China on Taiwan, particularly as Taiwan officials beginning in the 1990s increasingly emphasized Taiwan as an entity distinct and separate from China. In reaction, Chinese officials insisted on the recognition by Taiwan and others, including the United States, that Taiwan is part of one China. **Chen Shui-bian** of the **Democratic Progressive Party** was elected president of Taiwan in 2000 and reelected president in 2004 on a platform refusing to recognize this view of one China that would include Taiwan.

ONE CHINA POLICY. As US officials normalized and maintained official relations with the People's Republic of China while maintaining unofficial but extensive ties with and support for Taiwan, they were called upon repeatedly by Chinese officials to affirm support for a one China policy set forth in the **three joint communiqués** governing US policy toward China. Among other things, the policy recognized the People's Republic of China as the legitimate government of China, acknowledged that Taiwan was part of China, and determined that US relations with Taiwan would be unofficial.

ONE CHINA, ONE TAIWAN POLICY. Officials of the People's Republic of China (PRC) often accused the US government of following this policy that they said was designed to split Taiwan from China and treat Taiwan as a country separate from China. The PRC charges often were lumped together with charges that the US government was following a **two Chinas policy,** i.e. a policy that treated Beijing and Taipei as representing two separate and distinct Chinese governments. As Taiwan leaders at the start of the 21st century strengthened Taiwan's status as a country separate from China, PRC officials became more concerned about alleged US support for a one China, one Taiwan policy.

ONE COUNTRY, TWO SYSTEMS. This term referred to a proposal for reunifying Taiwan and China made by Chinese leaders beginning in the 1980s. It said that reunification would not affect Taiwan's political, economic, or social system. It also was used to govern China's approach to **Hong Kong**'s return to Chinese sovereignty in 1997. The proposal elicited some positive interest in the United States but little positive interest in Taiwan.

OPEN DOOR NOTES. Responding to the unexpected Japanese defeat of China in 1895, and European powers' extortion of leaseholds and **concessions** in the following three years, US Secretary of State **John Hay** used the work of State Department China expert **William Rockhill** and his British colleague from the **Chinese Imperial Maritime Customs Service**, **Alfred Hippisley**, as the basis for official US messages sent to all foreign powers concerned with China in September 1899. The notes sought the powers' agreement that even if they established special spheres in China, they would not discriminate against foreign **trade** or interfere with customs collection. They underlined US interests in preserving equal trade**, investment,** and other commercial access to China and the preservation of the integrity of the Chinese Customs Service, a crucial source of revenue for the struggling Chinese government. Though generally unenthusiastic about the US initiative, most concerned powers offered evasive and qualified responses, but all in effect endorsed the principles in the Open Door Notes.

As the United States and other foreign powers dispatched troops to crush the **Boxer uprising** and lift the siege of foreign legations in Peking, Hay in July 1900 sent a second round of Open Door Notes in which he expressed concern for preserving Chinese sovereignty. He depicted local Chinese authorities as responsible for law and order and the safety of foreigners in China. This helped the United States and other powers continue to work constructively with regional Chinese leaders in central and southern China who were maintaining law and order, and focus their anti-Boxer suppression more narrowly, in northern China. The foreign powers went along with Hay's notes.

OPEN DOOR POLICY. US policymakers repeatedly referred to the US Open Door Policy following the issuing of the **Open Door Notes** in 1899 and 1900. The **William H. Taft** administration interpreted the policy to extend beyond equal trade opportunity to include equal opportunity for **investment** in China. The **Woodrow Wilson** administration reacted to the Japanese **Twenty-One Demands** against China by refusing to recognize such infringements on the Open Door Policy. The related principles concerning US support for the territorial integrity of China were featured prominently in the **Nine Power Treaty** of the **Washington Conference** in the Warren Harding administration, and in the non-recognition of Japanese aggression in Manchuria during the **Herbert Hoover** administration. The **Harry Truman** administration sought Soviet Union leader **Joseph Stalin**'s promise that the Open Door Policy would be observed in the Soviet-influenced areas of Manchuria following the Soviet military defeat of Japanese forces there. In general, American political leaders dealing with China throughout the 20th century tended to refer to the Open Door Policy in positive terms, as a US attempt to prevent China from being carved up into commercially impenetrable foreign colonies. Chinese interpretations often emphasized that Americans were more concerned about maintaining their own commercial access, and were prepared to do little in practice in supporting Chinese integrity. *See also* NON-RECOGNITION DOCTRINE.

OPIUM WAR. The burgeoning **trade** in illegal opium entering China in the period before the Opium War (1839–1842) was carried out mainly by British merchants, though American merchants carried Turkish opium to China and held about 10 percent of the Chinese opium market. American opium along with British opium was confiscated and destroyed by Chinese authorities in Canton in 1839, leading to Great Britain's going to war. The US government took no part in the fighting.

OVERSEAS PRIVATE INVESTMENT CORPORATION (OPIC).
Though US foreign aid to the People's Republic of China remained restricted, this US government agency was able to provide guarantees for US **investment** in China. The agency's work in China was suspended for a time after the **Tiananmen crackdown**.

– P –

PAAL, DOUGLAS (1948–). This veteran Chinese affairs specialist who served as the senior National Security Council staff aide with responsibility for China in the **George H. W. Bush** administration achieved public prominence when he was appointed by the **George W. Bush** government as director of the **American Institute in Taiwan**. There he faced the difficult challenge of persuading Taiwan President **Chen Shui-bian** to avoid statements and actions favoring Taiwan independence or other issues seen as provocative by Beijing and contrary to US interest in maintaining stability in the **Taiwan Strait**.

PAGE ACT. Among federal laws passed in the 1870s making it more difficult for Chinese in the United States, this law passed in 1870 banned most **immigration** of Chinese women, hindering the creation of Chinese families in the United States. *See also* EXCLUSION MOVEMENT.

PANAMA CANAL. Amid wide-ranging anti-China charges in the Congress and the media, and residual concerns of some US groups over the return of the Panama Canal to Panama, charges were raised in the late 1990s by some members of Congress, including Senate Majority Leader Trent Lott, that recent agreements allowing a Hong Kong–based firm, **Hutchison Whampoa Limited** (HWL), to operate ports on either end of the canal posed a major security risk. Worth over $25 billion and already operating major ports in Europe and the Caribbean as well as Hong Kong and Shanghai, HWL was led by **Li Kashing**, who had close ties with senior Chinese leaders. The US critics alleged that Beijing would somehow use Li and his company to gain control of the canal in the event of a crisis with the United

States over Taiwan or for some other possible reason. Upon reflection, even some strong congressional critics of China found these accusations hard to believe.

The US agreement returning the Panama Canal to Panama figured earlier in US–China relations. President **Jimmy Carter** was unwilling to normalize diplomatic relations with China and break ties with Taiwan until the US Senate ratified the controversial treaty returning the canal to Panama. Carter needed Republican support for the two-thirds Senate vote of ratification and feared his China action might cost him votes on the Panama deal. Once the Senate approved the Panama treaty in spring 1978, Carter moved forward expeditiously with normalization with China.

PANAY. During the **Sino–Japanese War**, Japanese aircraft in December 1937 sank this US gunboat and machine-gunned its survivors near Nanking. US officials accepted Japan's apology and compensation, not choosing to make this an issue of confrontation with Japanese aggression in China.

PANCHEN LAMA (1937–1989). This Tibetan Buddhist leader was second only in prestige to the **Dalai Lama**. He remained in China dealing with Chinese authorities, unlike the Dalai Lama who fled abroad in 1959. When he died, a succession process took place among Tibetan monks who consulted secretly with the Dalai Lama. The Dalai Lama announced the choice of successor in 1995. Chinese authorities intervened, detained the chosen successor and others involved, and launched a new succession process announcing a choice acceptable to China. US media, **human rights** activists, Tibetan interest groups, and many in Congress were outraged by the Chinese actions.

PARKER, PETER (1804–1888). Among early American **missionaries** in China, Parker was a medical missionary in Canton in the 1830s. He helped **Caleb Cushing** to negotiate the **Treaty of Wang-hsia** in 1844. He was an interpreter and also helped to facilitate the talks by being on good terms with the chief Chinese government negotiator and his aides. Parker became US commissioner in China in 1856. He favored Britain's approach emphasizing firmness and appropriate use of force to advance foreign interests. He backed Commodore **James Armstrong**'s destruction of Chinese forts near Canton that had fired on US ships in 1956. Parker's ambitions regarding a US foothold on Taiwan and more active US naval presence in the region were not supported in Washington, however.

PATTEN, CHRISTOPHER (1944–). The last British governor of **Hong Kong**, Patten followed his 1992 appointment by pursuing a tougher, pro-democracy line in negotiations with Beijing that infuriated the Chinese authorities but was warmly received in the United States, especially in the Congress and media, and among **human rights** groups and other critics of China. Patten traveled regularly to Washington, seeking US support while urging the Congress to support annual renewal of **most-favored-nation (MFN) tariff status** for China, noting that Hong Kong's economy would suffer enormously if MFN were halted and US–China **trade** declined.

PEACE CORPS. The Chinese and US governments reached agreement in 1988 that the US Peace Corps would send 100 Americans to China's interior province of Sichuan to promote **education**, teaching English. About 4,000 American teachers had already taught in China under non-official auspices in the 1980s, and the numbers grew in following years, even with a dip caused by the **Tiananmen crackdown** of 1989.

PEACE MOVEMENT. This broad and largely grassroots American movement was identified by scholars as pursuing various initiatives in the period between the two world wars in order to reach international political agreements guaranteeing international peace while eschewing US involvement in arms races, power politics, and international conflicts that could draw the United States into war. It influenced US efforts at the **Washington Conference** in 1921–1922 to limit naval armaments and seek political agreements in support of US goals in China. It influenced US decisions to avoid military confrontation and seek political settlement and accommodation in the face of Chinese **Nationalist Party** forces challenging US rights in China in the latter 1920s. Peace activists helped to determine the largely symbolic US response to Japanese aggression against China in Manchuria in 1931–1932, and they helped to curb interest in the **Franklin D. Roosevelt** administration to take a more active role in helping China resist Japan following the outbreak of the **Sino–Japanese War** in 1937. *See also* NEUTRALITY LAWS.

PEACE PEARL. The **Ronald Reagan** administration agreed with the Chinese government in 1986 to upgrade Chinese F-8 jet fighters in a program with this name. The Grumman Corporation was the main US corporation involved in this effort, worth about $550 million. The project was frozen by President **George H. W. Bush** the day after the **Tiananmen crackdown**, was revived in a limited way by the president in October 1989, and ultimately ended without much being accomplished.

PEARL HARBOR. The Japanese attack on this US military base in Hawaii on 7 December 1941 prompted US entry into World War II. This signaled to leaders of the Chinese **Nationalist Party** and Chinese **Communist Party** and others in China that Japanese aggressors, whom China had been resisting for years, would likely be defeated, and that the United States would emerge as the most powerful foreign nation influencing developments in China.

PEKING, TREATIES OF (1860). British and French forces occupied Peking in 1860 and forced new treaties on the Chinese government that benefited foreigners, including Americans, in China.

PEKING UNION MEDICAL COLLEGE. The **Rockefeller Foundation** invested over $20 million from 1915–1947 for **education**, training doctors and nurses who engaged in teaching, research, and full-time hospital work, creating this modern medical center in China and bringing the advances of modern medicine to China.

PELOSI, NANCY (1940–). After the **Tiananmen crackdown**, this Democratic congresswoman from California was in the lead in congressional opposition to Chinese government **human rights** practices and to the **George H. W. Bush** administration's efforts to sustain moderation toward China. She worked closely with Senate Majority Leader **George Mitchell** and the incoming **William Clinton** administration's assistant secretary of state, **Winston Lord**, to establish the human rights conditions the Clinton administration would require before renewing **most-favored-nation (MFN) tariff status** for China. The terms worked out were widely welcomed in the United States in 1993, but by the next year business and other interests were unwilling to see MFN stopped even though the Chinese government had not significantly improved human rights practices. President Clinton decided to reverse the policy in May 1994. Pelosi opposed that decision, remained a strong critic of Chinese government practices, especially regarding human rights, and continued to work in subsequent years to attach strong conditions to the president's renewal of MFN tariff status for China. *See also* LINKAGE POLICY.

PENG DEHUAI (1898–1974). This seasoned Chinese **Communist Party** military commander led Chinese forces against American-led forces in the **Korean War**.

PEOPLE'S LIBERATION ARMY (PLA). This is the formal name of the armed forces of the Chinese **Communist Party** and the People's Republic of China.

PEOPLE'S REPUBLIC OF CHINA (PRC). With the military victory of **Communist Party** forces against the Chinese **Nationalist Party** forces on the Chinese mainland in 1949, **Mao Zedong** announced the formation of this new government of China on 1 October 1949. The Nationalists under **Chiang Kai-shek** retreated to Taiwan, where they continued to claim that their government, the Republic of China, represented the legitimate government of China. The United States sided with Chiang's Nationalists in the Cold War, strongly supporting their claim to be China's legitimate government, until President **Richard Nixon** began high-level contacts with the People's Republic of China, leading to the establishment of US–PRC relations and US recognition of the PRC as the government of China in 1979.

In the early 21st century, the PRC had a population of over 1.3 million people, a gross domestic product in nominal terms of over US $1 trillion, and annual foreign trade of about the same value. It had land borders with 14 nations. China's population and armed forces were the world's largest, while its geographic size was fourth in the world, slightly smaller than the United States. *See also* CULTURAL REVOLUTION; DENG XIAOPING; GREAT LEAP FORWARD; HU JINTAO; JIANG ZEMIN.

PERMANENT NORMAL TRADE RELATIONS (PNTR). After the United States agreed in late 1999 to China's joining the **World Trade Organization**, US legislation dealing with US **trade** with China passed and granted China permanent normal trade relations (PNTR) in 2000. This ended the need for annual presidential requests and congressional reviews regarding China's keeping normal trade relations tariff status, previously known as **most-favored-nation (MFN) tariff status**.

PERRY, WILLIAM J. (1927–). As undersecretary of defense in the **Jimmy Carter** administration, Perry in 1980 made an extensive trip to China, assessing Chinese military capabilities and options for US military assistance to China. As President **William Clinton**'s secretary of defense, Perry in 1993 resumed high-level military dialogue with China, suspended after the **Tiananmen crackdown**, by sending Assistant Secretary of Defense **Charles Freeman** to China, and Perry went to China in 1994. Perry supported a firm US stance in response to Chinese provocative military exercises in the **Taiwan Strait** in March 1996. After leaving office, he led important unofficial efforts to ease tensions in the Taiwan Strait, traveling to China and Taiwan.

PERSIAN GULF WAR. The rapid success in 1990–1991 of US technically capable and well-integrated military forces in defeating Iraqi forces that had invaded Kuwait vividly demonstrated to Chinese leaders the large gap in capabilities between Chinese and US military forces. It prompted more strenuous Chinese efforts at defense modernization while Chinese leaders tried to avoid military confrontation and conflict with the American superpower.

PESCADORES. The US defense commitment to defend these islands located west of Taiwan was reinforced by the **Formosa Resolution** of 1955.

PETHICK, ROBERT. An American linguist, Pethick provided translation services for visiting Americans in China in the last quarter of the 19th century while he worked as a tutor and private secretary for senior Chinese leader **Li Hung-chang**, who dominated Chinese foreign policymaking during this period. In 1879, he encouraged Li to use retired US President **Ulysses S. Grant**, then traveling in Asia, to intercede with Japan over a Sino–Japanese dispute over the **Liuch'iu (Ryukyu) Islands**.

PICKERING, THOMAS (1931–). Undersecretary of state at the time of the US bombing of the Chinese embassy in Belgrade in 1999, Pickering was made presidential special envoy and delivered the US explanation of the incident to Chinese officials in Beijing in June 1999. *See also* BELGRADE, US BOMBING OF CHINESE EMBASSY.

PIERCE, FRANKLIN (1804–1869). The administration of this US president, 1853–1857 showed very limited interest in China. This meant that ambitious plans for US actions by US commissioners in China, like **Humphrey Marshall**, and other Americans with an interest in China, were generally not followed by the US government.

PING PONG DIPLOMACY. While secret communications were underway between US and Chinese leaders, American table tennis players in April 1971 developed friendships with Chinese counterparts at an international meet in Japan. The Americans mentioned interest in visiting China. Chinese leaders agreed, and the team was warmly welcomed amid widespread media coverage in China and the West. **Zhou Enlai** received the guests on 14 April and spoke of a new chapter in China–US relations.

POTSDAM DECLARATION. The United States and its wartime allies used this declaration in July 1945 to reaffirm the statement made in the **Cairo Declaration** of 1943 that "Taiwan and territories stolen by Japan" would be returned after the war.

POWELL, COLIN (1937–). As secretary of state in the first term of the **George W. Bush** administration, Powell appreciated the multifaceted US–China relationship, with both common points and points of difference and conflict. On this basis, he endeavored to develop businesslike interaction with China that underlined US interests in relations with Japan and Taiwan, while seeking cooperation with China in a variety of areas, including in dealing with **North Korea's nuclear weapons development**.

PRISON LABOR. After the **Tiananmen crackdown, Hongda (Harry) Wu, Human Rights Watch–Asia**, congressional critics of China, and other US activists exposed the Chinese practice of having prisoners produce products for sale abroad, including the United States. Pressure in Congress and the media led the **George H. W. Bush** administration to negotiate a memorandum of understanding with China, signed 7 August 1992, whereby China agreed not to export prison labor products to the United States and agreed to permit inspections of suspected production sites by US officials. After disagreements and a halt by the Chinese to US inspections, another agreement was signed in 1994. This was not enough for Congress, particularly as China continued to resist US inspections. Provisions against prison labor were included in subsequent legislation, some of which became law.

PUTIN, VLADIMIR (1952–). As Russian president from 2000, Putin modified Russia's previous close public identification with China in opposition to US international dominance, and sought pragmatically to improve Russian relations with the United States. The Russian shift influenced China's leaders to make similar adjustments and seek more common ground with the United States by 2001. Russia and China continued to develop **trade** relations, and Chinese purchases of modern Russian arms were valued at $2 billion a year. Russia was China's main foreign arms supplier as a US-backed embargo against military sales to China persisted among US allies in the West after 1989.

– Q –

QIAN QICHEN (1928–). As foreign minister, state counselor, and vice premier, Qian was a leading architect and implementer of China's policy toward the United States in the period after the Tiananmen crackdown and the end of the Cold War. He met with most visiting senior US leaders and traveled regularly to the United

States. A close adviser of **Jiang Zemin**, he rose to greater prominence and power during Jiang's latter years as president and party
leader, supporting the senior leader in summit meetings with President **William Clinton** in 1997 and 1998. Qian demonstrated more
flexibility than other Chinese leaders in dealing with the United
States over Taiwan and other sensitive issues, and was held responsible and criticized after setbacks, notably **Lee Teng-hui**'s 1995 visit to
the United States. He was the first senior Chinese leader to travel to
Washington to meet with the **George W. Bush** administration, in
March 2001, a period of considerable uncertainty in China's approach toward the incoming US government.

QIAN XUESEN (1911–). This Chinese-born scientist played an important role in developing America's first missiles. When he attempted to return to China after the Communist victory there, his security clearance was removed and he was kept in the United States
against his will for several years. Returning to China in 1955, he
helped to develop China's first nuclear weapons and ballistic missiles.

QIAO SHI (1924–). This senior Chinese **Communist Party** leader
was a rival to **Jiang Zemin** in the struggle to succeed **Deng Xiaoping** as leader of China. Qiao adopted a notably hard line against the
United States over the Taiwan issue after **Lee Teng-hui**'s visit to the
United States in 1995, and was said to have led leaders sharply criticizing the way Jiang and Foreign Minister **Qian Qichen** handled US
and Taiwan affairs. Qiao eventually lost out to Jiang, and was forced
to retire from senior party posts in 1997, but various reports said he
continued periodically to attack Jiang for being too flexible and soft
in policy toward the United States over Taiwan, China's entry into the
World Trade Organization, and other issues.

QING (CH'ING) DYNASTY. This is the name given to the dynasty in
China, ruled by Manchu leaders, that was in power from 1644–1912.

QUARANTINE SPEECH. Responding to Japanese aggression
against China and other international military expansion, President
Franklin D. Roosevelt in a speech on 5 October 1937 called for a

quarantine of an "epidemic of world lawlessness." No specific US actions in Asia followed as the US government was not prepared to stand against Japan as it ruthlessly advanced in China.

QUEMOY. One large and some small islands near the China coast that remained under the control of **Nationalist Party** forces after 1949, Quemoy was the key fortress of **Chiang Kai-shek** along the China coast, occupied by hundreds of thousands of forces and figuring prominently in Nationalist–Communist military confrontations in the **Taiwan Strait** during the 1950s. *See also* MATSU; TAIWAN STRAIT CRISES.

– R –

RADIO FREE ASIA. Modeled on US-backed Radio Free Europe that was seen to have promoted challenge to Communist rule in Europe by giving people in Communist countries greater access to information and comment on developments in their countries, this US-backed enterprise focused in the post–Cold War period on China and other authoritarian Asian countries that endeavored to control information about developments in their countries. Support for greater Radio Free Asia efforts targeted against China increased in the strong anti-China atmosphere prevailing in Congress in the 1990s. Chinese officials condemned such steps as interference in Chinese affairs.

REAGAN, RONALD (1911–2004). A conservative Republican governor of California with a record of strong support for **Chiang Kai-shek** and the Chinese **Nationalist Party** government against the Chinese **Communist Party** government, Reagan competed for the 1976 presidential nomination. This curbed President **Gerald Ford**'s interest in moving forward with earlier promises to normalize US relations with the Communist government in China. Reagan ran against President **Jimmy Carter** in the 1980 election, asserting for a time that he would restore official relations with Taiwan. He backed away from this stance but claimed he would base his policy on the **Taiwan Relations Act** and avoided reference to the **US–China communiqué of 1978** requiring the United States to break all official ties with Taiwan and to recognize Beijing as China's legitimate government.

The Chinese government put heavy pressure on the Reagan administration, threatening serious deterioration in relations over various issues, but especially US arms sales to Taiwan. Viewing close China–US relations as a key element in US strategy against the Soviet Union, Secretary of State **Alexander Haig** led those in the Reagan administration who favored maintaining close China–US relations and he opposed US arms sales to Taiwan that might provoke China. The United States ultimately signed with China the **17 August 1982 communiqué** promising to reduce US arms sales to Taiwan. President Reagan registered private reservations about this arrangement, and his administration also took steps, notably in the **six assurances**, to reassure Taiwan's leader of continued US support.

With Haig's resignation in 1982 and the appointment of **George Shultz** as secretary of state, US policy shifted. There was less emphasis on China's strategic importance and less concern about China's possibly downgrading relations over Taiwan and other disputes. The Chinese leaders came to terms with the new US stance, seeing their interests best served by less pressure and more positive initiatives to the Reagan administration, seen notably in their warm welcome for the US president on his visit to China in 1984. In this atmosphere, the president's second term in office did not see repetition of the many China–US controversies that had marked Reagan's relations with China earlier in the 1980s.

RED STAR OVER CHINA. American journalist **Edgar Snow** visited the **Communist Party**–controlled areas of China and interviewed **Mao Zedong** and other Communist leaders in 1936. In this book published in 1938, Snow described the Chinese Communist movement and experiences, introducing the little-known Communists and their leaders to Western readers.

REED, WILLIAM (1806–1876). US minister to China in 1858, Reed followed the Anglo–French military forces that compelled the Chinese government to grant foreign diplomats rights of residency in Peking, to open the Yangtze River for foreign **trade**, and to protect foreign **missionaries** and converts. Chinese officials in vain appealed to Reed to mediate for China with the British and French. Reed's successors were able to claim and gain the same rights as those granted to Britain and France without directly engaging in combat and coercion.

REINSCH, PAUL (1869–1923). The US minister in China during World War I, Reinsch endeavored to encourage a reluctant US government to take stronger actions in the face of Japan's **Twenty-One Demands** grossly infringing on Chinese sovereignty in 1915. He supported President **Woodrow Wilson**'s subsequent efforts to encourage US banks to arrange loans to China in competition with Japan. Wilson ultimately turned to American bankers of a consortium that had been involved in lending to China in previous US administrations, a group Wilson had rejected at the outset of his administration. Reinsch opposed this step, judging that the group would come to be dominated by Japan. Reinsch reacted with concern to notes resulting from 1917 meetings between Japanese envoy Ishii Kikujiro and Secretary of State **Robert Lansing** that acknowledged Japan's "special interests" in China. President Wilson accepted Japanese claims to the former German **concessions** in China's Shantung province in the **Versailles Peace Treaty of 1919**. The agreement prompted mass demonstrations in China which Reinsch joined, resigning his post. *See also* SHANTUNG LEASEHOLD.

REPUBLIC OF CHINA (ROC). This government was established in China during the fall of the **Qing dynasty** in 1911. Self-seeking or weak military and political leaders were succeeded by a more effective regime under **Chiang Kai-shek** in the late 1920s that attempted to carry out nation building while fending off Japanese encroachment and suppressing **Communist Party** and warlord resistance. Chiang's government was driven into the interior by invading Japanese armies at the start of the **Sino–Japanese War** in 1937, held out until the tide of war turned against Japan, and was restored as the legitimate government of China with Japan's defeat in 1945. Defeated by the Chinese Communists in the **Chinese Civil War**, Chiang's forces in 1949 retreated to Taiwan and moved the Republic of China to Taiwan, where it remained into the 21st century. At that time, the government ruled over territory slightly smaller than Maryland and Delaware combined, a population of 23 million, an economy and foreign trade ranking among the top 20 in the world, and armed forces numbering over 300,000. Because of opposition from the People's Republic of China, the ROC had official relations with less than 30 mainly small countries and had no official ties with the **United Nations** and most international organizations that required statehood for membership. It was a member of such important economic groups as the **World Trade Organization**, the **Asian Development Bank**, and the **Asia Pacific Economic Cooperation** forum.

RESIST AMERICA–AID KOREA. As **Mao Zedong** and the Chinese **Communist Party** regime launched forces to battle US-led forces in the **Korean War**, they emphasized this mass campaign that had the effect of driving out and destroying American influence in higher **education**, research, and cultural and religious activities in China. American **missionaries**, universities, and foundations that worked in China were forced to leave, while Chinese institutions and programs receiving American support cut ties to the United States.

RIDGWAY, MATTHEW (1895–1993). Replacing **Douglas MacArthur** as US commander in the **Korean War** in 1951, Ridgway led US forces to drive Chinese forces back to the 38th parallel without the military escalation and direct attacks on China that MacArthur had called for.

RIGHTS RECOVERY MOVEMENT. This Chinese movement in the first decade of the 20th century sought to counter foreign **concessions** to build railways and other activities in China, and endeavored to buy back the foreign rights. In this context, senior leader **Chang Chih-tung** arranged in 1905 to redeem the **American China Development Company**'s contract to build a **Hankow–Canton Railway**.

ROBERTS, EDMUND (1794–1836). Sent by the Andrew Jackson administration to find new commercial opportunities in Asia, Roberts reached Canton in 1832 but failed to establish communications with Chinese authorities or to place US relations with China on a treaty basis.

ROBERTS, ISSACHAR J. (1802–1871). The founder of the **Taiping Rebellion**, **Hung Hsiu-ch'uan**, saw himself as the younger brother of Jesus Christ. He came to his own unique views of Christianity, though he studied for three months in 1837 with an American missionary in Canton, Issachar Roberts.

ROBERTSON, WALTER (1893–1970). Assistant secretary of state for East Asian affairs in the 1950s, Robertson was a strong supporter of the Chinese **Nationalist Party** administration on Taiwan and advocated a tough US stance against the **Communist Party** government in China.

ROCKEFELLER FOUNDATION. *See* PEKING UNION MEDICAL COLLEGE.

ROCKHILL, W. W. (1854–1914). The State Department's leading China specialist at the end of the 19th century, Rockhill drafted along with British colleague **Alfred Hippisley** material used by Secretary of State **John Hay** in the US **Open Door Notes** of 1899 and he was consulted by Hay in releasing a second round of such notes in 1900. Rockhill served as the American representative at the international negotiations in Peking in 1900–1901 dealing with results of the **Boxer uprising**. He was minister in China during the Chinese **anti-American boycott** of 1905, and dealt with Chinese actions against US exclusion of Chinese immigrants, Chinese violence against US **missionaries**, and related issues. Over the years, Rockhill worked to support progress in Chinese governance and institutions, the territorial integrity of China, and an overall moderate US policy seeking to advance American missionary, **trade**, and other interests with a regard for Chinese concerns. *See also* EXCLUSION MOVEMENT; IMMIGRATION.

ROCK SPRINGS MASSACRE. In September 1885, mobs of white people attacked Chinese in the Wyoming town of Rock Springs, killing 28 in an outburst of burning, looting, and mayhem. The incident caused the Union Pacific Railroad to halt hiring of Chinese workers and reinforced efforts to exclude Chinese **immigration** into the United States. *See also* EXCLUSION MOVEMENT.

ROOSEVELT, FRANKLIN D. (1882–1945). The long tenure of President Franklin D. Roosevelt saw US policy reluctant at first to offer support to **Chiang Kai-shek**'s **Nationalist Party** government struggling in the face of Japanese intimidation and, after 1937, all-out military aggression in the **Sino–Japanese War**. The US resolve to help

China and oppose Japan stiffened in the year prior to **Pearl Harbor** and American entry into the war. The **American Volunteer Group** provided air defense for Nationalist Chinese areas and **lend-lease aid** was approved for China.

After Pearl Harbor, China remained low on the list of US wartime priorities and US material aid to the Chinese Nationalists was hampered because surface supply routes were cut by the Japanese forces. US financial and other aid continued and President Roosevelt was in the lead in insuring that the Chinese Nationalist government was treated as one of the Allied great powers that would guide world affairs after the defeat of the Axis powers. Friction between Chiang Kai-shek and the US military commander in China saw the President send special envoy **Patrick Hurley** to China in late 1944. The President backed Hurley's stance of strong support for Chiang Kai-shek that subordinated US interests with the rival Chinese **Communist Party** forces. Dealing with the many hundreds of thousands of Japanese forces in China and uncertainties there caused by Nationalist–Communist rivalry, the president established arrangements in the **Far Eastern Agreement** at the **Yalta Conference** in early 1945 that called for Soviet forces to play the leading role in defeating Japanese forces in China and to obtain port, railway, and other benefits in post-war China.

ROOSEVELT, THEODORE (1858–1919). President Theodore Roosevelt generally dealt pragmatically with continued foreign encroachment on China in the first decade of the 20th century. He saw American interests in China threatened by Russian expansion in Manchuria, and was glad when Japan, Russia's chief rival in Manchuria, attacked Russia in 1904 and defeated Russia in 1905. Roosevelt won the Nobel Peace Prize for mediating the peace agreement between Japan and Russia. Following Japan's victory over Russia, Roosevelt was not prepared to confront the rising power of Japan for the sake of American interests in China or other concerns. After leaving office, Roosevelt advised his successor, **William H. Taft**, against that US administration's active pursuit of US **investment** and other schemes to counter Japanese expansion in Manchuria.

Blatantly discriminatory US laws and measures against Chinese **immigration** grew during the Roosevelt administration, leading to a grassroots Chinese **anti-American boycott** in 1905 that seriously damaged US **trade** in China for months. The boycott prompted the Roosevelt administration and some in Congress to consider reforms and other measures to ease the harsh US exclusion policies and practices against Chinese immigrants, but as the boycott waned by 1906, so did the reform efforts and the US **exclusion movement** against the Chinese remained intact.

ROOT, ELIHU (1845–1937). As secretary of state during the **Theodore Roosevelt** administration, Root followed the administration's policy in protesting Japanese and other discrimination against American **trade** in Manchuria or other parts of China, while avoiding more strenuous efforts that could lead to confrontation or conflict with Japan. The priority of the administration to avoid conflict with Japan over China or other issues was seen in the exchange of notes by Secretary Root and the Japanese Ambassador **Takahira Kogoro** in 1908, know as the **Root–Takahira Agreement,** which reaffirmed US commitment to the status quo in the Pacific and ruled out American challenge to Japanese interests in China. Root was a member of the US delegation to the **Washington Conference**, 1921–1922, where he played an important role in negotiating the **Nine Power Treaty** dealing with China.

ROOT–TAKAHIRA AGREEMENT. While Chinese officials were seeking US financial and political support to counter Japanese expansion in Manchuria, Secretary of State **Elihu Root** and Japanese Ambassador **Takahira Kogoro** exchanged notes on 30 November 1908 that underlined US commitment to the status quo in the Pacific region, including China; US desire to maintain friendly relations with Japan; and lack of US interest in considering any Chinese-inspired scheme to challenge Japanese interests in Manchuria.

ROTH, STANLEY (1954–). An aide and close adviser of Congressman **Stephen Solarz**, the most prominent congressional member dealing with China policy issues in the 1980s and early 1990s, Roth became the senior National Security Council staff person with responsibility for China in the first term of the **William Clinton** administration and was assistant secretary of state for East Asian affairs in the Clinton administration's second term. In these posts, he played important roles supporting his superiors in various initiatives in the often fast-changing circumstances in US–China relations during this time.

ROY, J. STAPLETON (1935–). A Chinese and Asian affairs specialist in the US State Department, Roy worked over the years to improve US–China relations, capping his role in policymaking regarding China by serving as US ambassador in Beijing during the difficult years of 1991–1995. Though the **William Clinton** administration's initially tough approach to China, including applying strict **human rights** conditions to US annual renewal of **most-favored-nation tariff status** for China, moderated in 1994 when the President dropped the conditions, relations entered their most serious crisis of the 1990s when the president allowed the Taiwan president to visit the United States in 1995. Roy had warned in vain against the visit and departed Beijing for the ambassadorship in Indonesia amid growing US–China friction and confrontation.

RUBIN, ROBERT (1938–). A close adviser of President **William Clinton**, Rubin served as the head of the president's National Economic Council, and later as secretary of the Treasury Department. He worked closely with Chinese leaders in managing the fallout of the 1997–1998 **Asian economic crisis**, urging China to maintain the value of its currency and to pursue policies conducive to reviving Asian economic growth. A supporter of the Clinton administration's **engagement policy** with China, Rubin nonetheless weighed in against accepting a draft US–China accord on China's entry into the **World Trade Organization** that was prepared at the time of Chinese Premier **Zhu Rongji**'s April 1999 visit to Washington. The president agreed, embarrassing Zhu, though ultimately an agreement was worked out along similar lines by November.

RUMSFELD, DONALD (1932–). Secretary of defense during the **George W. Bush** administration, Rumsfeld and his department remained wary of China's strategic intentions. He enhanced US military cooperation with Taiwan, built US and associates' military capabilities in the Asian region, and was slow to develop military exchanges with

China. The **EP-3 incident** of 1 April 2001 deepened Defense Department antagonism toward China, though the terrorist attack on America on 11 September 2001 and subsequent US military focus in Southwest Asia diverted primary Defense Department attention from security problems seen posed by China.

RUSK, DEAN (1909–1994). This career State Department officer with broad experience dealing with Asia sought to keep Taiwan out of Communist hands at the end of the **Chinese Civil War**, and he took a tough public line against **Mao Zedong** and his **Communist Party** regime at the outset of the **Korean War**. As secretary of state for President **John Kennedy** and President **Lyndon Johnson**, Rusk showed little interest in US moderation toward China. He came to see China becoming armed with nuclear weapons as a threat to Asian neighbors and world stability. Rusk supported deepening US involvement in **Vietnam** in part to meet the challenge he saw posed to the United States by Maoist China and its support for insurgencies against US allies.

RUSSELL AND COMPANY. Founded in 1824, this firm emerged as the leading American trading firm in China in the 19th century. Dealing with the opium **trade**, it also dealt with a wide range of goods in trading in Canton prior to the **Opium War**. It expanded with the subsequent opening of China to foreign trade, notably managing the Shanghai Steam Navigation Company involved in coastal China trade. But profits in China declined, while those in the United States increased, and the company leaders scaled back China investment and closed in 1891.

– S –

SASSER, JAMES (1936–). A former senator from Tennessee, Sasser found his appointment by the **William Clinton** administration as ambassador to China delayed by the Chinese government as a signal of Chinese government opposition to the visit of the Taiwan president to the United States in 1995. His tenure in Beijing saw notable progress, with Sino–US summits in 1997 and 1998, but he left the position amid a major downturn as Chinese demonstrators attacked, damaged, and destroyed US diplomatic properties in China in response to the US bombing of the Chinese embassy in Belgrade in May 1999. *See also* BELGRADE, US BOMBING OF CHINESE EMBASSY.

SATO, EISAKU (1901–1975). As Japanese prime minister, Sato in 1969 signed the **Nixon–Sato communiqué** that indicated US support for a greater Japanese role in Asian affairs and noted explicit Japanese security interests in Korea and Taiwan. Eliciting public statements of concern in Beijing, the communiqué strengthened Chinese strategic interest in seeking closer understanding with the United States over the future order in Asia. That interest helped to lead to secret preparations for the US–China opening announced by President **Richard Nixon** in July 1971. That step came as a shock to Japan, contradicted Japan's policy toward China, and led to the downfall of the prime minister.

SCALAPINO, ROBERT (1919–). This University of California Asian affairs specialist remained prominent as an educator, commentator, public policy researcher, and adviser to Congress and the administration from the 1950s through the early 21st century. He urged moderation in US China policy in periods when many urged extremes, and he supported a realistic appreciation of American interests in China at times when many exaggerated those interests, whether negative or positive.

SCHLESINGER, JAMES (1929–). As secretary of defense in the **Gerald Ford** administration, Schlesinger supported consideration of developing closer US–China military ties in opposition to the Soviet Union. Chinese officials and commentary welcomed his firm views on the Soviet Union at a time when they saw the Ford administration as overly solicitous in seeking better relations with the Soviet Union. Chinese officials judged such US–Soviet **détente** as weakening China's position against the Soviet Union.

SCHURMAN, JACOB G. (1854–1942). As US minister to China in the Warren Harding administration, Schurman advocated restoration of Chinese tariff autonomy and some other rights taken by foreign powers in the previous century. He was skeptical of **Sun Yat-sen**. When Sun turned to the Soviet Union and received support for a revived **Nationalist Party**–led movement, Schurman informed President Calvin Coolidge of Sun's new power, but the minister still viewed the Nationalist leader as contrary to US interests. Schurman and his colleague and replacement as minister in 1925, **John V. A. MacMurray**, judged that significant US gestures to China, especially the end of **extraterritoriality**, would have to wait until stable governance was restored in China.

SCOTT ACT, 1888. This legislation was named for Congressman William Scott of Pennsylvania. It restricted Chinese laborers' entry, and denied them reentry, into the United States. *See also* EXCLUSION MOVEMENT; IMMIGRATION.

SCOWCROFT, BRENT (1925–). Scowcroft helped to manage US–China policy as President **Gerald Ford**'s national security adviser, working closely with Secretary of State **Henry Kissinger**, the leading US official dealing with China at that time. As national security adviser for President **George H. W. Bush**, Scowcroft supported the president's view of China's long-term strategic importance for the United States and the need to maintain close ties with Chinese leaders. He differed with Ambassador **Winston Lord** over the invitation of prominent dissident **Fang Lizhi** to a banquet hosted by President Bush while visiting Beijing in February 1989. In bids to maintain high-level contact with Chinese leaders in the aftermath of the **Tiananmen crackdown**, President Bush sent Scowcroft and Deputy Secretary of State **Lawrence Eagleburger** on secret missions for meetings with Chinese leaders in Beijing in July and December 1989. The visits caused an uproar in the Congress and the media at a time of strong US opposition to Chinese leaders over the Tiananmen events.

SELF-STRENGTHENING MOVEMENT. During and after the suppression of mid-century rebellions and new Chinese treaty agreements with foreign powers in 1860, Chinese government leaders pursued with mixed results various arrangements with foreign governments, businesses, and other groups to bring to China Western technical knowledge and equipment in order to help develop Chinese wealth and power. US organizations participated in these self-strengthening efforts and the US government tended to welcome and cooperate with them.

SERVICE, JOHN S. (1909–1999). A junior US diplomat stationed in China, Service played an important role as a member of the **American Military Observer Group** sent to **Yenan** in 1944, notably meeting with and reporting the views of **Mao Zedong** and other **Communist Party** leaders. Like many other US officials in China at this time, Service was critical of **Chiang Kai-shek**'s **Nationalist Party** regime and was positive about the role the Communists could play in the war against Japan and in furthering US interests in China. Service was arrested in 1945 on charges of passing classified documents critical of Chiang Kai-shek and US Ambassador to China **Patrick Hurley** to the leftist magazine, *Amerasia*. The charges against Service were dropped. Service became a prime target of the investigations of Senator **Joseph McCarthy** in the early 1950s seeking to uncover Communists in the State Department undermining US policy toward China and elsewhere. Along with several other State Department China specialists dismissed or pressured to resign at this time, Service was dismissed from the State Department as a security risk.

SEVENTH FLEET. This is the designation for US naval forces in the western Pacific that were sent to intervene in the **Taiwan Strait** at the start of the **Korean War** in 1950 and represented the key US naval forces available for dealing with China-related military crises and contingencies into the 21st century. *See also* TAIWAN STRAIT CRISES.

SEWARD, WILLIAM (1801–1872). Secretary of state in the 1860s, Seward pursued a policy of cooperation with the foreign powers seeking implementation of treaty arrangements reached with the Chinese government in 1860, ánd cooperation with Chinese government efforts to reach out to the United States and other foreign powers for constructive interaction and support. Seward signed the **Burlingame Treaty** with China in 1868. Among other provisions in the treaty, the

United States said it would not interfere in the internal development of China, China recognized the right of its people to emigrate, and the United States gave Chinese immigrants the right to enter the United States. The latter pledge would soon be challenged by anti-Chinese **immigration** advocates in the United States.

SHANGHAI COMMUNIQUE. Signed on 28 February 1972 at the end of President **Richard Nixon**'s visit to China, the communiqué registered both sides' opposition to **"hegemony"**—a codeword for Soviet expansion, laid out differences on a variety of Asian and other issues, and set forth US intention to pull back militarily from Taiwan and to support a "peaceful settlement of the Taiwan question by the Chinese themselves."

SHANTUNG LEASEHOLD. Though US and Chinese delegations worked closely at the peace conference ending World War I to free China from restrictions on her sovereignty, and Chinese negotiators were particularly interested in regaining control of the former German **concessions** in China's Shantung province, President **Woodrow Wilson** in the end felt compelled to accept Japan's claim to the former German concessions, gravely disappointing Chinese patriots. The provision dealing with Shantung in the **Versailles Peach Treaty of 1919** was a catalyst for demonstrations in Beijing on 4 May 1919 that led to intellectual reform campaigns and radical, anti-imperialist political movements known collectively as the **May Fourth Movement**. US delegates working with others succeeded in getting Japan to agree to withdraw from Shantung under terms of agreements at the **Washington Conference** in 1921–1922.

SHATTUCK, JOHN (1943–). Assistant secretary of state for **human rights** and humanitarian affairs in the **William Clinton** administration, Shattuck supported a firm US position against a variety of Chinese government human rights policies and practices. When visiting China in February 1994, he met with leading Chinese dissident **Wei Jingsheng**, who had been released a few months earlier after a long prison sentence. Chinese authorities arrested Wei again in March 1994. Shattuck's tough stance on Chinese human rights practices remained a feature of State Department and US policy, though it had less influence following President Clinton's May 1994 decision to end linkage of human rights and **trade** issues regarding the granting of **most-favored-nation tariff status** to China, and his subsequent emphasis on an **engagement policy** with China. *See also* LINKAGE POLICY.

SHUFELDT, ROBERT (1822–1895). Charged with negotiating a US treaty opening Korea, Commodore Shufeldt eventually sought the assistance of Chinese leader **Li Hung-chang**. Li endeavored to use the US–Korean treaty, signed in 1882, as a model for other foreign arrangements with the Chinese tributary and a means to fend off more expansionist designs on Korea by Japan and Russia.

SHULTZ, GEORGE (1920–). In response to President **Ronald Reagan**'s initial strong statements of support for Taiwan, the Chinese government put heavy pressure on the Reagan administration, threatening serious deterioration in relations over various issues, but especially US arms sales to Taiwan. Viewing close China–US relations as a key element in US strategy against the Soviet Union, Secretary of State **Alexander Haig** led those in the Reagan administration who favored maintaining close China–US relations and opposed US arms sales to Taiwan that might provoke China. The United States ultimately signed the **17 August 1982 communiqué** with China, promising to reduce US arms sales to Taiwan.

Succeeding Haig as secretary of state, George Shultz shifted US policy beginning in 1983. There was less emphasis on China's strategic importance and less concern about China's possibly downgrading relations over Taiwan and other disputes. US policy gave top priority in Asia to developing strategic relations with Japan. The Chinese leaders came to terms with the new US stance, judging that their interests were best served by less pressure and more positive initiatives to the Reagan administration, seen notably in their warm welcome for the US president on his visit to China in 1984. In this atmosphere, Reagan's second term in office did not see the repeated China–US controversies that had marked Reagan's relations with China earlier in the 1980s.

SIGUR, GASTON (1924–1995). A prominent Asian affairs specialist with a focus on Japan in academic and non-government organizations, Sigur was the senior **Ronald Reagan** administration National Security Council aide in charge of Asia in 1982 and 1983. This period saw US policy in Asia shift from previous emphasis on soliciting Chinese support and accommodating Chinese demands to one that downgraded China's priority in US policy while focusing more on the strategic importance of US–Japan relations. Sigur worked closely with Assistant Secretary of State **Paul Wolfowitz** and with the Defense Department's Asian policy specialist **Richard Armitage**, under the broad leadership of Secretary of State **George Shultz**. The policy shift proved successful for US interests and Sigur continued to support it when he moved to the State Department as assistant secretary for East Asian affairs later in the Reagan administration.

SIHANOUK, NORODOM (1922–). The US and Chinese governments cooperated in support of this Cambodian leader in the wake of the Soviet-backed invasion of **Cambodia** by **Vietnam** in 1978. Although Sihanouk had been affiliated with the **Khmer Rouge** regime toppled by the Vietnamese invasion, he broke with the Khmer Rouge and became the focal point of international efforts strongly backed by the United States, China, and the Southeast Asian governments that rejected the legitimacy of the Vietnamese-created Cambodian regime and supported armed resistance against it. In the 1980s, this international united front, including the United States and China, pushed for a Vietnamese withdrawal, a provisional coalition of Cambodian factions, and elections to produce a new Cambodian government. The goals were reached in settlements endorsed by the United States and China in the early 1990s, and Sihanouk was placed as the new Cambodian head-of-state.

SILVER PURCHASE PROGRAM. In 1934, the US government inaugurated primarily for domestic reasons increased buying of silver that caused great turmoil in the Chinese economy as massive amounts of silver left China by 1935. In response, the US government under the leadership of Secretary of the Treasury **Henry Morgenthau** initiated a silver purchase program for the **Nationalist Party** government in China, paying it hundreds of millions of dollars in gold or US dollars for 500 million ounces of silver.

SINO–AMERICAN COOPERATION ORGANIZATION (SACO). In 1942, a small US **Naval Group China**, under the leadership of Navy Commander **Milton Miles**, worked with General **Dai Li**, head of **Chiang Kai-shek**'s secret police, to establish the Sino–American Cooperation Organization. It funneled military aid to the **Nationalist Party** regime with little oversight by senior US officers, assisting General Dai in fighting **Communist Party** supporters in China.

SINO–JAPANESE WAR, 1894–1895. Japan defeated **Qing dynasty** forces in a war in 1894–1895.

SINO–JAPANESE WAR, 1937–1945. Japan's launch of full-scale military offensives in China in 1937 was seen as the formal start of a Sino–Japanese war, which ended with Japan's defeat in 1945.

SINO–SOVIET ALLIANCE. The alliance was established with the **Sino–Soviet Friendship Treaty** of February 1950. The two powers cooperated closely for less than a decade.

SINO–SOVIET FRIENDSHIP TREATY, 1945. This accord was signed in August 1945 between the governments of the Soviet Union and the **Nationalist Party** regime in China. It implemented understandings reached by US, Soviet, and British leaders in the **Far Eastern Agreement** at the **Yalta Conference** in February 1945 regarding Soviet territorial and other rights and interests in China and Mongolia, and Soviet recognition and support of the Nationalist Chinese government.

SINO–SOVIET FRIENDSHIP TREATY, 1950. This accord of February 1950 established the Cold War alliance between the Soviet Union and the newly established People's Republic of China, reinforcing deep divisions between the United States and China at this time.

SINO–SOVIET SPLIT. Serious public differences between China and the Soviet Union emerged by 1960, seen notably in the abrupt withdrawal of Soviet aid from China. Though US policymakers were seeking to split China from the Soviet Union, they were slow to capitalize on the situation as China remained more hostile than the Soviet Union to the United States and deepening US involvement in **Vietnam** exacerbated US–China frictions. *See also* WEDGE STRATEGY.

SIX ASSURANCES. As the United States signed the **17 August 1982 communiqué** with China agreeing to reduce with a goal of eventually ending US arms sales to Taiwan, the **Ronald Reagan** administration assured the Taiwan government of the following points. The United States would (1) not set a specific date to end arms sales to Taiwan, (2) would not hold talks with China regarding US arms sales to Taiwan, (3) would not play a mediating role between China and Taiwan, (4) would not revise the **Taiwan Relations Act**, (5) would not change the US position on the sovereignty of Taiwan, and (6) would not pressure Taiwan to negotiate with China.

SMITH, ARTHUR (1845–1932). An influential spokesperson for **missionaries** in China, Smith was pessimistic about China's future amid the anti-missionary violence and chaos leading to the **Boxer uprising** of 1899–1900. His book, *Chinese Characteristics,* published in the 1890s, was widely read by US officials and other Americans interested in China. It portrayed Chinese society negatively, with backward-looking, morally deficient people. Later, Smith was impressed by subsequent reforms in China, and by 1907 was publishing works lauding Chinese attributes and prospects, and urging the United States to take a sympathetic attitude toward Chinese nationalism and reverse the evils of US exclusion of Chinese **immigration** and discrimination against Chinese in the United States. *See also* EXCLUSION MOVEMENT.

SMITH, CHRISTOPHER (1953–). This Republican congressman from New Jersey was prominent in sharply criticizing Chinese government **human rights** practices during the period after the **Tiananmen crackdown**. As a chairman of a congressional subcommittee dealing with human rights and in numerous legislative initiatives, he exposed or highlighted Chinese practices on abortion, suppression of religious freedom, prison labor, human organ trafficking, and other issues that often shocked Americans and added to sentiment in the

Congress and the country to curb economic and other interaction with the **Communist Party** regime.

SNOW, EDGAR (1905–1972). A journalist, Snow visited **Communist Party**–held areas of China in the 1930s and wrote about his interviews with **Mao Zedong** and other senior Communist leaders in his book *Red Star over China*, making Mao and the Communists better known in the West. Snow visited China several times after Mao's victory and the establishment of the People's Republic of China in 1949. His visit in October 1970, when he appeared together with Mao in pictures prominently displayed in Chinese media and heard the Chinese leader discuss a possible visit by President **Richard Nixon**, signaled a significant thaw in official Chinese attitudes toward the United States.

SOLARZ, STEPHEN (1940–). This Democratic congressman from New York used his prominent position on a congressional subcommittee dealing with Asian affairs and frequent travel to China, Taiwan, and nearby areas to foster an array of legislative and other initiatives dealing with US–China relations in the 1980s and the first half of the 1990s. A strong advocate of **human rights**, he strongly supported democratization in Taiwan and helped to lead the upsurge in congressional antipathy toward China after the **Tiananmen incident**. Frequent hearings and other activities of his subcommittee represented the most important means of congressional oversight of various aspects of US–China relations during the 1980s.

SOLOMON, RICHARD (1937–). An academic China specialist who served on the staff of National Security Adviser **Henry Kissinger** at the time of the **Richard Nixon** administration's opening to China, Solomon favored forward movement in US relations with China. As assistant secretary of state, he implemented President **George H. W. Bush**'s **engagement policy** with Chinese leaders after the **Tiananmen crackdown**. He obtained Chinese cooperation in dealing with the **Khmer Rouge** and other difficulties in leading the US effort to reach a peace agreement on **Cambodia** in 1991.

SOONG MAYLING (1898–2003). Also known as **Madame Chiang Kai-shek**, Soong was a close adviser of the Chinese **Nationalist**

Party leader who used her US **education** and command of English to highlight positive features of the Chinese government in the face of many difficulties. She won US support for China during and after the **Sino–Japanese War, 1937–1945.** She toured the United States from November 1942 to May 1943, addressed Congress in February 1943, and stayed at the White House during her Washington visit. She appealed for US support for Chiang Kai-shek's government in the **Chinese Civil War**, and after his defeat on the mainland and retreat to Taiwan in 1949.

SOONG, T. V. (1894–1971). A Harvard-educated brother-in-law of **Chiang Kai-shek**, Soong served the **Nationalist Party** government as finance minister, foreign minister, and in other capacities from the late 1920s. He traveled often to the United States, was used repeatedly by Chiang to appeal for more US support, and built friendships and economic relationships with influential Americans who tended to support Chiang's Nationalists in the war against Japan and in opposition to the Chinese **Communist Party** forces.

SOUTHEAST ASIA TREATY ORGANIZATION (SEATO). In order to shore up **containment** of Chinese-backed Communist expansion in Southeast Asia following the French withdrawal from Indochina, the United States agreed with Britain, France, Thailand, and the Philippines in September 1954 to establish this multinational security body.

SOUTHWEST ASSOCIATED UNIVERSITY. This university was a cooperative venture of faculty and students from leading eastern Chinese universities seeking refuge from Japanese aggression in the Chinese Nationalist-controlled city of Kunming. It had a faculty of 200, half of whom had received doctoral degrees in the United States. The figure underlined the large numbers of Chinese, estimated at 36,000, who received advanced **education** in the United States prior to 1949.

"SPECIAL STATE-TO-STATE" RELATIONS. Taiwan President **Lee Teng-hui** increased tension in the **Taiwan Strait** when he declared to Western media in 1999 that Taiwan's relations with mainland China were "special state-to-state" relations. China sharply criticized this step as part of what it saw as Lee's moves toward Taiwan independence.

STALIN, JOSEPH (1879–1953). The leader of the Soviet Union during World War II, the **Chinese Civil War**, and the early stages of the Cold War, Stalin several times exerted important influence on US–China relations in interactions with the two nations. Most notably, as the United States prepared for the final battles against Japan in World War II, it sought Soviet military involvement to deal with the hundreds of thousands of Japanese forces in China, and in return it made concessions in the **Far Eastern Agreement** at the **Yalta Conference** in February 1945 that came at the expense of Chinese territorial integrity and interests.

In August 1945, Soviet forces entered China, and the Soviet Union signed the **Sino–Soviet Friendship Treaty** with **Chiang Kai-shek**'s **Nationalist Party** administration. At this time, Stalin tilted Soviet policy in favor of the Chinese Nationalists, prompting the Chinese **Communist Party** forces to join Chinese Nationalist–Chinese Communist peace talks backed by the United States. Stalin later sided more with the Chinese Communists, ensuring they gained military supplies held by Japanese forces in Manchuria. As the Chinese Communists defeated the Nationalists, Stalin eventually agreed to **Mao Zedong**'s requests for aid and signed the **Sino–Soviet Friendship Treaty** with Mao, creating the **Sino–Soviet Alliance** in February 1950 directed against the United States and allied powers. Stalin and Mao's support was important in **Kim Il Sung**'s decision in June 1950 to launch an assault against South Korea that ultimately led to over two years of US–China combat in the **Korean War** and 20 years of US military, economic, and political efforts to isolate and to promote **containment** of China in Asian and world affairs.

STANDARD OIL. This American business firm's well-organized and well-run operations in China saw the company sell over half the kerosene used in China prior to World War I, and resume sales momentum after the war. In 1910 the China market accounted for 15 percent of the company's overseas kerosene sales.

STARR FOUNDATION. This foundation and its chairman, **Maurice Greenberg**, leader of **American International Group (AIG)**, the world's leading international insurance organization, focused in the post–Cold War period on the **education** of China specialists in US universities, promoting US–China academic and policy exchanges and supporting research that deepened understanding between leaders and citizens of the two countries.

STEVENSON, ADLAI (1900–1965). As President **John Kennedy**'s ambassador to the **United Nations**, Stevenson questioned the administration's tough posture toward China and sought a more compromising approach.

STILWELL, JOSEPH (1883–1946). The US military commander in China after **Pearl Harbor** who was appointed to be **Chiang Kai-shek**'s chief-of-staff, General Stilwell had strong differences with Chiang and others, notably General **Claire Chennault**, regarding how the war against Japan should be carried out and the role of Chiang Kai-shek's **Nationalist Party** forces in the war. Stilwell and his staff came to negative views of Chiang and his senior commanders as self-serving and ineffective, and were interested in establishing relations with the Chinese **Communist Party** forces who seemed more willing to fight Japan. A crisis in 1944 caused the dispatch of US presidential envoy **Patrick Hurley** who sided with Chiang against Stilwell. Stilwell was soon recalled to the United States.

STIMSON DOCTRINE. *See* HOOVER–STIMSON DOCTRINE.

STIMSON, HENRY L. (1867–1950). As secretary of state in the **Herbert Hoover** administration, Stimson reflected that administration's preoccupation with dealing with the disastrous consequences of the Great Depression, and was reluctant to respond forcefully to Japan's aggression in Manchuria and its breach of US-backed security arrangements in the **Nine Power Treaty** of 1922 and the **Kellogg–Briand Pact** of 1928. In accord with the president, Stimson favored a stance of non-recognition of the changes brought on by Japan's aggression. This **Hoover–Stimson Doctrine** failed in 1932 as Japanese forces expanded their military aggression in China to include attacks on Chinese forces in Shanghai. The Hoover administration formally protested, sent additional forces to China, and Stimson appealed to the world not to recognize the Japanese aggression. The Japanese halted the assault on Shanghai, the

League of Nations adopted a resolution of non-recognition, but Japan created a puppet state of **Manchukuo** and withdrew from the League of Nations when it approved a report critical of Japan's actions.

As secretary of war during the **Franklin D. Roosevelt** administration, Stimson had dealings with China that saw him back Army Chief-of-Staff **George Marshall** in support of General **Joseph Stilwell**, the senior US officer in China, though he and Marshall also backed the selection of **Patrick Hurley** to mediate between Stilwell and Chinese leader **Chiang Kai-shek** in 1944. Hurley sided with Chiang, leading to Stilwell's recall from China.

STRAIGHT, WILLARD (1880–1918). As US consul general in Mukden, Manchuria, during the **Theodore Roosevelt** administration, Straight attempted to work with Chinese officials to use American investments to counter growing Japanese dominance in Manchuria. The president and Secretary of State **Elihu Root** were more interested in seeking accommodation with Japan, leading to the **Root–Takahira Agreement**, an exchange of notes to this effect in 1908.

The **William H. Taft** administration was prepared to take a stand more in line with Straight's view. Straight left the US government and worked with Chinese officials and US and foreign bankers to promote plans to build a Manchurian railroad, the **Chinchow–Aigun Railroad**. He signed an agreement with Chinese authorities in Manchuria in October 1909 to have an American banking group finance a railroad between these two cities. Before moving forward with the deal, the Chinese authorities in Peking awaited US efforts to deal with expected Japanese and Russian anger over this challenge to their spheres of influence in Manchuria. Secretary of State **Philander Knox** proposed a bold scheme to internationalize all railroads in Manchuria. Japan and Russia rejected Knox's plan and warned against the Chinchow–Aigun railway, which also failed to get Chinese government approval.

STRAITS EXCHANGE FOUNDATION (SEF). An ostensibly private organization established in Taiwan in 1991 to manage contacts with China, SEF and its Chinese counterpart, the **Association for Relations Across the Taiwan Strait (ARATS)** held numerous consultations and meetings in the 1990s that were welcomed by the US government as a means to ease cross-strait tensions. The contacts were halted by China in 1999 amid tensions stemming from President **Lee Teng-hui**'s public assertion that Taiwan was a state separate from China and that China and Taiwan had **"special state-to-state" relations**. *See also* KOO CHEN-FU.

STRATEGIC ARMS LIMITATION TALKS/ STRATEGIC ARMS REDUCTION TALKS (SALT I, SALT II). These US–Soviet **arms control** negotiations and agreements from the 1960s into the 1990s figured in US–China relations. Some US leaders in the late 1960s through the early 1980s endeavored to use improved US relations with China as a means to prompt more positive Soviet positions in the SALT talks. Other US leaders argued against this tactic, judging that the United States would benefit more from straightforward bargaining with the Soviet Union and that playing the **China "card"** would lead to stiff Soviet resistance and preclude successful negotiations. Against this background, Chinese officials sometimes complained about US willingness to accommodate and "appease" the Soviet Union over arms control and other issues. They said this left China more vulnerable in the face of the expanding Soviet threat. Chinese officials also resisted occasional US consideration of concurrent Chinese reductions in strategic nuclear weapons as the United States and the Soviet Union reduced their arsenals under terms of these negotiations and agreements.

STUART, JOHN LEIGHTON (1876–1962). In 1949, during the final months of the **Chinese Civil War** on mainland China, US Ambassador Stuart was instructed by Secretary of State **Dean Acheson** to seek contacts with **Communist Party** leaders. He stayed in the **Nationalist Party** capital of Nanking after Nationalist forces retreated, and he made contact with **Huang Hua**, a former student of Stuart's who was sent by the Communist leaders to investigate US intentions. Stuart was invited to meet Communist leaders in Peking, but President **Harry Truman** blocked the visit.

SUN YAT-SEN (1866–1925). Sun was known as a founder of the Republic of China and of the Chinese **Nationalist Party**. After the **Qing**

dynasty was overthrown, he became the provisional president of the Republic of China in January 1912, but he subsequently abdicated to avoid civil war in China. He sought support from the United States and other powers, but became disappointed with the West and turned to the Soviet Union for advice and supplies to build his Nationalist Party and reunite China, then divided among various warlords. Sun's political philosophy became known as the **Three Principles of the People** and provided the ideological basis of the Nationalist Party and its rule in the Republic of China on the Chinese mainland and later on Taiwan.

– T –

TAFT, WILLIAM H. (1857–1930). During the Taft administration, 1909–1913, the president and Secretary of State **Philander Knox** tried to use schemes involving US **investment** to prevent Russia and Japan from dominating Manchuria. They tried to encourage major American investments in railroads as a means to counterbalance Japanese and Russian spheres of influence centered on Manchurian railroads, and they called for a plan to neutralize or internationalize all railway projects in Manchuria. As Japan and Russia objected and US investors showed little enthusiasm, such so-called **dollar diplomacy** failed. The administration subsequently adopted a more moderate stance emphasizing cooperation with European powers, and ultimately Russia and Japan, in an international consortium dealing with loans to China. *See also* CHINCHOW-AIGUN RAILROAD; HUKWANG RAILWAY.

TAIPEI ECONOMIC AND CULTURAL REPRESENTATIVE OFFICE (TECRO). As part of the US **Taiwan policy review** in 1994, it was agreed that Taiwan's unofficial mission to the United States, then known as the **Coordination Council for North American Affairs**, would change its name to Taipei Economic and Cultural Representative Office, a name more favored by the Taiwan government.

TAIPING REBELLION. This massive rebellion in China during 1850–1864 caused US officials to cooperate with British officials in trying to maintain order and ensure functioning customs in Shanghai, and to see US interests better served by continued **Qing dynasty** rule rather than the rebels. The Americans also shared the inclination of the British and French to use the opportunity to revise the existing treaties to their advantage, although the United States, unlike the Europeans, generally was not willing to use force to back its demands.

TAIWAN. This island of 13,885 square miles located 90 miles off the coast of southeastern mainland China saw Portuguese and then Dutch settlement at the turn of the 16th century, until 1662 when Chinese forces loyal to the defeated Ming dynasty drove out the Dutch. The newly founded **Qing dynasty** brought Taiwan under Chinese rule in 1683. Taiwan was ceded to Japan in 1895, and came under the rule of the Republic of China in 1945. **Chiang Kai-shek** and his **Nationalist Party** administration retreated to Taiwan after being defeated by **Mao Zedong** and his **Communist Party** forces on the Chinese mainland in 1949. The island was a base of US military operations in the 1950s and 1960s. US forces were withdrawn along with the US defense treaty and other official bonds with the Republic of China government on Taiwan as part of the US's establishing official relations with the People's Republic of China in the 1970s. US political, economic, and security interests in Taiwan remained strong, however. The US government established a legal basis for ostensibly unofficial ties with Taiwan in the **Taiwan Relations Act** of 1979. US arms sales and military contacts remained active and grew beginning in the 1990s. Consistent with its **one China policy,** the US government did not support Taiwan independence advocated by increasing numbers of citizens in Taiwan in the early 21st century.

TAIWAN INDEPENDENCE MOVEMENT. Oppositionists to the **Nationalist Party** government in Taiwan that was dominated by officials who came from mainland China with **Chiang Kai-shek** in 1949 often advocated independence for Taiwan. They favored the overthrow of the Nationalist regime dominated by **mainlander Chinese** and the establishment of a democratic government led by **Taiwanese**, people whose roots on the island went back to before 1949. Given martial law and severe repression prevailing in Taiwan until the late 1980s, most such oppositionists remained abroad, pursuing various efforts that were known in general terms as the Taiwan Independence Movement. With greater liberalization, **human rights**, and democracy in Taiwan beginning in the 1980s, many oppositionists returned to the island and joined with indigenous oppositionists in the **Democratic Progressive Party** and more extreme political parties in pushing for greater self-determination and independence for Taiwan. US policy supported greater democracy for Taiwan but did not support Taiwan independence, which went against the US **one China policy** and was seen as likely to cause a military attack by China against Taiwan.

TAIWAN POLICY REVIEW. Encouraged by pro-Taiwan advocates at home and abroad, the **William Clinton** administration carried out a review of Taiwan policy in 1993–1994, which resulted in slight upgrades in US relations with Taiwan. The changes angered the Chinese government but were seen as too timid by many in Taiwan and among the many supporters of Taiwan at this time in the US media and Congress, who moved ahead with bolder initiatives, notably efforts to allow Taiwan's president to visit the United States.

TAIWAN RELATIONS ACT (TRA). This legislation was passed by Congress in March 1979 and signed by President **Jimmy Carter** on 10 April 1979, becoming Public Law 96-8. The legislation was proposed by the Carter administration to govern US relations with Taiwan once official US ties were ended in 1979. Congress rewrote the legislation, notably adding or strengthening provisions on US arms sales, opposition to threats and use of force, **trade** and economic relations, **human rights**, and congressional oversight. Treating Taiwan as a separate entity that would continue to receive US military and other support, the law appeared to Chinese officials and other observers to contradict the US stance in the **United States–China communiqué of 1978**, which established official US–China relations on 1 January 1979. That document said that the United States recognized the People's Republic of China (PRC) as the sole legal government of China and acknowledged the Chinese position that there is one China and Taiwan is part of China. Subsequently, Chinese and Taiwan officials and their supporters in the United States competed to incline US policy toward the commitments in the US–China communiqué or the commitments in the TRA. US policy usually supported both, though it sometimes seemed more supportive of one set of commitments than the other.

TAIWAN SECURITY ENHANCEMENT ACT. As originally proposed in 1999, this bill called for the sales of very sophisticated US military equipment (e.g., naval destroyers with **AEGIS seaborne systems**) to Taiwan, and required the US administration to develop closer military training and related relations with Taiwan and to report thoroughly on the US arms relationship with Taiwan. Trying to dampen a cross-strait crisis prompted by Taiwan President **Lee Teng-hui**'s public assertion in July 1999 that Taiwan and the mainland were two states having **"special state-to-state" relations**, the **William Clinton** administration strongly opposed the bill. The US House of Representatives passed a much milder version of the bill in February 2000.

TAIWAN STRAIT. This body of water west of Taiwan is 85 miles wide at its narrowest point and separates Taiwan from mainland China. It saw US naval forces intervene in June 1950 to prevent Chinese **Communist Party** forces from attacking Taiwan, other US military deployments including regular patrols of the strait until the 1970s, and subsequent occasional passages of US naval ships underscoring American interest in preserving peace in this sensitive area. *See also* TAIWAN STRAIT CRISES.

TAIWAN STRAIT CRISES. The United States was involved in military conflicts or confrontations between Taiwan and China in the Taiwan Strait notably in 1954–1955, 1958, and 1996. The first two crises occurred as **Mao Zedong** and the Chinese **Communist Party** leaders confronted, reacted to, and probed for weaknesses in the US alliance with Taiwan and broader US **containment** against China. The 1996 crisis occurred as US leaders felt compelled to send two US aircraft carrier battle groups to the Taiwan area in reaction to months of provocative Chinese military exercises in the Taiwan area in the period prior to the Taiwan presidential election in 1996. *See also* UNITED STATES–REPUBLIC OF CHINA DEFENSE TREATY.

TAIWANESE. This term was used to describe the large majority of people in Taiwan whose roots on the island went back before officials, soldiers, and others from the Chinese mainland retreated there with **Chiang Kai-shek**'s **Nationalist Party** regime after the victory of **Communist Party** forces in the **Chinese Civil War** on mainland China in 1949. While the latter group, known as **mainland Chinese,** represented only about 15 percent of Taiwan's population, they nonetheless tended to dominate the government and related positions of power as the Nationalist regime consolidated and maintained its position in Taiwan. The majority Taiwanese, 85 percent of the total population, had little political power for decades. By the 1980s, demographic and democratic changes gradually saw Taiwanese rise to prominence within the Nationalist Party and in the main opposition party, the **Democratic Progressive Party.** By the 1990s, they dominated Taiwan politics and increasingly challenged Taiwan's status as part of China. In the process, they antagonized the Chinese government and upset US policy that sought to support democracy in Taiwan without supporting Taiwan independence, seen as likely to cause China to attack Taiwan with military force. *See also* TAIWAN INDEPENDENCE MOVEMENT.

TAKAHIRA, KOGORO (1854–1926). *See* ROOT–TAKAHIRO AGREEMENT.

T'ANG SHAO-YI (TANG SHAOYI) (1860–1938). A governor in Manchuria who was close to regional leader **Yuan Shih-kai**, Tang studied in the United States and worked with Yuan and others in encouraging the United States government and US business to become more involved with railway building in Manchuria as a means to counter Japanese expansion there. After seeking support from US financial backers and officials in China, Tang traveled to Washington in 1908 where he met with Secretary of State **Elihu Root**, who underlined the **Theodore Roosevelt** administration's lack of interest in confronting Japan in Manchuria by sharing with Tang the yet unpublished **Root–Takahira Agreement.**

TAO-KUANG (DAO-GUANG) (1782–1850). This **Qing dynasty** emperor favored a policy of appeasement in dealing with foreign powers after the **Opium War**, including granting to the Americans the most-favored-nation clause in the **Treaty of Wang-hsia,** allowing them to have the benefits Great Britain gained as a result of the Opium War.

TATNALL, JOSIAH (1796–1871). When British and French forces in 1859 advanced toward Peking, they came under attack from Chinese forts, driving them back. US Commodore Tatnall was an ostensible neutral on the scene but had his forces intervene to assist the British combatants.

TEHERAN CONFERENCE. Though disillusioned with **Chiang Kai-shek** and the performance of his political and military forces in the war with Japan, President **Franklin D. Roosevelt** insisted at this meeting of the Allied powers in 1944 that China would play a great-power role in the future **United Nations** security council. *See also* CAIRO DECLARATION; POSTSDAM DECLARATION.

TERRANOVA CASE. In 1821, Francesco Terranova, a Sicilian sailor on an American ship, was accused of the murder of a boatwoman selling fruit to the ship in Canton. He and his shipmates denied the charge. A standoff resulted, with Chinese authorities cutting off American trade until Terranova was handed over. The American merchants and shipowners gave in, Terranova was handed over, tried in secret under Chinese procedures with no Americans present, convicted, and executed.

TERRORISM, WAR ON. The 11 September 2001 terrorist attack on America and subsequent US-led international campaign against terrorism diverted officials in the **George W. Bush** administration that were focused on China as an emerging strategic threat to the United States. Chinese leaders worked to cooperate with the United States in the War on Terrorism, building common ground in US–China relations. US–China relations subsequently developed more smoothly and without the major frictions seen in the early months of the Bush administration.

THEATER MISSILE DEFENSE (TMD). Beginning in the 1990s, Chinese officials and media objected to US plans to develop and deploy anti-ballistic missile systems, especially in areas near China. China also objected to Japan's cooperation with the United States in developing such theater missile defenses for Japan, and Chinese officials warned strongly against US sales of such theater ballistic missile defense systems to Taiwan. *See also* BALLISTIC MISSILE DEFENSE.

THOMPSON, FRED (1942–). This Republican senator from Tennessee in the late 1990s used his committee chairmanship to investigate **William Clinton** administration fund-raising that allegedly involved illegal contributions from Chinese backers in return for the administration's turning a blind eye to Chinese illegal trading practices and Chinese espionage activities in the United States.

THREE GORGES DAM. This large project was attacked by some environmental and **human rights** groups in the United States, and the controversy became part of the multifaceted US debate on China in the 1990s. Some environmentalists judged that the negative impact of the dam on China's environment was offset to some degree as the energy it would produce substituted for coal-fired furnaces that added to China's air pollution and global warming. Meanwhile, Chinese officials supported the dam as a means to control floods along the Yangtze River and to gain needed hydroelectric power.

THREE JOINT COMMUNIQUES. Chinese and US officials repeatedly emphasized that understandings in these three documents provided a foundation of US–China relations from the late 20th century into the 21st century. They were the **Shanghai communiqué** of 1972, the **United States–China communiqué of 1978** establishing formal US–China diplomatic relations, and the **17 August 1982 communiqué** governing US arms sales to Taiwan. US officials but not Chinese officials usually added the **Taiwan Relations Act** of 1979 to the list of documents said to govern US–China policy at this time.

THREE LINKS. This refers to direct transportation, **trade**, and postal services between mainland China and Taiwan across the **Taiwan Strait**. They were repeatedly discussed after Chinese leaders offered these links in 1979. Taiwan was wary of the Chinese offer, though US policy favored such cross-strait interchange. *See also* LETTER TO TAIWAN COMPATRIOTS.

THREE PRINCIPLES OF THE PEOPLE. These ideas from the writings of **Sun Yat-sen** represented the core of the official ideology of the **Nationalist Party** and the Republic of China. The three principles were nationalism, democracy, and people's livelihood. In general, the Nationalist government of **Chiang Kai-shek** focused on nationalism and nation building, did not emphasize democracy, and was often lagging in dealing with people's livelihood, leading to criticism from American officials and other observers.

THREE NOS. Speaking in Shanghai in June 1998 during his visit to China, President **William Clinton** affirmed that the United States does not support Taiwan independence; or two Chinas, or one Taiwan, one China; and that the United States does not believe Taiwan should be a member of an organization where statehood is required. The Clinton administration claimed the statement was a reaffirmation of longstanding US policy, but it was roundly criticized in the Congress and US media as undermining Taiwan. The **George W. Bush** administration refrained from repeating the three nos. *See also* ONE CHINA, ONE TAIWAN POLICY; TAIWAN INDEPENDENCE MOVEMENT; TWO CHINA POLICY.

THUNDER OUT OF CHINA. Journalist **Theodore White**, a wartime correspondent in China, described a callous and self-serving **Nationalist Party** regime in this book, published in 1946, about the suffering of China during World War II.

TIANANMEN CRACKDOWN. Mass demonstrations, especially by students critical of government practices and calling for political reforms and other changes, grew in Beijing and other Chinese cities following the death of **Communist Party** leader **Hu Yaobang** on 15 April 1989. A divided Chinese leadership ultimately decided, under the direction of senior leader **Deng Xiaoping**, to use strong military force to end the demonstrations, centered on Beijing's Tiananmen Square, and crack down on dissent throughout the country. The military attack on the square on 4 June 1989 and subsequent repression, which involved hundreds of deaths and even more arrests, caused international outrage, especially in the United States, marking the most important turning point in US–China relations since President **Richard Nixon** traveled to China in 1972, beginning the process of normalizing US relations with China.

TIBET. Amid a Tibetan uprising and Chinese crackdown in 1959, the **Dalai Lama** and many thousands of Tibetans fled to India. Backing the Dalai Lama's cause, the US government clandestinely supported armed resistance to Chinese rule in Tibet during the 1960s. US interest in supporting Tibetan interests against Chinese rule declined with the US reconciliation with China in the 1970s and 1980s, but it revived with the upsurge in US criticism of Chinese **human rights** practices in Tibet and other areas following the **Tiananmen crackdown** of 1989. That year, the Dalai Lama, admired around the world as the spiritual leader of Tibet, was awarded the Nobel Peace Prize. Subsequently, US presidents and senior officials met regularly with the Dalai Lama, Congress passed legislation recognizing Tibet as an independent country and condemning Chinese policies and practices in Tibet, and the State Department with strong congressional prodding established a special office to deal with Tibet. In the 1990s, US movies and movie stars brought the plight of Tibetans to a wider American public and reinforced pro-Tibet sentiment in the Congress and US media.

TIENTSIN, TREATIES OF. Backed by British and French forces, the foreign powers, including the United States, demanded in the late 1850s revision of treaties with China. To underline their determination after a month of fruitless negotiations, the British and French forces attacked and damaged Chinese defenses near the northern Chinese city of Tientsin. The Chinese then gave in to foreign demands and signed new treaties in Tientsin in 1858, but when British and French envoys returned in 1859 to exchange ratification, a battle resulted where the Chinese drove off the foreigners. The American envoy managed to exchange ratification, however. The British and French returned in 1860 and marched to Peking before setting forth new conditions in the treaties of 1860. *See also* PEKING, TREATIES OF (1860).

TOURISM. American tourists were among the first non-government US visitors to China following President **Richard Nixon**'s visit in 1972. Their initially small numbers grew to many thousands and then hundreds of thousands as China opened to outside economic and cultural interchange in the decades following the death of **Mao Zedong** in 1976. The flow of US tourists waned in the years immediately after the **Tiananmen crackdown** of 1989, but revived with greater vigor amid advancing Chinese efforts to promote a wide-ranging tourist industry.

TRADE. Merchants seeking trading opportunities were among the first Americans to go to China at the start of the 19th century, and they have remained important advocates in US relations with China ever since. Although the importance of the China market waned during and after the American Civil War, protecting American trading opportunities in China was an important imperative behind the US government's **Open Door notes** of 1899 and 1900, and the subsequent US government emphasis on an **Open Door Policy** toward China.

After the Chinese **Communist Party** government of **Mao Zedong** sent forces into the **Korean War** in 1950, the US government established a trade embargo against the People's Republic of China while encouraging US trade and economic exchange with the Republic of China on Taiwan. As part of the US opening to China, the United States eased and ended the embargo in the 1960s and 1970s. China's economic reforms and opening to international commerce beginning in the late 1970s saw US traders actively seek opportunities in the burgeoning China market. China came to export 30–40 percent of its exports to the United States, creating the largest trade deficit (over $150 billion in 2004, according to US government figures) with any country. In the 1990s, congressional and other US critics of Chinese government policies and practices advocated assiduously but with little overall effect for restrictions on US provision of **most-favored-nation tariff status** for China. The United States eventually granted China **permanent normal trade relations** and supported China's entry into the **World Trade Organization**, even though serious differences of **Intellectual Property Rights** and other trade issues persisted.

US trade interests with Taiwan and **Hong Kong** remained strong into the 21st century. While the People's Republic of China ranked among the top three or four US trading partners, Taiwan was among the top ten, and Hong Kong was among the top-20 US trading partners.

TRADE AND DEVELOPMENT PROGRAM (TDP). Though US foreign aid to the People's Republic of China remained restricted, this US Department of Commerce program was able to provide **trade** promotional activities for US exporters to China. The program's work in China was suspended for a time after the **Tiananmen crackdown**.

TREATY PORTS. The British agreement with China ending the **Opium War** in the 1842 **Treaty of Nanking** opened five Chinese ports for foreign residence. US and other foreign merchants and **missionaries** came, and foreign governments subsequently demanded and received expanded rights and more treaty ports, as well as the right to live in other parts of China. With expanded foreign rights and **concessions** of land, some areas in treaty ports, notably Shanghai, came to resemble large foreign enclaves, with Chinese playing only supporting roles to foreign residents.

TREATY SYSTEM. This term refers to the system of special rights and privileges for foreigners, including Americans, in China under terms of what Chinese patriots called the **unequal treaties** imposed on China by the foreign powers in the 19th and 20th centuries. The treaties gave foreigners **extraterritoriality**, the right to reside in China under their own laws and jurisdiction. They provided for **concessions** of land and development rights that made parts of Chinese ports, like Shanghai, into foreign-ruled enclaves. They allowed foreign military forces to patrol Chinese waterways and eventually to deploy ground forces in China to secure their interests. The treaties also marked the loss of substantial pieces of Chinese territory to foreign ownership. *See also* OPEN DOOR POLICY.

TRIBUTE SYSTEM. This system of Chinese foreign relations, in use when American traders first entered the China **trade**, emphasized the superiority of China and the emperor, and restricted foreign interaction with China, including trade. British, Americans, and others chafed under these restrictions and came to demand more open access for trade and the work of **missionaries**, and equal treatment in diplomatic and other interchange. *See also* CANTON SYSTEM.

TRIE, CHARLIE (1949–). This Arkansas businessman was a focal point of media, congressional, and other investigations into illegal political donations to the Democratic Party that allegedly involved connections to China during the **William Clinton** administration. In return for raising hundreds of thousands of dollars for the **Democratic National Committee**, Trie was permitted to take visiting Chinese businesspeople on tours of the White House. Under media and congressional pressure, and not sure of the source of Trie's and other donations, the Democratic National Committee returned three million dollars in donations of questionable origins from Trie and other donors. In 1999, Trie pled guilty to two counts of illegally funneling money into the Clinton campaign and was sentenced to three years' probation.

TRUMAN, HARRY S. (1884–1972). Becoming president with the death of President **Franklin D. Roosevelt** in 1945, Truman followed the broad China policy guidelines of his predecessor in supporting **Chiang Kai-shek**'s **Nationalist Party** administration and urging the Chinese **Communist Party** leaders to seek peace and alignment in a government led by Chiang as China prepared for the defeat of Japan. The arrangements with the Soviet Union regarding China in the **Far Eastern Agreement** at the **Yalta Conference** were adhered to despite emerging Cold War tensions between the United States and the Soviet Union.

The abrupt resignation of the US ambassador to China, **Patrick Hurley**, amid rising Nationalist–Communist tensions in November 1945 prompted Truman to appoint General **George Marshall** to mediate and prevent Chinese civil war. US policy continued to provide extensive military and other support to the Chinese Nationalists, sought to demobilize and repatriate Japanese troops in China, and avoided direct confrontation with Soviet forces in China. Marshall's extraordinary efforts backed by the president failed to bring peace as full-scale war emerged by late 1946. As many of the president's advisers had warned, the civil war turned against the Chinese Nationalists. Truman by 1948 sought ways to cut US aid to the Nationalists but felt pressured by US domestic politics to continue some support. Some of his aides sought to open communications with the rising Chinese Communists in 1949. US Ambassador **John Leighton Stuart** stayed in Nanking for this purpose while the Nationalists withdrew, but Truman would not allow him to pursue a Communist initiative and travel to Peking for talks.

Though many of his advisers in early 1950 favored US intervention to prevent Communist control of Taiwan, Truman supported Secretary of State **Dean Acheson** and others in the position that the United States should not prevent the expected Communist victory over the retreating Nationalists in Taiwan. With the outbreak of the **Korean War** in June 1950, Truman reversed this policy, sending US forces to protect Taiwan as the United States confronted Communist aggression in Korea. Truman supported the decision that US forces, victorious in South Korea, advance into North Korea in order to create a unified state under **United Nations** auspices. Though wary of possible Chinese intervention, he did not respond to Chinese warnings and by the end of 1950 faced a protracted armed struggle with Chinese armies on the peninsula for the rest of his administration.

TSENG KUO-FAN (ZENG GUOFAN) (1811–1872). This senior Chinese leader led armies from his regional base in Hunan province and elsewhere to defeat the **Taiping Rebellion**. He was a dominant figure in Chinese government policy in the 1860s when Chinese leaders endeavored to work cooperatively with the United States and other foreign powers, seeking material and technological advances from the West to help develop Chinese national wealth and power.

TSUNLI YAMEN. This body, a subcommittee of the **Qing dynasty**'s Grand Council, was established in 1861 to exchange official calls and correspondence with US and other foreign governments and the foreign legations that were established in Peking as a result of the treaties signed in 1860. It served as a foreign office until one was established in 1901.

TUNG, CHEE HWA (1937–). Selected by Chinese leaders and elected by a **Hong Kong** provisional legislature approved by China, this Hong Kong shipping tycoon served as the chief executive of Hong Kong after its return to Chinese sovereignty in 1997. He adhered to Chinese government guidelines and resisted growing demands for greater democracy among Hong Kong people, which were backed by US media and congressional and executive branch officials. He resigned his position in 2005.

TWENTY-ONE DEMANDS. Allied with Great Britain and siding with the Allies in World War I, Japan occupied German **concessions** in China's Shantung province in 1914. In January 1915, Japan presented the Chinese government with five sets of secret demands that became known as the Twenty One Demands. The demands were leaked and the resulting controversy compelled Japan to defer the more outrageous ones. However, they resulted in May 1915 in Sino–Japanese treaties and notes confirming Japan's dominant position in Shantung, southern Manchuria, and eastern Inner Mongolia, and Japan's special interests in an industrial area in central China. US officials debated how to respond. Secretary of State **William Jennings Bryan** at first reaffirmed US support for China's territorial integrity and equal commercial access to China, but also acknowledged Japan's "special relations" with China. President **Woodrow Wilson** subsequently warned that the United States would not accept infringements on its rights, and Bryan said the United States would not recognize infringements on US rights, Chinese sovereignty, or the **Open Door Policy**. In a bid to expand US leverage, Wilson then reversed an earlier decision and supported American banks' lending money to China through an international consortium as a means to balance Japanese expansion in China. *See also* NON-RECOGNITION DOCTRINE.

TWO CHINAS POLICY. As the United States dealt with competing Chinese regimes of the Chinese **Communist Party** on the Chinese mainland and the Chinese **Nationalist Party** on Taiwan in the last half of the 20th century, it often was said to follow a policy that sought relations with both governments. This policy also was known as a **one China, one Taiwan** policy. Such a stance was unacceptable to the Chinese Communist government which insisted that it represented the only legitimate government of China. The Chinese Nationalists on Taiwan stuck to a similar rigid stance, though they became more flexible in the 1990s under President **Lee Teng–hui** and were willing to accept the legitimacy of two Chinese governments, one based in Beijing and one based in Taipei. With the end of Nationalist Party rule in Taiwan in 2000, Taiwan leaders of the **Democratic Progressive Party** said they accepted the legitimacy of the Chinese Communist government as the government of China, but they argued that Taiwan was a separate legitimate state, not falling within the "China" scope of that government.

TZ'U-HSI. *See* EMPRESS DOWAGER TZ'U-HSI.

– U –

UNEQUAL TREATIES. Chinese patriots called unequal treaties those treaties imposed on China by the foreign powers in the 19th and 20th centuries. The treaties gave foreigners **extraterritoriality**, the right to reside in China under their own laws and jurisdiction. They provided for **concessions** of land and development rights that made parts of Chinese ports, like Shanghai, into foreign-ruled enclaves. They allowed foreign military forces to patrol Chinese waterways and eventually to deploy on the ground in China to secure their interests. The treaties also marked the loss of substantial pieces of Chinese territory to foreign ownership. *See also* TREATY SYSTEM.

UNITED DEMOCRATS OF HONG KONG. *See* DEMOCRATIC PARTY (HONG KONG).

UNITED NATIONS. This international organization was established after World War II to replace the **League of Nations**. A founding conference was held in San Francisco in 1945 attended by 51 countries that had declared war on Germany or Japan. The **Nationalist Party** government of **Chiang Kai-shek**, the Republic of China, held China's seat as one of the five permanent members of the UN Security Council until 1971. The United Nations supported the US-led military actions against North Korean aggression and Chinese intervention in the **Korean War**. The **Communist Party** government of **Mao**

Zedong, the People's Republic of China, was excluded from the United Nations until it took the China seat in 1971 and the Republic of China government, then based in Taiwan, was expelled.

The People's Republic of China continued to block efforts by the Republic of China to gain representation in the United Nations and related agencies. Beginning in 1980, it worked closely with the **World Bank,** the **International Monetary Fund**, and other UN agencies to gain economic assistance and technical advice in advancing China's economy. It also signed a number of UN-supported **human rights** accords and **arms control** agreements and arrangements that brought China's international policies and commitments somewhat more into line with internationally accepted standards.

UNITED NATIONS FOURTH CONFERENCE ON WOMEN. Held in Beijing in September 1995 amid strong criticism in the United States and the West over the Chinese government's coercive birth control policies and broader issues of **human rights**, the event saw Chinese authorities endeavor to separate more vocal non-government organization representatives from the proceedings. **Hilary Clinton** attended the conference and gave a speech defending the right of the non-government representatives to participate and supported their criticisms of government regimes that violate women's reproductive rights and broader human rights.

UNITED NATIONS HUMAN RIGHTS COMMISSION. China participated in this body beginning in 1982. After the **Tiananmen crackdown**, the United States in most years led efforts to consider a resolution examining Chinese **human rights** practices. Chinese officials resisted such efforts strenuously, and never failed in having the US-led efforts defeated by the commission.

UNITED NATIONS POPULATION FUND. Through US congressional and executive branch actions beginning in the 1980s, the United States government repeatedly restricted US funding for this **United Nations organization** because of the group's connection with China's family planning policies and practices that were widely seen in the United States as coercive and abusive of **human rights**.

UNITED NATIONS RELIEF AND REHABILITATION ADMINISTRATION. Hundreds of millions of dollars of US economic aid were sent to China after the defeat of Japan through this agency. The aid went overwhelmingly to areas controlled by the **Nationalist Party** administration of **Chiang Kai-shek**. The areas of China controlled by **Mao Zedong** and the **Communist Party** forces held a third of the population of China in 1946 but received only a small fraction of the assistance.

UNITED STATES–CHINA COMMUNIQUE OF 1978. This communiqué, announced in December 1978, established official US relations with the People's Republic of China (PRC) under conditions whereby the United States recognized the PRC as the government of China, acknowledged that Taiwan was part of China, ended official US relations with the Republic of China government on Taiwan, and terminated the **United States–Republic of China defense treaty.**

UNITED STATES–CHINA BUSINESS COUNCIL. Beginning in the 1970s, this group represented several hundred US firms in pursuing **trade** and other economic relations with China.

UNITED STATES–CHINA PEOPLE'S FRIENDSHIP ASSOCIATION. Beginning in the 1970s, this group was active among a wide range of American audiences in promoting sympathetic understanding of Chinese practices and policies through lectures, publications, and guided trips to China.

UNITED STATES–JAPAN DEFENSE GUIDELINES. The convergence of US–Japanese interests in reaffirming strategic cooperation evident in the **Clinton–Hashimoto Declaration** of April 1996 saw the two powers work together to come up with guidelines that would specify how they would cooperate in dealing with regional contingencies, especially regarding North Korea. Chinese officials were concerned by this upswing in US–Japan strategic cooperation and pointedly warned against any such cooperation regarding Taiwan.

UNITED STATES–JAPAN SECURITY TREATY. This US defense alliance with Japan, in effect since 1951, was a key element in US **containment** efforts against China in the 1950s and 1960s, and was duly condemned by Chinese officials. Chinese leaders came to support the treaty as a useful bulwark against expansion by the Soviet Union in Asia in the 1970s and 1980s. With the collapse of the Soviet Union and rise of US pressure against China in the 1990s, Chinese officials viewed with suspicion US and Japanese efforts to strengthen the alliance, seeing such efforts as directed against Chinese interests, notably regarding Taiwan. *See also* CLINTON–HASHIMOTO DECLARATION; UNITED STATES–JAPAN DEFENSE GUIDELINES.

UNITED STATES–REPUBLIC OF CHINA DEFENSE TREATY. This treaty was signed on 2 December 1954 and committed both countries, the United States and the Republic of China, to each other's assistance in the event of war or the threat of war. The treaty was part of a number of treaties and alliances established by the United States to surround and pursue a policy of **containment** against the People's Republic of China. The treaty mentioned US commitments to only Taiwan and the **Pescadores** islands, but the scope was subsequently extended to include the offshore islands of **Quemoy** and **Matsu** under terms of the **Formosa Resolution** of 1955. As part of the **United States–China communiqué of 1978** establishing official US diplomatic relations with China, President **Jimmy Carter** gave notification of US intent to terminate the treaty and it ended 1 January 1980.

UNITED STATES–TAIWAN BUSINESS COUNCIL. Known earlier as the USA–ROC Economic Council, this group represented over 200 firms dealing with Taiwan and endeavored to promote **trade** and other economic US–Taiwan relations following the break in US official relations with Taiwan.

UNIVERSAL TRADING CORPORATION. This company was controlled by supporters of **Chiang Kai-shek** and received US credits to support Chiang Kai-shek's **Nationalist Party** forces resisting Japan prior to **Pearl Harbor**.

– V –

VANCE, CYRUS (1917–2002). Secretary of state during the **Jimmy Carter** administration, Vance traveled to China in 1977 but failed to make progress in normalizing US–China relations. Emphasizing the importance of US **arms control** and other arrangements with the Soviet Union, Vance tried to counter the arguments of National Security Adviser **Zbigniew Brzezinski** who urged normalization with China as a means to pressure the Soviet Union, but President Carter sided with Brzezinski.

VERSAILLES, TREATY OF 1919. US and Chinese delegations worked closely at the peace conference ending World War I to free China from restrictions on her sovereignty, and Chinese negotiators were particularly interested in regaining control of the former German **concessions** in China's Shantung province. Nevertheless, Japan earlier signed secret agreements with European powers that bound them to support Japanese claims to the **Shantung leasehold**, and the Chinese government's position was weakened by agreeing as part of the **Twenty-One Demands** in 1915 to accept German–Japanese agreement on the concessions. President **Woodrow Wilson** in the end felt compelled to accept Japan's claim to the former German concessions, gravely disappointing Chinese patriots. The provision was a catalyst for demonstrations in Peking on 4 May 1919 that led to both intellectual reform campaigns and radical, anti-imperialist political movements that spread throughout China in following years and became known collectively as the **May Fourth Movement**.

VIETNAM. The People's Republic of China provided a wide range of military and other support to the Vietnamese Communist insurgents opposed to US-backed French forces in Vietnam and other parts of Indochina in the early 1950s. The Chinese government competed with the Soviet Union in backing the Vietnamese Communist insurgency in South Vietnam and the Communist government of North Vietnam against the large-scale escalation of US military force in South Vietnam and air attacks against North Vietnam in the 1960s and early 1970s. President **Richard Nixon**'s opening to China coincided with steady withdrawals of US troops from Vietnam. China was more pleased than North Vietnam with the January 1973 compromise peace agreement on the Vietnam War. China was publicly supportive but privately alarmed by Soviet-backed North Vietnam's successful assault against the US-supported South Vietnamese government in 1975. China and Vietnam fought a short border war in 1979 after the Vietnamese army, supported by the Soviet Union, attacked and overthrew the Chinese-backed Cambodian government of the **Khmer Rouge**. China and the United States worked together for over a decade to promote resistance to the Vietnamese occupation of **Cambodia**. Vietnam and China, and the United States and Vietnam, resumed more normal relations following a Vietnamese military withdrawal and peace agreement on Cambodia in 1991. *See also* GENEVA ACCORDS.

VINCENT, JOHN CARTER (1900–1972). A leading State Department official dealing with China policy in the 1940s, Vincent was attacked by Senator **Joseph McCarthy** along with other China specialists in the early 1950s for insufficient support for **Chiang Kai-shek** and possible pro-Communist leanings. He was fired by Secretary of State **John Foster Dulles**.

VOICE OF AMERICA. Periodic jamming by Chinese authorities of the broadcasts of this US government radio station in the years after the **Tiananmen crackdown** was resented by US officials. It became an issue in US–China leadership discussions and in US policy determining conditions for renewing **most-favored-nation tariff status** for China.

– W –

WALLACE, HENRY (1888–1965). This US vice president was sent to China in June 1944 to press **Chiang Kai-shek** to negotiate with the Chinese **Communist Party** leaders and to insist that an American military and diplomatic observer team be allowed through the blockade of **Nationalist Party** forces to the Communist headquarters in **Yenan**. *See also* AMERICAN MILITARY OBSERVER GROUP (YENAN).

WALSH, JAMES (1891–1981). The Chinese authorities released this US cleric, imprisoned in China since the 1950s, in July 1970, a sign of improved US–China relations during this period.

WANG DAN (1969–). During the **Tiananmen crackdown**, this Chinese dissident was arrested and sentenced to a four-year term for his role in the pro-democracy demonstrations. He was sentenced to a longer sentence in 1996, and was released on medical parole and sent to the United States in March 1998. Throughout this period, he was a focal point of US criticism of China's **human rights** practices and an issue in high-level US–China discussions.

WANG DAOHAN (1916–). Former mayor of Shanghai and mentor of **Jiang Zemin**, Wang was head of the **Association for Relations Across the Taiwan Strait (ARATS)**, China's ostensibly unofficial body to deal with Taiwan on cross-strait issues. He held talks with his Taiwan counterpart **Koo Chen-fu** in Singapore in 1993, which both sides viewed as positive. Trying to ease cross-strait tensions caused by **Lee Teng-hui**'s US visit in 1995 and the Chinese provocative military exercises against Taiwan in 1995–1996, Koo traveled to China and talked with Wang as well as Jiang Zemin in 1998. Talks between ARATS and its Taiwan counterpart, the **Straits Exchange Foundation**, were suspended following Lee Teng-hui's statement in 1999 asserting that the mainland and Taiwan have **"special state-to-state" relations**, but Wang and his entourage continued to engage in various more informal discussions with US and other representatives seeking ways to enhance cross-strait ties.

WANG-HSIA, TREATY OF. Signed by US envoy **Caleb Cushing** and Chinese government negotiator **Ch'i-ying** in 1844, the treaty agreed that all Chinese benefits provided to other nations would apply to the United States as well. It also opened the **treaty ports** to Americans and guaranteed **extraterritoriality** for Americans. *See also* MOST-FAVORED-NATION PRINCIPLE.

WARD, ANGUS (1893–1969). This US consul general in Mukden was placed under house arrest by **Communist Party** forces in late 1948, and was not released for a year, souring US relations with the Communists.

WARD, FREDERICK TOWNSEND (1831–1862). This American commanded a small Sino–foreign mercenary force, the **Ever-Victorious Army**, which helped to defeat rebels in the Shanghai area in the early 1860s.

WARD, JOHN (1814–1902). American minister to China, Ward managed in 1859 to exchange ratification with Chinese authorities of the US revised treaty with China of 1858. In contrast, when they sought to exchange ratifications with Chinese authorities of their revised treaties with China, British and French envoys confronted the Chinese and were repelled, though they returned with greater military support the following year, marching to Peking and forcing new treaties on China. *See also* PEKING, TREATIES OF (1860); TIENTSIN, TREATIES OF.

WARSAW AMBASSADORIAL TALKS. *See* AMBASSADORIAL TALKS.

WASHINGTON CONFERENCE, 1921–1922. The US government took the lead in calling a major conference to include powers with interests in the western Pacific, including China but not the Soviet Union, to deal with relevant security issues. The result was the Washington Conference of 1921–1922 that saw passage of a **Nine Power Treaty** supporting non-interference in Chinese internal affairs, and other agreements including one concerning Japan's withdrawal from China's Shantung province. *See also* SHANTUNG LEASEHOLD.

WATERGATE SCANDAL. A politically motivated break-in and cover-up involved President **Richard Nixon** in criminal activity. As congressional investigation led toward impeachment, Nixon resigned in August 1974. As he fended off charges in the previous year, Nixon paid less attention to China, and his promise to normalize US relations with China in his second term ended with his resignation.

WEDEMEYER, ALBERT (1897–1989). Succeeding General **Joseph Stilwell** as the senior US military officer in China after Stilwell's recall in 1944, Wedemeyer supported the US policy strongly backing **Chiang Kai-shek**'s **Nationalist Party** government. When the US embassy staff sent a message on 28 February 1945 that challenged Ambassador **Patrick Hurley**'s policy of supporting Chiang while keeping the **Communist Party** leaders at a distance, Wedemeyer worked with Hurley in rebutting the embassy staff assessment in a meeting with President **Franklin D. Roosevelt**. Roosevelt supported Hurley and his approach, Hurley remained in his post, and dissident embassy staff members were transferred to other posts.

As the war with Japan ended, Wedemeyer judged that Chiang's Nationalists were not strong enough to reunify China without direct US intervention. Later, he was sent on a special mission to China in 1947, and returned advocating large-scale economic and military aid for the Nationalists provided they undertook significant reforms. His recommendations were used by pro-Chiang advocates in the media and the Congress to demand that the **Harry Truman** administration continue aid to Chiang Kai-shek and his Nationalist Party government, even though many in the administration saw them as a losing cause.

WEDGE STRATEGY. US leaders sought ways to drive a wedge between the Soviet Union and China and weaken the **Sino–Soviet alliance**. Some scholars contrasted President **Dwight Eisenhower** with Secretary of State **John Foster Dulles**. They said that the president was prepared to use soft tactics in order to woo China to the US side and away from the USSR, while Dulles favored using hard tactics against China, forcing it to make demands that Moscow could not meet and thereby splintering the Sino–Soviet alliance. In practice, Eisenhower pursued with less enthusiasm than Dulles and others in his administration the US government's stated **containment** policy against China. It involved an economic embargo, political isolation, subversion, and the strong support of US defense allies and friends around China's periphery; it was backed by large-scale US military deployments in Asia. Eisenhower was more open than his secretary of state and others to being flexible regarding **trade** with China, and was sympathetic to British and Japanese complaints about US-imposed restrictions on their trade with China.

WEI JINGSHENG (1950–). In the United States, Wei was the most famous dissident in post–**Mao Zedong** China. He was arrested in

1979 after the so-called **Democracy Wall movement** was suppressed by Chinese authorities and he was given a long prison sentence. US interest in his case rose markedly after the **Tiananmen crackdown**. Chinese authorities released Wei in 1993, six months shy of his full 15-year sentence. He wrote in Western media urging a strong US stand against **human rights** abuses in China. In 1994, he met with the visiting US assistant secretary of state in charge of human rights affairs, **John Shattuck**. He was arrested again and sentenced to 14 years in prison. His case was raised repeatedly in congressional deliberations over China policy, in US government interaction with China, and in US media. As a result of long US–China negotiations, Wei was released on medical parole and sent to the United States on 16 November 1997. Wei persisted in criticizing the US **engagement policy** with China, as well as Chinese policies, even during a meeting with President **William Clinton** on 8 December 1997.

WEINBERGER, CASPAR (1917–). Secretary of defense in the **Ronald Reagan** administration, Weinberger disagreed with Secretary of State **Alexander Haig**'s emphasis on China as a strategic counterweight to the Soviet Union, arguing for greater American defense preparations. He also favored strong US support for Taiwan. He visited China in 1983 and was successful in resuming US–China strategic cooperation and military exchanges, including advancing the sale of US weapons and defense equipment to China.

WEI YUAN (1794–1856). An important Chinese scholar of foreign relations in the period after the **Opium War**, Wei adopted a positive view of the United States as a country with commercial interests less threatening to China than those of Great Britain and with a history at odds with Britain. He judged that China could use relations with the United States as a means to offset more aggressive and demanding powers, a view that was to prevail in Chinese leaders' thinking through the rest of the **Qing dynasty**.

WHITE TERROR. This term is used to describe the violent suppression of **Communist Party** members and radicals by **Chiang Kai-shek** and like-minded **Nationalist Party** leaders as Chiang and conservative forces in 1927 moved to gain control of the Nationalist Party and establish a viable Chinese government.

WHITE, THEODORE (1915–1986). A journalist in wartime China, White wrote a sharp critique of self-serving officials in the ruling **Nationalist Party** government in the midst of the massive misery of the Chinese people. The book was entitled *Thunder Out of China* and was published in 1946.

WILLIAMS, S. WELLS (1812–1884). A mainstay at the US legation in China, Williams worked for over 20 years for the US government, 1855–1876, as translator, interpreter, and temporary head of the US mission on eight separate occasions. He came to China along with other American **missionaries**, but pursed publications and scholarship. He wrote a major book about China, *The Middle Kingdom* (1848). He accompanied and influenced the US envoy negotiating a treaty in 1858 to insure that wording allowed missionary work in China.

WILSON, WOODROW (1856–1924). In 1913, the first year of his presidency, Wilson decided that the United States would withdraw from a consortium of foreign banks that were planning and carrying out loans to the Chinese government. The new US government viewed the consortium process as demeaning to China. Wilson and his administration endeavored to support China in 1915. US officials spoke out against Japanese demands levied against China. The so-called **Twenty-One Demands** were modified as a result of US and other foreign pressure, though the weak Chinese government was compelled to accept most of the Japanese conditions, which the Wilson administration said for the record that the United States would not recognize.

US and Chinese delegations worked closely at the peace conference ending World War I to free China from restrictions on her sovereignty, and Chinese negotiators were particularly interested in regaining control of the former German **concessions** in China's Shantung province. Nevertheless, Japan earlier signed secret agreements with European powers that bound them to support Japanese claims to the **Shantung leasehold**, and the Chinese government's position was weakened by agreeing as part of the Twenty-One Demands in 1915 to accept German–Japanese agreement on the concessions. President Wilson in the end felt compelled to accept Japan's claim to the former German concessions, gravely disappointing Chinese patriots. Wilson also was instrumental in the establishment of the **League of Nations** to govern world affairs after World War I and was very disappointed in US refusal to join the world body. *See also* NON-RECOGNITION DOCTRINE; WILLIAM JENNINGS BRYAN.

WOLFOWITZ, PAUL (1943–). As director of policy planning in the State Department during the **Ronald Reagan** administration, Wolfowitz was at odds with Secretary of State **Alexander Haig** and the priority he gave to meeting Chinese concerns over Taiwan and other issues. After Haig's departure in 1982, Wolfowitz became assistant secretary for East Asian affairs. He worked closely with the State Department's new secretary, **George Shultz**, a Defense Department Asian affairs policymaker, **Richard Armitage**, and the senior National Security Council staff aide on Asian affairs, **Gaston Sigur**, in order to shift US policy to a less solicitous and accommodating stance toward China while giving much higher priority to US relations with Japan.

Wolfowitz served in a senior Defense Department post in the **George H. W. Bush** administration, and as deputy defense secretary in the **George W. Bush** administration. He was occasionally prominent in China policymaking, notably supporting the approach of Defense Secretary **Donald Rumsfeld** in the George W. Bush administration that emphasized strong support for Taiwan and wariness regarding China's military intentions and US–China military exchanges.

WOMEN'S INTERNATIONAL LEAGUE FOR PEACE AND FREEDOM. This and other peace groups reacted to the Japanese military assault on China in 1937 by urging that Americans be evacuated from the war zone to avoid US involvement in the **Sino–Japanese War**. Pressure from these groups limited the willingness of the **Franklin D. Roosevelt** administration to support China against Japan.

WOODCOCK, LEONARD (1911–2001). The head of the US **liaison office** in Beijing during the **Jimmy Carter** administration, Woodcock was the main US negotiator with Chinese officials, including senior leader **Deng Xiaoping**, over the agreement set forth in the

United States–China communiqué of December 1978 establishing official relations between the two powers.

WORLD BANK. Despite various international sanctions after the **Tiananmen crackdown** that had a temporary effect on China's relations with the World Bank, China in 1992 became the largest recipient of World Bank funds. By 1999, China's cumulative borrowings from the World Bank were about $33 billion. The US government was very supportive of closer China–World Bank relations after China decided to join the bank and the **International Monetary Fund** in 1980. The US government favored the close advisory role the bank played as China moved to reform its economy during the 1980s. US policy was constrained to some degree by legislative and other sanctions imposed after the Tiananmen crackdown, but the US government did not block the growth of Chinese–World Bank cooperation.

WORLD TRADE ORGANIZATION (WTO). The most influential international organization dealing with world **trade**, WTO, and its predecessor before 1995, the **General Agreement on Tariffs and Trade (GATT)**, dealt with China for almost two decades before granting full membership. GATT granted China permanent observer status in 1984. In 1986, China applied for full membership in the organization. Chinese officials initially thought that China's rapidly growing economy, dynamic economic reforms, and burgeoning foreign trade would assure quick acceptance; but the **Tiananmen crackdown** added to serious economic issues to slow the process. The United States took the lead among the organization's contracting parties in protracted negotiations (1986–1999) to reach agreements with China on a variety of trade-related questions before Chinese accession could move forward. Those talks concluded in 1999 and China became a WTO member in 2001.

WU, HARRY (1937–). Harry Wu spent many years in Chinese prisons before emigrating to the United States in 1986. Wu achieved prominence in US–China relations following the **Tiananmen crackdown**. He worked from the United States to expose and force change in Chinese prison and penal practices. In this effort, he led **Laogai Research Foundation**, an organization linked with the **American**

Federation of Labor–Congress of Industrial Organizations (AFL–CIO). Wu was arrested in June 1995 trying to enter China and was held for interrogation. This caused a serious controversy with many in Congress, the administration, and the media calling publicly or working privately for his release. The controversy subsided in August 1995 when Wu was tried, sentenced to 15 years in prison, and deported to the United States.

WU T'ING-FANG (WU TINGFANG) (1842–1922). A protégé of Li Hung-chang, the dominant Chinese foreign policy decision maker in the last three decades of the 19th century, Wu rose in the Chinese foreign affairs bureaucracy, served as minister in the Chinese legation in the United States in the late 1890s, and advocated closer Chinese reliance on the United States against the more voracious demands of European powers and Japan.

– Y –

YALTA CONFERENCE. US President Franklin D. Roosevelt, British Prime Minister Winston Churchill, and Joseph Stalin, the leader of the Soviet Union, met in this Crimean city in February 1945 to discuss the final stages of World War II. They reached agreement on the war against Japan and related conditions in China in the Far Eastern Agreement of 11 February 1945.

YE JIANYING (1897–1986). A Communist Party leader and military commander, Ye got along well with US officers sent to Yenan in 1944 as part of the American Military Observer Group (Yenan). He played an important role in the struggle for power during the Cultural Revolution, providing support as one of China's senior military leaders for Zhou Enlai's pragmatic policy initiatives, including the opening to the United States, in the face of more extreme positions by Defense Minister Lin Biao and the radical Gang of Four. Ye was the first and most senior Chinese official to greet Dr. Henry Kissinger on his arrival at Beijing airport on his secret mission in July 1971. Kissinger arrived in the middle of a life-and-death Chinese leadership struggle that saw the death of Lin Biao and arrest and life imprisonment of top members of the Chinese high command two months later. As president of China, Ye in September 1981 issued a nine-point program for cross-strait relations and exchanges that envisioned an eventual settlement under which Taiwan would accept the sovereignty of the People's Republic of China and would be permitted to maintain its own armed forces and maintain its economic and social systems. Chinese leaders endeavored to win the support of US leaders for the plan.

YEH MING-CH'EN (YE MINGCHEN (1785–1858). This governor-general at Canton in the 1850s deflected foreign demands for treaty revision, circumvented Chinese obligations under existing treaties, and incited local resistance to foreigners. British forces eventually captured Canton and Yeh, shipping him to Calcutta before going north with French forces to Tientsin in 1858 to compel China to agree to new treaties meeting foreign demands for legations in Peking, diplomatic equality, access for **missionaries** beyond the **treaty ports**, and **trade** opportunities. *See also* TIENTSIN, TREATIES OF.

YENAN. Headquarters of **Communist Party** forces in China during the **Sino–Japanese War** and World War II, Yenan was rarely visited by Americans because of a blockade maintained by Chinese **Nationalist Party** forces until 1944. That year US pressure on **Chiang Kai-shek** led to permission to dispatch the **American Military Observer Group (Yenan)**. US Ambassador to China **Patrick Hurley** visited Yenan in November 1944.

YIN HE. In 1993, this Chinese ship was suspected by the United States of transporting ingredients for chemical weapons to Iran. It was tracked by US Navy forces and the United States demanded inspection. Inspection in Saudi Arabia found no chemical weapons or related ingredients. The episode caused Chinese resentment against the United States.

YOUNG MEN'S CHRISTIAN ASSOCIATION (YMCA). Soon after its founding in the United States, this group extended operations to China in the 1890s. Its offices in Tientsin and Shanghai attracted recent US college graduates devoted to urban reform and social services.

YUAN SHIH-K'AI (YUAN SHIKAI) (1859–1916). A protégé of **Li Hung-chang**, Yuan emerged as the most important military and political leader in China in the early 20th century until his death in 1916. His base of power was in northern China and he was closely involved with efforts to stem the decline of Chinese influence and control in Manchuria in the face of Russian and Japanese advances. He supported Chinese approaches to the **Theodore Roosevelt** administration seeking US investment and other support to counter Japanese expansion in Manchuria. Seeking good relations with the United States, he argued for suppression of the **anti-American boycott** in China in 1905. Removed from power in 1908, Yuan returned to power three years later and saw the initially vigorous **dollar diplomacy** of the **William H. Taft** administration wane.

The dominant leader of the newly founded Republic of China, Yuan endeavored to use expressions of sympathy and support from the **Woodrow Wilson** administration to his and China's advantage. However, Wilson withdrew US government backing for the international consortium that Yuan used to obtain funding for his government. And US support for Yuan's government in the face of Japan's **Twenty-One Demands** in 1915 was weak and mainly symbolic.

YUNG WING (1828–1912). The leader of the **Hartford Education Mission**, 1872–1881, Yung settled in the United States, worked with the Chinese legation, and served as senior Chinese leader **Chang Chih-tung**'s financial agent in the United States during the **Sino–Japanese War, 1894–1895**. He later advised Chang to use American capital in building railways in China, as in his view Americans posed less political risk than other foreign investors.

– Z –

ZENG QINGHONG (1939–). A close adviser to **Jiang Zemin**, Zeng worked behind the scenes, and his influence on China's policy toward the United States appeared only occasionally. He facilitated back-channel communications between President **George H. W. Bush** and senior Chinese leaders after the **Tiananmen crackdown**. He encouraged the revival of informal high-level cross-strait dialogue, sought by the United States, resulting in Taiwan leader **Koo Chen-fu**'s meetings with **Wang Daohan** and **Jiang Zemin** during a visit to China in 1998. As vice president of China, Zeng hosted US Vice President **Richard Cheney** during his visit to China in 2004.

ZHAO ZIYANG (1919–2005). As Chinese premier and later **Communist Party** general secretary in the 1980s, this economic and political reformer followed the broad foreign policy guidelines of senior leader **Deng Xiaoping**. He duly pressed the **Ronald Reagan** administration on Taiwan in the early 1980s, and adopted a more relaxed and accommodating stance following the shift of US and Chinese policy seen at the time of Reagan's visit to China in 1984. He hosted President **George H. W. Bush** on his visit to China in early 1989. Zhao split with Deng and many of his colleagues in arguing for flexibility and accommodation to deal with demonstrators in Tiananmen square; he was removed from power and placed under house arrest as Deng led the violent **Tiananmen crackdown**.

ZHOU ENLAI (1898–1976). Zhou was the most senior Chinese **Communist Party** official responsible for foreign affairs for 40 years. Aligned closely with **Mao Zedong**, who often set broad guidelines and intervened on particular issues in Chinese Communist foreign policy, Zhou represented the Communists in interaction with US officials and other Americans in China's World War II capital **Chungking**. He interacted closely with US mediators **Patrick Hurley**, in 1944–1945, and **George Marshall**, in 1945–1946. As premier and foreign minister of the **People's Republic of China**, Zhou adhered to China's tough revolutionary line in the early 1950s, and then switched by 1955 to a policy emphasizing peaceful coexistence and dialogue with the United States.

Facing turmoil and destruction in Chinese cities during the early years of the **Cultural Revolution** and a growing Soviet strategic threat to Chinese territorial integrity, Zhou endeavored to restore conventional governance and foreign policy after the widespread violence and turmoil brought about by the Cultural Revolution. The Foreign Ministry under his guidance tried in late 1968 to reach out to the incoming **Richard Nixon** administration, but was brought up short by domestic opposition, notably from leadership groups led by Defense

Minister **Lin Biao** and the **Gang of Four**. Enhanced Soviet military pressure on China and an accommodating Nixon administration eventually led to the Sino–US breakthrough seen in Nixon's visit to China in 1972. Zhou endeavored to move relations forward with mixed results on account of continued domestic resistance and his own failing health. He died in 1976.

ZHU RONGJI (1928–). This senior Chinese leader in the decade after the **Tiananmen crackdown** focused mainly on domestic issues, especially management and reform of the Chinese economy and international issues affecting China's economy. When he was appointed premier in 1998, he did not follow the practice of his predecessor, **Li Peng**, in playing a primary foreign policy role, preferring to follow the leadership of **Communist Party** general secretary and national president, **Jiang Zemin**.

Zhu played a leading role in managing China's response to the **Asian economic crisis** of 1997–1998, interacting closely with US officials and agreeing with their advice that China should not devalue its currency and should endeavor to sustain growth. Zhu visited Washington in April 1999 hoping to reach agreement with the United States on China's entry into the **World Trade Organization (WTO)**. An agreement was reached and disclosed by the Americans, only to be turned down by President **William Clinton**. Recovering quickly from the setback, Zhu was able to complete the US–China negotiations in 1999, paving the way for China's entry into the WTO and US provision of **permanent normal trade relations** to China.

Appendix A

United States Presidents and Secretaries of State 1789–2005

President	Secretary of State
George Washington 1789–1797	Thomas Jefferson March 1790–December 1793 Edmund Randolph January 1794–August 1795 Timothy Pickering December 1795–March 1797
John Adams 1797–1801	Timothy Pickering March 1797–May 1800 John Marshall June 1800–February 1801
Thomas Jefferson 1801–1809	James Madison May 1801–March 1809
James Madison 1809–1817	Robert Smith March 1809–April 1811 James Monroe April 1811–September 1814, February 1815–March 1817
James Monroe 1817–1825	John Quincy Adams September 1817–March 1825
John Quincy Adams 1825–1829	Henry Clay March 1825–March 1829
Andrew Jackson 1829–1837	Martin Van Buren March 1829–March 1831 Edward Livingston May 1831–May 1833 Louis McLane May 1833–June 1834 John Forsyth July 1834–March 1837
Martin Van Buren 1837–1841	John Forsyth March 1837–March 1841
William Henry Harrison 1841	Daniel Webster March 1841

(*continued*)

President	Secretary of State
John Tyler 1841–1845	Daniel Webster April 1841–May 1843 Abel P. Upshur July 1843–February 1844 John C. Calhoun April 1844–March 1845
James Polk 1845–1849	James Buchanan March 1845–March 1849
Zachary Taylor 1849–1850	John M. Clayton March 1849–July 1850
Millard Fillmore 1850–1853	Daniel Webster July 1850–October 1852 Edward Everett November 1852–March 1853
Franklin Pierce 1853–1857	William L. Marcy March 1853–March 1857
James Buchanan 1857–1861	Lewis Cass March 1857–December 1860 Jeremiah S. Black December 1860–March 1861
Abraham Lincoln 1861–1865	William H. Seward March 1861–April 1865
Andrew Johnson 1865–1869	William H. Seward April 1865–March 1869
Ulysses S. Grant 1869–1877	Elihu B. Washburne March 1869 Hamilton Fish March 1869–March 1877
Rutherford B. Hayes 1877–1881	William M. Evarts March 1877–March 1881
James Garfield 1881	James G. Blaine March 1881–December 1881
Chester Arthur 1881–1885	Frederick T. Frelinghuysen December 1881–March 1885
Grover Cleveland 1885–1889	Thomas F. Bayard March 1885–March 1889
Benjamin Harrison 1889–1893	James G. Blaine March 1889–June 1892 John W. Foster June 1892–February 1893
Grover Cleveland 1893–1897	Walter Q. Gresham March 1893–May 1895 Richard Olney June 1895–March 1897

President	Secretary of State
William McKinley 1897–1901	John Sherman March 1897–April 1898 William R. Day April 1898–September 1898 John Hay September 1898–September 1901
Theodore Roosevelt 1901–1909	John Hay September 1901–July 1905 Elihu Root July 1905–January 1909 Robert Bacon January 1909–March 1909
William H. Taft 1909–1913	Philander C. Knox March 1909–March 1913
Woodrow Wilson 1913–1921	William Jennings Bryan March 1913–June 1915 Robert Lansing June 1915–February 1920 Bainbridge Colby March 1920–March 1921
Warren Harding 1921–1923	Charles Evans Hughes March 1921–March 1923
Calvin Coolidge 1923–1929	Charles Evans Hughes March 1923–March 1925 Frank B. Kellogg March 1925–March 1929
Herbert Hoover 1929–1933	Henry L. Stimson March 1929–March 1933
Franklin D. Roosevelt 1933–1945	Cordell Hull March 1933–November 1944 Edward R. Stettinius, Jr. December 1944–June 1945
Harry Truman 1945–1953	James F. Byrnes July 1945–January 1947 George C. Marshall January 1947–January 1949 Dean G. Acheson January 1949–January 1953
Dwight Eisenhower 1953–1961	John Foster Dulles January 1953–April 1959 Christian A. Herter April 1959–January 1961
John F. Kennedy 1961–1963	Dean Rusk January 1961–November 1963

(*continued*)

President	Secretary of State
Lyndon Johnson 1963–1969	Dean Rusk November 1963–January 1969
Richard Nixon 1969–1974	William P. Rogers January 1969–September 1973
	Henry A. Kissinger September 1973–August 1974
Gerald Ford 1974–1977	Henry A. Kissinger August 1974–January 19, 1977
Jimmy Carter 1977–1981	Cyrus Vance January 1977–April 1980
	Edmund Muskie May 1980–January 1981
Ronald Reagan 1981–1989	Alexander Haig, Jr. January 1981–July 1982
	George P. Shultz July 1982–January 1989
George H. W. Bush 1989–1993	James A. Baker, III January 1989 –August 1992
	Lawrence S. Eagleburger December 1992–January 1993*
William J. Clinton 1993–2001	Warren M. Christopher January 1993–January 1997
	Madeleine Albright January 1997–January 2001
George W. Bush 2001–	Colin L. Powell January 2001–2005
	Condoleezza Rice January 2005–

*Served as Acting Secretary of State, August–December 1992.

Appendix B

China Presidents and Prime Ministers, 1912–present

Republic of China 1912–1949

President	Prime Minister
Sun Yat–sen 　January 1912–March 1912	
Yuan Shikai 　March 1912–June 1916	
Li Yuanhong 　June 1916–July 1917	
Feng Guozhang 　July 1917–October 1918	
Xu Shichang 　Oct 1918–June 1922	Ch'in Nong–hsun 　October 1918–June 1919
	Kung Hsin–chan 　June 1919–September 1919
	Chin Jun–p'ong 　September 1919–May 1920
	So Chon–ping 　May 1920–August 1920
	Chin Jun–p'ong 　August 1920–January 1921
	Jon Hui–ch'ing 　January 1921–April 1922
	Chou Tsu–ch'i 　April 1922–June 1922
Li Yuanhong 　June 1922–June 1923	Jon Hui–ch'ing 　June 1922–August 1922
	T'ang Schao–ji 　August 1922–September 1922
	Wang Ch'ung–hui 　September 1922–November 1922
	Wang Ta–hsieh 　November 1922–December 1922
	Chang Schao–ts'ong 　January 1923–June 1923

(continued)

President	Prime Minister
Zhang Shaozeng June 1923–September1923 Gao Lingwei September 1923–October 1923 Cao Kun October 1923–November 1924	Kao Ling–wei June 1923–January 1924 Sun Pao–ch'i January 1924–July 1924 Ku Wei–chun July 1924–September 1924 Jon Hui–ch'ing September 1924–October 1924
Huang Fu November 1924 Duan Qirui November 1924–April 1926	Huang Fu November 1924–December 1925 Hsu Shih–jing December 1925–February 1926 Chia To–jao February 1926–April 1926
Hu Weide April 1926–May 1926 Yan Huiqing May 1926–June 1926 Du Xigui June 1926–October1926 Gu Weijun October 1926–June 1927 Zhang Zuolin June 1927–June 1928 Chiang Kai–shek June 1928–December 15, 1931	Hu Wei–te April 1926–May 1926 Jon Hui–ch'ing May 1926–June 1926 Tu Tsi–kuei June 1926–October 1926 Ku Wei–chun October 1926–June 1927 P'an Fu June 1927–June 1928 T'an Jon–k'ai October 1928–September 1930 Sung Tso–won September 1930–November 1930 Chiang Kai–shek December 1930–December 1931
Lin Sen January 1932–May 1943	Sun Fo December 1931–January 1932 Wang Ching–wei January 1932–December 1935 Chiang Kai–shek December 1935–December 1937 Kung Hsiang–hsi January 1938–November 1939 Chiang Kai–shek November 1939–May 1945

President	Prime Minister

Chiang Kai–shek
  May 1943–January 1949
	Sung Tso–won
	  May 1945–March 1947
	Chang chun
	  April 1947–May 1948
	Sun Fo
	  November 1948–March 1949
	Ho Jing–chen
	  March 1949–April 1949

People's Republic of China

President	Prime Minister

Mao Zedong
  October 1949–April 1959
Liu Shaoqi
  April 1959–October 1968
Dong Biwu
  October 1968–January 1975
Zhu De
  January 1975–July 1976
Ye Jianying
  March 1978–June 1983
Li Xiannian
  June 1983–March 1993
Jiang Zemin
  March 1993–March 2003
Hu Jintao
  March 2003–
	Zhou Enlai
	  October 1949–January 1976
	
	Hua Guofeng
	  February 1976–September 1980
	Zhao Ziyang
	  September 1980–November 1987
	Li Peng
	  November 1987–March 1998
	Li Peng
	  March 1998–March 2003
	Wen Jiabao
	  March 2003–

Presidents, Republic of China (on Taiwan, 1949–)

Chiang Kai–shek, 1949–1975
Yen Chia–kan, 1975–1978
Chiang Ching–kuo, 1978–1988
Lee Tung–hui, 1988–2000
Chen Shui–bian, 2000–

BIBLIOGRAPHY

The scholarly literature dealing with US–China relations is large and growing rapidly, especially regarding relations in recent years. Major turning points in relations brought on by such important developments as the Western and Japanese expansion in 19th-century China, the collapse of China's imperial order, war and revolution in 20th-century China, US–China confrontation and reconciliation during the Cold War, and post–Cold War adjustments in US–China relations prompt the approach used below of grouping selected scholarly works under chronological headings.

The first section of the bibliography contains general works providing overviews dealing with the full range of US–China developments or with somewhat more narrow topics over the course of US–China relations. For readers seeking clearly written and cogent introductions, the best overview treatments include Warren I. Cohen, *America's Response to China: A History of Sino–American Relations*, and Michael Schaller, *The United States and China: Into the Twenty-First Century*. Both have useful sections suggesting further readings on various topics. Michael H. Hunt, *The Making of a Special Relationship: The United States and China to 1914* provides a masterful assessment with extensive treatment of source materials regarding relations up to the early 20th century.

Scholarly works on US–China relations in the late 18th and 19th centuries make up the second section of the bibliography. They tend to focus on the activities and importance of American missionaries and merchants in China. Such works include those by John K. Fairbank and those published with his support by the Harvard University Press that were in the lead among publications about the US and other Christian missions in China. Other excellent works in this field include Daniel H. Bays, ed. *Christianity in China* (Stanford, 1996). Also listed in this section are salient works in a growing field of historical scholarship dealing with US restrictions on Chinese immigration, US discrimination against Chinese, and their impact on US–China relations beginning in the latter decades of the 19th century.

Scholarly works listed in the third section of the bibliography deal with some of the twists and turns in US–China relations amid often chaotic developments in China in the period from China's defeat by Japan in 1895 to the Japanese attack on Pearl Harbor and US entry in to the war against Japan in 1941. Highlights include the treatment of US–China relations over Manchuria in Michael H. Hunt, *Frontier Defense and the Open Door: Manchuria in Chinese–American Relations, 1895–1911*, and the works of Akira Iriye and Dorothy Borg dealing with American policy toward China in the first four decades of the 20th century.

With the American entry into World War II, the United States became an ally of China and would emerge as the most important foreign power in China. Although Japan was defeated and China freed, US policy by the end of the decade failed in the face of major challenges. The fourth section of the bibliography focuses on this decade. Among the notable accounts listed are those dealing with US–China relations during World War II. Highlights include Liu Xiaoyuan, *A Partnership for Disorder: China, the United States, and Their Policies for the Postwar Disposition of the Japanese Empire*, Michael Schaller, *The US Crusade in China, 1938–1945*, and Barbara Tuchman, *Stilwell and the American Experience in China, 1911–1945*. The period after Japan's surrender is treated in such classic works as Tang Tsou, *America's Failure in China, 1941–1950,* and Dorothy Borg and Waldo Heinrichs, eds. *Uncertain Years: Chinese–American Relations, 1947–1950*, as well as in more recent works including Harry Harding and Yuan Ming, eds. *Sino–American Relations, 1945–1955*, and Akira Iriye and Warren I. Cohen, eds. *American, Chinese, and Japanese Perspectives on Wartime Asia, 1939–1949*.

The fifth section of the bibliography deals with scholarly literature on US–China relations during the first two decades of the Cold War. Assessments of this period are undergoing revision as scholars obtain increased access to US, Chinese, and other documents. Perhaps the best overview is provided in Robert S. Ross and Jiang Changbin, eds. *Reexamining the Cold War*. Among works providing notable insights for contemporary scholarship are those by Robert M. Blum, Chen Jian, Thomas Christensen, and John Garver listed in this section of the bibliography.

Historians, political scientists, and journalists long have been fascinated by the abrupt turn toward US–China reconciliation begun by President Richard Nixon and Chinese Communist Party Chairman Mao Zedong, and the zigzag pattern of improved US–China relations during the remainder of the Cold War. The accounts of various participants in the process, especially on the American side, provide important insights and are listed among scholarly works in the sixth section of the bibliography. A. Doak Barnett was the leading American non-government specialist writing on these developments, and many of his works are listed. Also listed are the most influential scholarly treatments of the period by Harry Harding and Robert Ross, as well as important accounts by journalists, of which Jim Mann, *About Face: A History of America's Curious Relationship with China, From Nixon to Clinton*, is highly recommended. The US Congress played an important role in the making of US policy toward China in this period, and listed in this section of the bibliography are a number of important reports and documents. A highlight is US Congress, House, Committee on Foreign Affairs, *Executive-Legislative Consultations over China Policy, 1978–1979*.

The Chinese government crackdown on pro-democracy demonstrators in Tiananmen Square and other parts of China in June 1989 and the subsequent collapse of Communist regimes in Eastern Europe and, ultimately, the Soviet Union had a major impact on US–China relations. American policy became erratic and subject to major domestic debate that did not diminish until the 11 September 2001 terrorist attack on America diverted US attention from China. Scholarly works dealing with US–China relations since 1989 are listed in the seventh section of the bibliography. An excellent overview of the period to the end of the Clinton administration can be obtained by reading the best scholarly assessment, David M. Lampton, *Same Bed, Different Dreams: Managing US–China Relations, 1989–2000*, and the best assessment by a US policy practitioner, Robert L. Suettinger, *Beyond Tiananmen: The Politics of US–China Relations, 1989–2000*.

Keeping track of recent developments in US–China relations is aided by informative Internet resources and publications. Among the most useful are articles dealing with China and the United States contained in the quarterly electronic journal *Comparative Connections* that can be accessed at the website of the Center for Strategic and International Studies, Pacific Forum, Honolulu, Hawaii, www.csis.org/pacfor; also the annual review of the United States, China, and other powers' relations in Asia is published under the title *Strategic Asia* by the National Bureau of Asian Research, Seattle, Washington, and available at the organization's website at www.nbr.org.

CONTENTS

1. GENERAL WORKS AND REFERENCE WORKS

Arkush, R. David, and Leo O. Lee. *Land Without Ghosts: Chinese Impressions of America from the Mid-Nineteenth Century to the Present*. Berkeley, Cal.: University of California Press, 1989.

Chan, Ming K. and Lo, S. H. *Historical Dictionary of Hong Kong and Macau*. Lanham, Md.: Scarecrow Press, 2006.

Cohen, Warren I. *America's Response to China: A History of Sino–American Relations*. New York: Columbia University Press, 2000.

———. ed. *New Frontiers in American–East Asian Relations*. New York: Columbia University Press, 1983.

———. ed. *Pacific Passage: The Study of American–East Asian Relations on the Eve of the Twenty-First Century*. New York: Columbia University Press, 1996.

Copper, John F. *Historical Dictionary of Taiwan (Republic of China)*. Lanham, Md.: Scarecrow Press, 2000

Dennett, Tyler. *Americans in Eastern Asia: A Critical Study of the Policy of the United States with Reference to China, Japan, and Korea in the 19th Century*. New York: Macmillan, 1922.

Fairbank, John K. *The United States and China*. Cambridge, Mass.: Harvard University Press, 1983.

Fairbank, John K., Edwin O. Reischauer, and Albert M. Craig. *East Asia: Tradition and Transformation*. Boston: Houghton Mifflin, 1973.

___. *East Asia: The Modern Transformation*. Boston: Houghton Mifflin, 1965.

Griswold, A. Whitney *The Far Eastern Policy of the United States*. New York: Harcourt Brace, 1938.

Hsu, Immanuel Chung-yueh. *The Rise of Modern China*. New York: Oxford University Press, 2000.

Hu, Sheng. *Imperialism and Chinese Politics*. Beijing: Foreign Language Press, 1985.

Hunt, Michael H. *The Making of a Special Relationship: The United States and China to 1914*. New York: Columbia University Press, 1983.

Iriye, Akira. *Across the Pacific: An Inner History of American–East Asian Relations*. New York: Harcort, Brace and World, 1967.

Issacs, Harold R. *Scratches on Our Minds: American Images of China and India*. New York: John Day, 1958.

Kitts, Charles R. *The United States Odyssey in China, 1784–1990*. Lanham, Md.: University Press of America, 1991.

Leung, Edwin Pak-wah. *Historical Dictionary of the Chinese Civil War*. Lanham, Md.: Scarecrow Press, 2000

Lyman, Stanford M. *Chinese Americans*. New York: Random House, 1974.

Mancall, Mark. *China at the Center: 300 Years of Foreign Policy.* New York: Free Press, 1984.

May, Ernest R., and John K. Fairbank, eds. *America's China Trade in Historical Perspective: The Chinese and American Performance.* Cambridge, Mass.: Harvard University Press, 1986.

Schaller, Michael. *The United States and China: Into the Twenty-First Century.* New York: Oxford University Press, 2002.

Spence, Jonathan D. *To Change China: Western Advisers in China, 1620–1960.* Boston: Little, Brown, 1969.

Sullivan, Lawrence R. *Historical Dictionary of the People's Republic of China. 2nd edition.* Lanham, Md.: Scarecrow Press, 2006.

Thomson, James C., Peter W. Stanley, and John C. Perry. *Sentimental Imperialists: The American Experience in East Asia.* New York: Harper and Row, 1981.

Twitchett, Denis and John K. Fairbank, eds. *The Cambridge History of China.* Cambridge, England: Cambridge University Press.

Vol. 10: *Late Ch'ing, 1800–1911, Part I,* ed. John K. Fairbank (1978).

Vol. 11: *Late Ch'ing, 1800–1911, Part 2,* eds. John K. Fairbank and Kwang-Ching Liu (1980).

Vol. 12: *Republican China, 1912–1949, Part 1,* ed. John K. Fairbank (1983).

Vol. 13: *Republican China, 1912–1949, Part 2,* ed. John K. Fairbank and Albert Feuerwerker (1986).

Vol. 14: The *People's Republic, Part 1: The Emergence of Revolutionary China, 1949–1965,* eds. Roderick MacFarquhar and John K. Fairbank (1987).

Vol. 15: The *People's Republic, Part 2: Revolutions Within the Chinese Revolution, 1966–1982,* eds. Roderick MacFarquhar and John K. Fairbank (1991).

2. RELATIONS IN THE 19TH CENTURY

Anderson, David L. *Imperialism and Idealism: American Diplomats in China, 1861–1898.* Bloomington, Ind.: University of Indiana Press, 1985.

Bays, Daniel H. ed. *Christianity in China.* Stanford, Cal.: Stanford University Press, 1996.

Bennett, Adrian A. *Missionary Journalist in China: Young J. Allen and His Magazines, 1860–1883.* Athens, Ga.: University of Georgia Press, 1983.

Boardman, Eugene P. *Christian Influence upon the Ideology of the Taiping Rebellion, 1850–1864.* Madison, Wis.: University of Wisconsin Press, 1952.

Breslin, Thomas A. *China, American Catholicism, and the Missionary.* College Station, Penn.: Pennsylvania State University Press, 1980.

Coates, P. D. *China Consuls: British Consular Officers, 1843–1943.* New York: Oxford University Press, 1988.

Downs, Jacques M. *The Golden Ghetto: The American Commercial Community in Canton and the Shaping of American China Policy, 1784–1844.* Bethlehem, Penn.: Lehigh University Press, 1997.

Drake, Fred W. *China Charts the World: Hsu Chi-yu and His Geography of 1848.* Cambridge, Mass.: Harvard University Press, 1975.

Fairbank, John K., ed. *The Missionary Enterprise in China and America.* Cambridge, Mass.: Harvard University Press, 1974.

———. *Trade and Diplomacy on the China Coast: The Opening of the Treaty Ports, 1842–1854.* Cambridge, Mass.: Harvard University Press, 1953.

Fairbank, John K. and Suzanne W. Barnett, eds. *Christianity in China.* Cambridge, Mass.: Harvard University Press, 1985.

Fay, Peter Ward. *Opium War, 1840–1842: Barbarians in the Celestial Empire in the Early Part of the Nineteenth Century and the War by Which They Forced Her Gates Ajar.* Chapel Hill, N.C.: University of North Carolina Press, 1997.

Goldstein, Jonathan. *Philadelphia and the China Trade.* University Park, Penn.: Pennsylvania State University Press, 1978.

Gulick, Edward V. *Peter Parker and the Opening of China.* Cambridge, Mass.: Harvard University Press, 1973.

Hao Yen-ping. *The Commercial Revolution in Nineteenth-Century China: The Rise of Sino–Western Mercantile Capitalism.* Berkeley, Cal.: University of California Press, 1986.

Hevia, James L. *Cherishing Men from Afar: Qing Guest Ritual and the Macartney Embassy of 1793.* Durham, N.C.: Duke University Press, 1995.

Higham, John. *Strangers in the Land.* New Brunswick, N.J.: Rutgers University Press, 1955.

Hing, Bill Ong. *Making and Remaking Asian America through Immigration Policy, 1850–1900.* Stanford, Cal.: Stanford University Press, 1993.

Hou Chi-ming. *Foreign Investment and Economic Development in China, 1840–1937.* Cambridge, Mass.: Harvard University Press, 1965.

Hyatt, Irwin. *Our Ordered Lives Confess: Three Nineteenth-Century American Missionaries in East Shantung.* Cambridge, Mass.: Harvard University Press, 1976.

Iriye, Akira. *Pacific Estrangement: Japanese and American Expansionism, 1879–1911.* Cambridge, Mass.: Harvard University Press, 1972.

LaFeber, Walter. *American Search for Opportunity, 1865–1913.* New York: Cambridge University Press, 1993.

———. *The New Empire: An Interpretation of American Expansion, 1860–1898.* Ithaca, N.Y.: Cornell University Press, 1963.

Latourette, Kenneth S. *The History of Early Relations Between the United States and China, 1784–1844.* New Haven, Conn.: Yale University Press, 1917.

Lukin, Alexander. *The Bear Watches the Dragon: Russia's Perceptions of China and the Evolution of Russian–Chinese Relations since the Eighteenth Century.* Armonk, N.Y.: M.E. Sharpe, 2003.

Lutz, Jessie Gregory. *China and the Christian Colleges, 1850–1950.* Ithaca, N.Y.: Cornell University Press, 1971.

McKee, Delber. *Chinese Exclusion Versus the Open Door Policy, 1900–1906.* Detroit, Mich.: Wayne State University Press, 1977.

Miller, Stuart Creighton. *The Unwelcome Immigrant: The American Image of the Chinese, 1785–1882.* Berkeley, Cal.: University of California Press, 1969.

Morse, Hosea B. and Harley F. MacNair. *Far Eastern International Relations.* Boston: Houghton Mifflin, 1931.

Neils, Patricia, *United States Attitudes Toward China: The Impact of American Missionaries.* Armonk, N.Y.: M. E. Sharpe, 1990.

Paine, S.C.M. *Imperial Rivals: China, Russia, and Their Disputed Frontier.* Armonk, N.Y.: M.E. Sharpe, 1996.

Peyrefitte, Alain. *The Collision of Two Civilizations: The British Expedition to China in 1792–1794.* London: Harvill, 1993.

Phillips, Clifton Jackson. *Protestant America and the Pagan World: The First Half Century of the American Board of Commissioners for Foreign Missions, 1810–1860.* Cambridge, Mass.: Harvard University Press, 1969.

Polachek, James. *The Inner Opium War.* Cambridge, Mass.: Council on East Asian Studies, Harvard University Press, 1992.

Ptak, Roderich. *China and the Asian Seas: Trade, Travel and Visions of the Other (1400–1750).* Brookfield, Vt.: Ashgate, 1998.

———. *China's Seaborne Trade with South and Southeast Asia, 1200–1750.* Brookfield, Vt.: Ashgate, 1999.

Rabe, Valentin. *The Home Base of American China Missions, 1880–1920.* Cambridge, Mass.: Harvard University Press, 1978.

Swisher, Earl. *China's Management of the American Barbarians: A Study of Sino–American Relations, 1841–1861.* New Haven, Conn.: Far Eastern Publications for the Far Eastern Association, 1951.

Takaki, Ronald. *Strangers from a Different Shore: A History of Asian Americans.* Boston: Little, Brown, 1998.

Tikhvinsky, Sergei L. *Chapters from the History of Russo–Chinese Relations, 17th–19th Centuries.* Moscow: Progress Publishers, 1985.

Wakeman, Frederick, *Strangers at the Gate.* Berkeley, Cal.: University of California Press, 1966.

Wang, Gungwu. *Anglo–Chinese Encounters since 1800: War, Trade, Science, and Governance.* New York: Cambridge University Press, 2003.
Williams, S. Wells *The Middle Kingdom.* New York: J. Wiley, 1851.

3. FOREIGN DOMINATION, DECLINE, AND REVOLUTION, 1895–1941

Anderson, David L. *Imperialism and Idealism: American Diplomats in China, 1861–1898.* Bloomington, Ind.: Indiana University Press, 1985.
Anderson, Irvine H. *The Standard-Vacuum Oil Company and United States East Asian Policy, 1933–1941.* Princeton, N.J.: Princeton University Press, 1975.
Barnhart, Michael. *Japan Prepares for Total War: The Search for Economic Security, 1931–1941.* Ithaca, N.Y.: Cornell University Press, 1987.
Borg, Dorothy. *American Policy and the Chinese Revolution, 1925–1928.* New York: Macmillan, 1947.
———. *The United States and the Far Eastern Crisis of 1933–1938.* Cambridge, Mass.: Harvard University Press, 1964.
Borg, Dorothy, and Shumpei Okamoto, eds. *Pearl Harbor as History: Japanese–American Relations, 1931–1941.* New York: Columbia University Press, 1973.
Brandt, Conrad. *Stalin's Failure in China, 1924–1927.* Cambridge, Mass.: Harvard University Press, 1958.
Buck, Pearl. *The Good Earth.* New York: John Day, 1931.
———. *My Several Worlds.* New York: John Day, 1954.
Buck, Peter. *American Science and Modern China, 1876–1936.* Cambridge, England: Cambridge University Press, 1980.
Buckley, Thomas H. *The United States and the Washington Conference, 1921–1922.* Knoxville, Tenn.: University of Tennessee Press, 1970.
Buhite, Russell D. *Nelson T. Johnson and American Policy toward China, 1925–1941.* East Lansing, Mich.: Michigan State University Press, 1968.
Bullock, Mary Brown. *An American Transplant: The Rockefeller Foundation and Peking Union Medical College.* Berkeley, Cal.: University of California Press, 1980.
Butow, Robert J. C. *The John Doe Associates: Backdoor Diplomacy for Peace.* Stanford, Cal.: Stanford University Press, 1974.
———. *Tojo and the Coming of the War.* Princeton, N.J.: Princeton University Press, 1961.
Campbell, Charles S. *Special Business Interests and the Open Door Policy.* New Haven, Conn.: Yale University Press, 1951.

Carlson. Evans F. *Twin Stars of China.* New York: Dodd, Mead and Co., 1940.

Chang, Iris. *Rape of Nanking: The Forgotten Holocaust of World War II.* New York: Basic Books, 1997.

Chi, Madeleine. *China Diplomacy, 1914–1918.* Cambridge, Mass.: Harvard University Press, 1970.

Chow Tse-tsung. *The May Fourth Movement: Intellectual Revolution in Modern China.* Cambridge, Mass.: Harvard University Press, 1960.

Clubb, O. Edmund. *Communism in China as Reported from Hankow in 1932.* New York: Columbia University Press, 1968.

Cochran, Sherman. *Big Business in China: Sino–American Rivalry in the Cigarette Industry.* Cambridge, Mass.: Harvard University Press, 1980.

Cohen, Paul. *History in Three Keys: The Boxers as Event, Experience, and Myth.* New York: Columbia University Press, 1997.

Cohen, Warren I. *The Chinese Connection: Roger S. Greene, Thomas W. Lamont, George E. Sokolsky and American–East Asian Relations.* New York: Columbia University Press, 1978.

———. *Empire Without Tears.* New York: McGraw-Hill, 1987.

Crow, Carl. *Four Hundred Million Customers.* New York: Harper, 1937.

Crowley, James. *Japan's Quest for Autonomy.* Princeton, N.J.: Princeton University Press, 1966.

Curry, Roy W. *Woodrow Wilson and Far Eastern Policy, 1913–1921.* New York: Octagon Books, 1968.

Dayer, Roberta Allbert. *Bankers and Diplomats in China, 1917–1925: The Anglo–American Relationship.* London: Frank Cass, 1981.

Dingman, Roger. *Power in the Pacific: The Origins of Naval Limitations, 1914–1922.* Chicago: University of Chicago Press, 1976.

Eastman, Lloyd. *The Abortive Revolution: China Under Nationalist Rule, 1927–1937.* Cambridge, Mass.: Harvard University Press, 1974.

Edmonds, Richard Louis, and Steven Goldstein, eds. *Taiwan in the Twentieth Century.* New York: Cambridge University Press, 2001.

Edwards, E. W. *British Diplomacy and Finance in China, 1895–1914.* New York: Oxford University Press, 1987.

Elleman, Bruce A. *Diplomacy and Deception: The Secret History of Sino–Soviet Diplomatic Relations, 1917–1927.* Armonk, N.Y.: M.E. Sharpe, 1997.

Esherick, Joseph. *The Origins of the Boxer Uprising.* Berkeley, Cal.: University of California Press, 1987.

Feis, Herbert. *The Road to Pearl Harbor: The Coming of the War Between the United States and Japan.* Princeton, N.J.: Princeton University Press, 1950.

Ferrell, Robert H. *American Diplomacy in the Great Depression.* New Haven, Conn.: Yale University Press, 1957.

Fifield, Russell H. *Woodrow Wilson and the Far East: The Diplomacy of the Shantung Question.* New York: Crowell, 1952.

Fishel, Wesley R. *The End of Extraterritoriality in China.* Berkeley, Cal.: University of California Press, 1952.

Fogel, Joshua A. *The Cultural Dimension of Sino–Japanese Relations: Essays on the Nineteenth and Twentieth Centuries.* Armonk, N.Y.: M.E. Sharpe, 1995.

Garrett, Shirley S. *Social Reformers in Urban China: The Chinese YMCA, 1895–1962.* Cambridge, Mass.: Harvard University Press, 1970.

Garver, John W. *Chinese–Soviet Relations, 1937–1945: The Diplomacy of Chinese Nationalism.* New York: Oxford University Press, 1988.

Gilbert, Rodney. *What's Wrong with China.* New York: Frederick A. Stokes, 1926.

Heinrichs, Waldo H. *Threshold of War: Franklin D. Roosevelt and American Entry into World War Two.* New York: Oxford University Press, 1988.

Hilton, James. *Lost Horizon.* New York: Grosset and Dunlap, 1933.

Holden, Reuben. *Yale in China: The Mainland, 1901–1951.* New Haven, Conn.: Yale in China Association, 1964.

Hou Chi-ming. *Foreign Investment and Economic Development in China, 1840–1937.* Cambridge, Mass.: Harvard University Press, 1965.

Hu Chiao-mu. *Thirty Years of the Communist Party of China: An Outline History.* London: Lawrence and Wishart, 1951.

Hunt, Michael H. *Frontier Defense and the Open Door: Manchuria in Chinese–American Relations, 1895–1911.* New Haven, Conn.: Yale University Press, 1973.

Hunt, Michael H., and Niu Jun, eds. *Toward a History of Chinese Communist Foreign Relations, 1920s–1960s: Personalities and Interpretive Approaches.* Washington, D.C.: Woodrow Wilson International Center for Scholars, 1993.

Hunter, Jane. *The Gospel of Gentility: American Women Missionaries in Turn-of-the Century China.* New Haven, Conn.: Yale University Press, 1984.

Iriye, Akira. *After Imperialism: The Search for a New Order in the Far East, 1921–1931.* Cambridge, Mass.: Harvard University Press, 1965.

———. *Pacific Estrangement: Japanese and American Expansionism, 1879–1911.* Cambridge, Mass.: Harvard University Press, 1972.

Isaacs, Harold. *The Tragedy of the Chinese Revolution.* Stanford, Cal.: Stanford University Press, 1951.

Israel, Jerry. *Progressivism and the Open Door: America and China, 1905–1921.* Pittsburgh, Penn.: University of Pittsburgh Press, 1971.

Keenan, Barry. *The Dewey Experiment in China: Education Reform and Political Power in the Early Republic.* Cambridge, Mass.: Harvard University Press, 1977.

Kirby, William C. *Germany and Republican China.* Stanford, Cal.: Stanford University Press, 1974.

LaFeber, Walter. *American Search for Opportunity, 1865–1913.* New York: Cambridge University Press, 1993.

Langer, William L. *The Diplomacy of Imperialism.* New York: Knopf, 1950.

Li, Tien-yi. *Woodrow Wilson's China Policy, 1913–1917.* New York: Twayne, 1952.

Link, Arthur. *Wilson: The Struggle for Neutrality, 1914–1915.* Princeton, N.J.: Princeton University Press, 1963.

Lutz, Jessie Gregory. *China and the Christian Colleges, 1850–1950.* Ithaca, N.Y.: Cornell University Press, 1971.

McClellan, Robert. *The Heathen Chinese: A Study of American Attitude Toward China, 1895–1905.* Columbus, Ohio: Ohio State University Press. 1971.

McCormick, Thomas. *China Market: America's Quest for Informal Empire, 1893–1901.* Chicago: Quadrangle, 1967.

McKee, Delber, *Chinese Exclusion Versus the Open Door Policy, 1900–1906.* Detroit, Mich.: Wayne State University Press, 1977.

Morley, James W. *China Quagmire: Japan's Expansion on the Asian Continent, 1933–1941.* New York: Columbia University Press, 1983.

Morrison, Elting E. *Turmoil and Tradition: A Study of the Life and Times of Henry L. Stimson.* Boston: Houghton Mifflin, 1960.

Neils, Patricia. *China Images in the Life and Times of Henry Luce.* Lanham, Md.: Rowman and Littlefield, 1990.

Peck, Graham. *Two Kinds of Time.* Boston: Houghton Mifflin, 1967.

Pollard, Robert L. *China's Foreign Relations, 1917–1931.* New York: Macmillan, 1933.

Preston, Diana. *Besieged in Peking: The Story of the 1900 Boxer Rising.* London: Constable, 1999.

Pugach, Noel H. *Paul S. Reinsch: Open Door Diplomat in Action.* Millwood, N.Y.: KTO Press, 1979.

Quigley, Harold S., and George H. Blakeslee. *The Far East.* Boston: World Peace Foundation, 1938.

Reed, James. *The Missionary Mind and American East Asia Policy, 1911–1915.* Cambridge, Mass.: Harvard University Press, 1983.

Reinhold, Christine. *Studying the Enemy: Japan Hands in Republican China and Their Quest for National Identity.* New York: Routledge, 2001.

Remer, Charles F. *Foreign Investments in China.* New York: Macmillan, 1933.

Reynolds, Douglas R. *China, 1898–1912: The Xinzheng Revolution and Japan.* Cambridge. Mass.: Harvard University Press, 1993.

Rosenberg, Emily. *Financial Missionaries to the World: The Politics and Culture of Dollar Diplomacy.* Cambridge, Mass: Harvard University Press, 1999.

Salisbury, Harrison E. *The Long March: The Untold Story.* New York: Harper and Row, 1985.

Scholes, Walter, and Mary Scholes. *The Foreign Policies of the Taft Administration.* Columbia, Mo.: University of Missouri Press, 1970.

Schwartz, Benjamin. *Chinese Communism and the Rise of Mao.* Cambridge, Mass.: Harvard University Press, 1958.

Seagrave, Sterling. *The Soong Dynasty.* New York: Harper and Row, 1985.

Shaw, Yu-ming. *An American Missionary in China: John Leighton Stuart and Chinese–American Relations.* Cambridge, Mass.: Harvard University Press, 1992.

Sheridan, James E. *China in Disintegration: The Republican Era in Chinese History, 1912–1949.* New York: The Free Press, 1975.

Shewmaker, Kenneth E. *Americans and the Chinese Communists, 1927–1945: A Persuading Encounter.* Ithaca, N.Y.: Cornell University Press, 1971.

Snow, Edgar. *Red Star over China.* New York: Random House, 1938.

Stimson, Henry L., and McGeorge Bundy. *On Active Service in Peace and War.* New York: Harper, 1948.

Stuart, John Leighton. *Fifty Years in China.* New York: Random House, 1954.

Sun, You-Li. *China and the Origins of the Pacific War, 1931–1941.* New York: St Martin's Press, 1993.

Takaki, Ronald. *Strangers from a Different Shore: A History of Asian Americans.* Boston: Little, Brown, 1998.

Thomson, James C. Jr. *While China Faced West: American Reformers in Nationalist China, 1928–1937.* Cambridge, Mass.: Harvard University Press, 1968.

Thorne, Christopher. *The Limits of Foreign Policy: The West, the League, and the Far Eastern Crisis of 1931–1933.* New York: G.P. Putman, 1972.

Tuchman, Barbara. *Stilwell and the American Experience in China, 1911–1945.* New York: Macmillan, 1971.

Unterberger, Betty M. *America's Siberian Expedition, 1918–1920.* Durham, N.C.: Duke University Press, 1956.

Utley, Jonathan. *Going to War with Japan, 1937–1941.* Knoxville, Tenn.: University of Tennessee Press, 1985.

Van Slyke, Lyman. *Enemies and Friends.* Stanford, Cal.: Stanford University Press, 1967.

Varg, Paul A. *The Making of a Myth: The United States and China, 1897–1912.* East Lansing, Mich.: Michigan State University Press, 1968.

———. *Missionaries, Chinese and Diplomats: The American Protestant Missionary Movement in China, 1890–1952.* Princeton, N.J.: Princeton University Press, 1958.

———. *Open Door Diplomat: The Life of W. W. Rockhill.* Urbana, Ill.: University of Illinois Press, 1952.

Vevier, Charles. *The United States and China, 1906–1913: A Study of Finance and Diplomacy.* New Brunswick, N.J.: Rutgers University Press, 1955.

Vinson, J. Chalmers. *Parchment Peace.* Athens, Ga.: University of Georgia Press, 1956.

Wakeman, Frederick Jr. *Policing Shanghai, 1927–1937.* Berkeley, Cal.: University of California Press, 1995.

———. *The Shanghai Badlands: Wartime Terrorism and Urban Crime, 1937–1941.* New York: Cambridge University Press, 1996.

Wang, Gungwu. *Anglo–Chinese Encounters Since 1800: War, Trade, Science, and Governance.* New York: Cambridge University Press, 2003.

West, Philip. *Yenching University and Sino–Western Relations, 1916–1952.* Cambridge, Mass.: Harvard University Press, 1976.

White, John A. *The Siberian Intervention.* Princeton: Princeton University Press, 1950.

Whiting, Allen S. *Soviet Policies in China, 1917–1921.* New York: Columbia University Press, 1954.

Wilbur, C. Martin. *Missionaries of Revolution: Soviet Advisers and Nationalist China, 1920–1927.* Cambridge, Mass.: Harvard University Press, 1989.

Young, Arthur N. *China and the Helping Hand, 1937–1945.* Cambridge, Mass.: Harvard University Press, 1963.

———. *China's Wartime Finance and Inflation, 1937–1945.* Cambridge, Mass.: Harvard University Press, 1965.

Young, Ernest. *The Presidency of Yuan Shih-kai: Liberalism and Dictatorship in Early Republican China.* Ann Arbor, Mich.: University of Michigan Press, 1977.

Young, Marilyn B. *The Rhetoric of Empire: American China Policy, 1895–1901.* Cambridge, Mass.: Harvard University Press, 1968.

4. WORLD WAR II, CHINESE CIVIL WAR, 1941–1949

Acheson, Dean. *Power and Diplomacy.* Cambridge, Mass.: Harvard University Press, 1958.

———. *Present at the Creation.* New York: W.W. Norton, 1969.

Barrett, David D. *Dixie Mission: The US Army Observer Group in Yenan, 1944.* Berkeley, Cal.: University of California Press, 1970.

Beal, John R. *Marshall in China.* Garden City, N.Y.: Doubleday, 1970.

Belden, Jack. *China Shakes the World.* New York: Harper and Row, 1949.

Borg, Dorothy, and Waldo Heinrichs, eds. *Uncertain Years: Chinese–American Relations, 1947–1950.* New York: Columbia University Press, 1980.

Buhite, Russell D. *Patrick J. Hurley and American Foreign Policy.* Ithaca, N.Y.: Cornell University Press, 1973.

Carter, Carol. *Mission to Yenan: American Liaison with the Chinese Communists, 1944–1947.* Lexington, Ky.: University of Kentucky Press, 1997.

Chennault, Claire Lee. *Way of a Fighter: The Memoirs of Claire Lee Chennault, Major General US Army (ret.)*. New York: Putnam, 1949.

Chiang Kai-shek. *China's Destiny*. New York, Macmillan, 1947.

Davies, John Patton. *Dragon by the Tail*. New York: Norton, 1972.

Dittmer, Lowell. *Sino–Soviet Normalization and Its International Implications, 1945–1990*. Seattle, Wash.: University of Washington Press, 1992.

Dower, John. *War Without Mercy: Race and Power in the Pacific War*. New York: Pantheon Books, 1986.

Eastman, Lloyd. *Seeds of Destruction: Nationalist China in War and Revolution, 1937–1949*. Stanford, Cal.: Stanford University Press, 1984.

Edmonds, Richard Louis, and Steven Goldstein, eds. *Taiwan in the Twentieth Century*. Cambridge, England: Cambridge University Press, 2001.

Esherick, Joseph W. *Lost Chance in China: The World War II Dispatches of John S. Service*. New York: Random House, 1974.

Fairbank, Wilma. *America's Cultural Experiment in China, 1942–1949*. Washington, D.C.: US Government Printing Office, 1976.

Feis, Herbert. *The China Tangle: The American Effort in China from Pearl Harbor to the Marshall Mission*. Princeton, N.J.: Princeton University Press, 1953.

Gaddis, John L. *The United States and the Origins of the Cold War, 1941–1947*. New York: Columbia University Press, 1972.

Gallicchio, Mark. *The Cold War Begins in Asia: American East Asia Policy and the Fall of the Japanese Empire*. New York: Columbia University Press, 1988.

Garver, John W. *Chinese–Soviet Relations, 1937–1945: The Diplomacy of Chinese Nationalism*. New York: Oxford University Press, 1988.

Grasso, June M. *Truman's Two-China Policy*. Armonk, N.Y.: M.E. Sharpe, 1988.

Harding, Harry, and Yuan Ming, eds. *Sino–American Relations, 1945–1955*. Wilmington, Del.: Scholarly Resources, 1989.

Hess, Gary R. *The United States Emergence as a Southeast Asian Power, 1940–1950*. New York: Columbia University Press, 1987.

Hsiung, James, and Steven I. Levine, eds. *China's Bitter Victory*. Armonk, N.Y.: M.E. Sharpe, 1992.

Hunt, Michael H. *The Genesis of Chinese Communist Foreign Policy*. New York: Columbia University Press, 1996.

Hunt, Michael H., and Niu Jun, eds. *Toward a History of Chinese Communist Foreign Relations, 1920s–1960s: Personalities and Interpretive Approaches*. Washington, D.C.: Woodrow Wilson International Center for Scholars, 1993.

Iriye, Akira, and Warren I. Cohen, eds. *American, Chinese, and Japanese Perspectives on Wartime Asia, 1939–1949*. Wilmington, Del.: Scholarly Resources, 1990.

Jespersen, T. Christopher. *American Images of China, 1931–1949.* Stanford, Cal.: Stanford University Press, 1996.

Johnson, Chalmers. *Peasant Nationalism and Communist Power.* Stanford, Cal.: Stanford University Press, 1962.

Kahn, Ely J. Jr. *The China Hands.* New York: Random House, 1975.

Klehr, Harvey, and Ronald Radosh. *The Amerasia Spy Case: Prelude to McCarthyism.* Chapel Hill, N.C.: University of North Carolina Press, 1996.

Levine, Steven I. *The Anvil of Victory: The Communist Revolution in Manchuria, 1945–1948.* New York: Columbia University Press, 1987.

Lindsay, Michael. *North China Front.* London: China Campaign Committee, 1944.

Liu, Frederick F. *A Military History of Modern China, 1924–1949.* Princeton, N.J.: Princeton University Press, 1956.

Liu, Xiaoyuan. *A Partnership for Disorder: China, the United States, and Their Policies for the Postwar Disposition of the Japanese Empire.* New York: Cambridge University Press, 1996.

MacKinnon, Janice, and Stephen MacKinnon. *Agnes Smedley: The Life and Times of an American Radical.* Berkeley, Cal.: University of California Press, 1988.

MacKinnon, Stephen, and Oris Friesen. *China Reporting: An Oral History of American Journalism in the 1930s and 1940s.* Berkeley, Cal.: University of California Press, 1987.

Matray, James I. *The Reluctant Crusade: American Foreign Policy in Korea, 1941–1950.* Honolulu: University of Hawaii Press, 1985.

May, Ernest R. *The Truman Administration and China, 1945–1949.* New York: Lippincott, 1975.

Melby, John. *The Mandate of Heaven: Record of a Civil War in China, 1945–1949.* Toronto.: University of Toronto Press, 1968.

Neils, Patricia. *China Images in the Life and Times of Henry Luce.* Lanham, Md.: Rowman and Littlefield, 1990.

Newman, Robert P. *Owen Lattimore and the Loss of China.* Berkeley, Cal.: University of California Press, 1992.

Peck, Graham. *Two Kinds of Time.* Boston: Houghton Mifflin, 1950.

Pepper, Suzanne. *Civil War in China: The Political Struggle, 1945–1949.* Berkeley, Cal.: University of California Press, 1978.

Reardon-Anderson, James. *Yenan and the Great Powers: The Origins of Chinese Communist Foreign Policy, 1944–1946.* New York: Columbia University Press, 1980.

Romanus, Charles F., and Riley Sunderland. *Stilwell's Command Problems.* Washington, D.C.: Department of the Army, 1956.

——. *Stilwell's Mission to China.* Washington, D.C.: Department of the Army, 1953.

——. *Time Runs Out on CBI*. Washington, D.C.: Department of the Army, 1959.

Schaller, Michael. *The American Occupation of Japan: The Origins of the Cold War in Asia*. New York: Oxford University Press, 1985.

——. *The US Crusade in China, 1938–1945*. New York: Columbia University Press. 1979.

Schroeder, Paul W. *The Axis Alliance and Japanese–American Relations, 1941*. Ithaca, N.Y.: Cornell University Press, 1958.

Seagrave, Sterling. *The Soong Dynasty*. New York: Harper and Row, 1985.

Service, John S. *Lost Chance in China*. New York: Vintage, 1975.

Shaw, Yu-ming. *An American Missionary in China: John Leighton Stuart and Chinese–American Relations*. Cambridge, Mass.: Harvard University Press, 1992.

Shewmaker, Kenneth E. *Americans and the Chinese Communists, 1927–1945: A Persuading Encounter*. Ithaca, N.Y.: Cornell University Press, 1971.

Spector, Ronald. *Eagle Against the Sun: The American War with Japan*. New York: Free Press, 1985.

Stilwell, Joseph W. *The Stilwell Papers*. New York: Sloane Associates, 1948.

Stimson, Henry L., and McGeorge Bundy. *On Active Service in Peace and War*. New York: Harper, 1948.

Strong, Tracy B., and Helene Keyssar. *Right in Her Soul: The Life and Times of Anna Louise Strong*. New York: Random House, 1983.

Stuart, John Leighton. *Fifty Years in China*. New York: Random House, 1954.

Stueck, William W. *The Road to Confrontation: American Policy toward China and Korea, 1947–1950*. Chapel Hill, N.C.: University of North Carolina Press, 1981.

Taylor, Jay. *The Generalissimo's Son: Chiang Ching-kuo and the Revolutions in China and Taiwan*. Cambridge, Mass.: Harvard University Press, 2000.

Tsou, Tang. *America's Failure in China, 1941–1950*. Chicago: University of Chicago Press, 1963.

Tuchman, Barbara. *Stilwell and the American Experience in China, 1911–1945*. New York: Macmillan, 1971.

Tucker, Nancy B. *China Confidential: American Diplomats and Sino–American Relations, 1945–1996*. New York: Columbia University Press, 2001.

——. *Patterns in the Dust: Chinese–American Relations and the Recognition Controversy, 1949–1950*. New York: Columbia University Press, 1983.

US Congress. Senate. Committee on Armed Services and Committee on Foreign Relations. *Military Situation in the Far East, Hearings*. 82d Congress, 1st session, 5 parts. Washington, D.C.: US Government Printing Office, 1949.

US Congress. Senate. Committee on Foreign Relations. Subcommittee of the Committee on Foreign Relations. *State Department Employee Loyalty Investigation, Hearings*. 81st Congress, 2d session, 3 parts. Washington, D.C., US Government Printing Office, 1950.

US Department of State, *United States Relations with China with Special Reference to the Period 1944–1949*. Washington, D.C.: US Government Printing Office, 1949.

Van Slyke, Lyman P., ed. *The Chinese Communist Movement: A Report of the United States War Department, July 1945*. Stanford, Cal.: Stanford University Press, 1968.

Varg, Paul A. *The Closing of the Door: Sino–American Relations, 1936–1946*. East Lansing, Mich.: Michigan State University Press, 1973.

Vincent, John C. *The Extraterritorial System in China: Final Phase*. Cambridge, Mass.: Harvard University Press, 1969.

Wei, C. X. George. *Sino–American Economic Relations, 1944–1949*. Westport, Conn.: Greenwood Press, 1997.

Wells, Sumner. *Seven Decisions That Shaped History*. New York: Harper, 1950.

Westad, Odd Arne. *Brothers in Arms: The Rise and Fall of the Sino–Soviet Alliance, 1945–1963*. Stanford, Cal.: Stanford University Press, 1998.

———. *Cold War and Revolution: Soviet–American Rivalry and the Origins of the Chinese Civil War, 1944–1946*. New York: Columbia University Press, 1993.

White, Theodore H. *In Search of History*. New York: Harper and Row, 1978.

White, Theodore H., and Annalee Jacoby. *Thunder Out of China*. New York: Sloan Associates, 1946.

Young, Arthur N. *China and the Helping Hand, 1937–1945*. Cambridge, Mass.: Harvard University Press, 1963.

———. *China's Wartime Finance and Inflation, 1937–1945*. Cambridge, Mass.: Harvard University Press, 1965.

Zi, Zhongyun. *Meiguo duihua zhengce de yuanqi he fazhan, 1945–1950* [The Origins and Development of American Policy toward China, 1945–1950]. Chongqing: Chongqing, 1987.

5. CONFLICT AND CONTAINMENT, 1950–1968

Accinelli, Robert. *Crisis and Commitment: United States Policy toward Taiwan, 1950–1955*. Chapel Hill, N.C.: University of North Carolina Press, 1996.

Acheson, Dean. *Power and Diplomacy*. Cambridge, Mass.: Harvard University Press, 1958.

———. *Present at the Creation*. New York: W.W. Norton, 1969.

Ambrose, Stephen E. *Eisenhower: The President*. New York: Simon and Schuster, 1984.

Bachrack, Stanley D. *The Committee of One Million: "China Lobby" Politics, 1953–1971*. New York: Columbia University Press, 1976.

Barnett, A. Doak. *Communist China and Asia: Challenge to American Policy*. New York: Harper and Brothers, 1960.

Barnouin, Barbara, and Yu Changgen. *Chinese Foreign Policy During the Cultural Revolution*. New York: Columbia University Press, 1997.

Beam, Jacob. *Multiple Exposure: An American Ambassador's Unique Perspective of East–West Issues*. New York: Norton, 1978.

Bird, Kai. *The Color of Truth: McGeorge Bundy and William Bundy, Brothers in Arms: A Biography*. New York: Simon and Schuster, 1998.

Blum, Robert. *The United States and China in World Affairs*. New York: McGraw-Hill, 1966.

Blum, Robert M. *Drawing the Line: The Origins of the American Containment Policy in East Asia*. New York: W.W. Norton, 1982.

——. *The United States and China in 1949 and 1950: The Question of Rapprochement and Recognition*. Washington, D.C.: US Government Printing Office, 1973.

Borg, Dorothy. *Historians and American Far Eastern Policy*. New York: Columbia University East Asian Institute, 1966.

Borg, Dorothy, and Waldo Heinrichs, eds. *Uncertain Years: Chinese–American Relations, 1947–1950*. New York: Columbia University Press, 1980.

Burles, Mark, and Abram N. Shulsky. *Patterns in China's Use of Force*. Santa Monica, Cal.: Rand, 2000.

Bush, Richard. *At Cross Purposes: US–Taiwan Relations since 1942*. Armonk, N.Y.: M.E. Sharpe, 2004.

Camillieri, Joseph. *Chinese Foreign Policy*. Seattle, Wash.: University of Washington Press, 1980.

Chang, Gordon. *Friends and Enemies: The United States, China, and the Soviet Union, 1948–1972*. Stanford, Cal.: Stanford University Press, 1990.

Chen, Jian. *China's Road to the Korean War*. New York: Columbia University Press, 1994.

——. *Mao's China and the Cold War*. Chapel Hill, N.C.: University of North Carolina Press, 2001.

Christensen, Thomas. *Useful Adversaries: Grand Strategy, Domestic Mobilization, and Sino–American Conflicts, 1949–1958*. Princeton, N.J.: Princeton University Press, 1996.

Clough, Ralph. *Island China*. Cambridge, Mass.: Harvard University Press, 1978.

Clubb, O. Edmund. *The Witness and I*. New York: Columbia University Press, 1974.

Cohen, Warren I. *Dean Rusk*. Totowa. N.J.: Cooper Square Publishers, 1980.

Cohen, Warren I., and Akira Iriye, eds. *The Great Powers in East Asia, 1953–1960.* New York: Columbia University Press, 1990.

Cohen, Warren I., and Nancy Bernkopf Tucker, eds. *Lyndon Johnson Confronts the World: American Foreign Policy, 1963–1968.* New York: Cambridge University Press, 1994.

Copper, John F. *Taiwan: Nation-State or Province.* Boulder, Colo.: Westview Press, 2003.

Cummings, Bruce. *The Origins of the Korean War.* Princeton, N.J.: Princeton University Press, 1990.

Dittmer, Lowell. *Sino–Soviet Normalization and Its International Implications, 1945–1990.* Seattle: University of Washington Press, 1992.

Divine, Robert A. *Eisenhower and the Cold War.* New York: Oxford University Press, 1981.

Dulles, Foster Rhea. *American Policy Toward Communist China, 1949–1969.* New York: Thomas Y. Crowell, 1972.

Edmonds, Richard Louis, and Steven Goldstein, eds. *Taiwan in the Twentieth Century.* Cambridge, England: Cambridge University Press, 2001.

Eisenhower, Dwight D. *Mandate for Change.* New York: New American Library, 1965.

Finkelstein, David. *Washington's Taiwan Dilemma, 1949–1950.* Fairfax, Va.: George Mason University Press, 1993.

Foot, Rosemary. *The Practice of Power: US Relations with China Since 1949.* New York: Oxford University Press, 1997.

——. *The Wrong War: American Conflict and the Dimensions of the Korean Conflict, 1950–1953.* Ithaca, N.Y.: Cornell University Press, 1985.

——. *A Substitute for Victory: The Politics of Peacemaking and the Korean Armistice Talks.* Ithaca, N.Y.: Cornell University Press, 1990.

Friedman, Edward, and Mark Selden, eds. *America's Asia.* New York: Pantheon, 1971.

Gaddis, John. *The Long Peace: Inquiries into the History of the Cold War.* New York: Oxford University Press, 1987.

——. *We Now Know: Rethinking Cold War History.* New York: Oxford University Press, 1997.

Garver, John W. *The Sino–American Alliance: Nationalist China and American Cold War Strategy in Asia.* Armonk, N.Y.: M.E. Sharpe, 1997.

George, Alexander. *The Chinese Communist Army in Action: The Korean War and Its Aftermath.* New York: Columbia University Press, 1969.

Goncharov, Sirgei N., John Lewis, and Xue Li Tai. *Uncertain Partners: Stalin, Mao and the Korean War.* Stanford, Cal.: Stanford University Press, 1993.

Grasso, June M. *Truman's Two-China Policy.* Armonk, N.Y.: M.E. Sharpe, 1988.

Griffith, William E. *Cold War and Coexistence: Russia, China, and the United States.* Englewood Cliffs, N.J.: Prentice Hall, 1971.

Guhin, Michael A. *John Foster Dulles: A Statesman and his Times.* New York: Columbia University Press, 1972.

Gurtov, Melvin. *First Vietnam Crisis: Chinese Communist Strategy and United States Involvement, 1953–1954.* New York: Columbia University Press, 1968.

Gurtov, Melvin, and Byong-Moo Hwang. *China Under Threat.* Baltimore, Md.: Johns Hopkins University Press, 1981.

Halperin, Morton H. *China and the Bomb.* New York: Praeger, 1965.

Halpern, Abraham M., ed. *Policies Toward China: Views from Six Continents.* New York: McGraw-Hill, 1965.

Harding, Harry, and Yuan Ming, eds. *Sino–American Relations, 1945–1955.* Wilmington, Del.: Scholarly Resources, 1989.

Hilsman, Roger. *To Move a Nation.* New York: Doubleday, 1967.

Hinton, Harold. *Bear at the Gate: Chinese Policymaking under Soviet Pressure.* Washington, D.C.: American Enterprise Institute, 1971.

——. *China's Turbulent Quest.* New York: Macmillan, 1972.

——. *Communist China in World Politics.* Boston: Houghton Mifflin, 1966.

Hoopes, Townsend. *The Devil and John Foster Dulles.* Boston: Little, Brown, 1973.

Hsieh, Alice Langley. *Communist China's Strategy in a Nuclear Era.* Englewood Cliffs, N.J.: Prentice Hall, 1962.

Hu Sheng, ed. *Zhongguo gongchandang de qishi nian* [70 Years of the Chinese Communist Party]. Beijing: Zhonggong Dangshi Chubanshe, 1991.

Hunt, Michael H. *The Genesis of Chinese Communist Foreign Policy.* New York: Columbia University Press, 1996.

Hunt, Michael H., and Niu Jun, eds. *Toward a History of Chinese Communist Foreign Relations, 1920s–1960s: Personalities and Interpretive Approaches.* Washington, D.C.: Woodrow Wilson International Center for Scholars, 1993.

Immerman, Richard, ed. *John Foster Dulles: Piety, Pragmatism and Power in US Foreign Policy.* Wilmington, Del.: Scholarly Resources, 1999.

Iriye, Akira. *The Cold War in Asia: A Historical Introduction.* Englewood Cliffs, N.J.: Prentice Hall, 1974.

——. *US Policy Toward China: Testimony Taken From the Senate Foreign Relations Committee Hearings, 1966.* Boston: Little, Brown, 1968.

Jacoby, Neil H. *US Aid to Taiwan.* New York: Praeger, 1966.

Jervis, Robert, and Jack Snyder, eds. *Dominos and Bandwagons: Strategic Beliefs and Great Power Competition in the Eurasian Rimland.* New York: Oxford University Press, 1991.

Jiang, Changbin, and Robert S. Ross, eds. *1955–1971 Nian de Zhong Mei Guanxi—Huanhe Zhigian: Lengzhan Chongtu yu Keshi de Cai Tantao*

[US–China Relations, 1955–1971 — Before Détente: An Examination of Cold War Conflict and Restraint]. Beijing: Shijie Zhishi Chubanshe, 1998.

———. *Cong Duizhi zouxiang Huanhe: Lengzhan Shiqi Zhong Mei Guanxi zai Tantao* [From Confrontation Toward Détente: A Reexamination of US–China Relations During the Cold War]. Beijing: Shijie Zhishi Chubanshe, 2000.

Johnson, Lyndon. *The Vantage Point.* New York: Holt, Rinehart and Winston, 1971.

Johnson, U. Alexis. *The Right Hand of Power.* Englewood Cliffs, N.J.: Prentice Hall, 1984.

Kahn, Ely J. Jr. *The China Hands.* New York: Random House, 1975.

Kalicki, Jan H. *The Pattern of Sino–American Crises: Political–Military Interactions in the 1950s.* London: Cambridge University Press, 1975.

Kennan, George F. M*emoirs.* Boston: Little, Brown, 1967.

———. *Realities of American Foreign Policy.* New York: W.W. Norton, 1966.

Klintworth, Gary. *New Taiwan, New China: Taiwan's Changing Role in the Asia–Pacific Region.* New York: St. Martins, 1995.

Knaus, John Kenneth. *Orphans of the Cold War: America and the Tibetan Struggle for Survival.* New York: Public Affairs, 1999.

Koen, Ross Y. *The China Lobby in American Politics.* New York: Harper and Row, 1974.

Kunz, Diane B., ed. *Diplomacy of the Crucial Decade: American Foreign Policy During the 1960s.* New York: Columbia University Press, 1994.

Kusnitz, Leonard. *Public Opinion and Foreign Policy: America's China Policy, 1949–1979.* Westport, Conn.: Greenwood Press, 1984.

Lall, Arthur. *How Communist China Negotiates.* New York: Columbia University Press, 1968.

Lewis, John L., and Xue Litai. *China Builds the Bomb.* Stanford, Cal.: Stanford University Press, 1988.

Li, Xiaobing, and Hongshan Li, eds. *China and the United States: A New Cold War History.* Lanham, Md.: University Press of America, 1998.

Liao, Kuang-shang. *Antiforeignism and Modernization in China, 1860–1980.* New York: St. Martins, 1984.

Lin, Qing. *Zhou Enlai zaixiang shengya* [The Career of Prime Minister Zhou Enlai]. Hong Kong: Changcheng Wenhua Chubanshe, 1991.

MacFarquhar, Roderick. ed. *Sino–American Relations, 1949–1971.* New York: Praeger, 1972.

Marks, Frederick W. III. *Power and Peace: The Diplomacy of John Foster Dulles.* Westport, Conn.: Praeger, 1993.

Matray, James I. *The Reluctant Crusade: American Foreign Policy in Korea, 1941–1950.* Honolulu: University of Hawaii Press, 1985.

Maxing, D.P., and Thomas W. Robinson. *Lin Biao on "People's War": China Takes a Second Look at Vietnam.* Santa Monica, Cal.: RAND, 1975.

Maxwell, Neville. *India's China War.* London: Jonathan Cape, 1970.

May, Earnest R., and James C. Thomson. *American–East Asian Relations: A Survey.* Cambridge, Mass.: Harvard University Press, 1972.

May, Gary. *China Scapegoat: The Diplomatic Ordeal of John Carter Vincent.* Washington, D.C.: New Republic Books, 1979.

Mayer, David Allan. *Cracking the Monolith: US Policy Against the Sino–Soviet Alliance, 1949–1955.* Baton Rouge: Louisiana State University Press, 1986.

Mozingo, David. *China's Foreign Policy and the Cultural Revolution.* Ithaca, N.Y.: Cornell University Press, 1970.

Newman, Robert P. *Owen Lattimore and the Loss of China.* Berkeley, Cal.: University of California Press, 1992.

Oshinski, Daniel M. *A Conspiracy So Immense: The World of Joe McCarthy.* New York: Free Press, 1989.

Pei, Jianzhang. *Yanjiu Zhou Enlai: Waijiao sixiang yu shijian* [Researching Zhou Enlai: Diplomatic Thought and Practice]. Beijing: Shijie Zhishi Chubanshe, 1989.

———. *Zhonghua renmin gongheguo waijiao shi, 1949–1956* [A Diplomatic History of the People's Republic of China, 1949–1956]. Beijing: Shijie Zhishi, 1994.

Rankin, Karl. *China Assignment.* Seattle: University of Washington Press, 1964.

Ross, Robert S., and Jiang Changbin, eds. *Reexamining the Cold War.* Cambridge, Mass.: Harvard University Press, 2001.

Rostow, Walt W. *The Diffusion of Power: An Essay in Recent History.* New York: Macmillan, 1972.

Rusk, Dean. *As I Saw It.* New York: Norton, 1990.

Ryan, Mark A. *Chinese Attitudes Toward Nuclear Weapons: China and the United States During the Korean War.* Armonk, N.Y.: M.E. Sharpe, 1989.

Schaller, Michael. *The American Occupation of Japan: The Origins of the Cold War in Asia.* New York: Oxford University Press, 1985.

———. *Douglas MacArthur: The Far Eastern General.* New York: Oxford University Press, 1989.

Schlesinger, Arthur, Jr. *A Thousand Days.* Boston: Houghton Mifflin, 1965.

Schoenbaum, Thomas J. *Waging Peace and War: Dean Rusk in the Truman, Kennedy and Johnson Years.* New York: Simon and Schuster, 1988.

Seagrave, Sterling. *The Soong Dynasty.* New York: Harper and Row, 1985.

Sheng, Michael. *Battling Western Imperialism.* Princeton, N.J.: Princeton University Press, 1997.

Solomon, Richard H. *The China Factor: Sino–American Relations and the Global Scene.* Englewood Cliffs, N.J.: Prentice Hall, 1982.

Soman, Appu K. *Double-Edged Sword: Nuclear Diplomacy in Unequal Conflicts; The United States and China, 1950–1958.* Westport, Conn.: Praeger, 2000.

Starr, John Bryan, ed. *The Future of US–China Relations*. New York: New York University Press, 1981.

Steele, Archibald T. *The American People and China*. New York: McGraw-Hill, 1966.

Stolper, Thomas E. *China, Taiwan, and the Offshore Islands*. Armonk, N.Y.: M.E. Sharpe, 1985.

Stueck, William W. *The Korean War: An International History*. Princeton, N.J.: Princeton University Press, 1997.

———. *The Road to Confrontation: American Policy Toward China and Korea, 1947–1950*. Chapel Hill, N.C.: University of North Carolina Press, 1981.

Su, Ge. *Meiguo: Dui hua Zhengce yu Taiwan wenti* [America: China Policy and the Taiwan Issue]. Beijing: Shijie Zhishi Chubanshe, 1998.

Sutter, Robert G. *China Watch: Toward Sino–American Reconciliation*. Baltimore: Johns Hopkins University Press, 1978.

Taylor, Jay. *The Generalissimo's Son: Chiang Ching-kuo and the Revolutions in China and Taiwan*. Cambridge, Mass.: Harvard University Press, 2000.

Truman, Harry S. *Memoirs*. New York: New American Library, 1965.

Tsou, Tang. *Chinese Policies in Asia and America's Alternatives*. Chicago: University of Chicago Press, 1968.

———. *The Embroilment over Quemoy: Mao, Chiang, and Dulles*. Salt Lake City, Ut.: University of Utah Press, 1959.

Tucker, Nancy B. *China Confidential: American Diplomats and Sino–American Relations, 1945–1996*. New York: Columbia University Press, 2001.

———. *Patterns in the Dust: Chinese–American Relations and the Recognition Controversy, 1949–1950*. New York: Columbia University Press, 1983.

———. *Taiwan, Hong Kong, and the United States, 1945–1992: Uncertain Friendships*. New York: Twayne, 1994.

US Congress. Senate. Committee on the Judiciary. Subcommittee to Investigate the Administration of the Internal Security Act and Other Internal Security Laws. *Institute of Pacific Relations, Hearings*. 82d Congress, 1st and 2nd sessions, 15 parts. Washington, D.C.: US Government Printing Office, 1951–1952.

———. *The Amerasia papers: A Clue to the Catastrophe of China*. Washington, D.C.: US Government Printing Office, 1970.

US Congress. Senate. Committee on Foreign Relations. Subcommittee of the Committee on Foreign Relations. *State Department Employee Loyalty Investigation, Hearings*. 81st Congress, 2d session, 3 parts. Washington, D.C.: US Government Printing Office, 1950.

Van Ness, Peter. *Revolution and Chinese Foreign Policy*. Berkeley, Cal.: University of California, 1970.

Wang, Bingnan. *Zhongmei huitan jiunian huigu* [Nine Years of Sino–American Ambassadorial Talks]. Beijing: Shijie Zhishi, 1985.

Wang, Taiping, et al., *Zhonghua renmin gongheguo waijiao shi, 1957–1969* [A Diplomatic History of the People's Republic of China, 1957–1969]. Beijing: Shijie Zhishi, 1998.

Westad, Odd Arne. *Brothers in Arms: The Rise and Fall of the Sino–Soviet Alliance, 1945–1963.* Stanford, Cal.: Stanford University Press, 1998.

Whiting, Allen S. *China Crosses the Yalu.* New York: Macmillan, 1960.

——. *The Chinese Calculus of Deterrence: India and Indochina.* Ann Arbor, Mich.: University of Michigan Press, 1975.

Yahuda, Michael. *The International Politics of the Asia–Pacific, 1945–1995.* New York: Routledge, 1996.

Young, Kenneth T. *Negotiating with the Chinese Communists: The United States Experience, 1953–1967.* New York: McGraw Hill, 1968.

Yuen, Foong Khong. *Analogies at War: Korea, Munich, Dien Bien Phu, and the Vietnam Decisions of 1965.* Princeton, N.J.: Princeton University Press, 1992.

Zagoria, Donald. *The Sino–Soviet Conflict, 1956–1961.* New York: Antheneum, 1964.

Zeiler, Thomas W. *Dean Rusk: Defending the American Mission Abroad.* Wilmington, Del.: Scholarly Resources, 2000.

Zhai, Qiang. *China and the Vietnam Wars, 1950–1975.* Chapel Hill, N.C.: University of North Carolina Press, 2000.

——. *The Dragon, the Lion, and the Eagle: Chinese–British–American Relations, 1949–1958.* Kent, Ohio: Kent State University Press, 1994.

Zhang, Shuguang. *Deterrence and Strategic Culture: Chinese–American Conflicts, 1949–1959.* Ithaca, N.Y.: Cornell University Press, 1992.

——. *Economic Cold War: American Embargo Against China and the Sino–Soviet Alliance.* Stanford, Cal.: Stanford University Press.

——. *Mao's Military Romanticism.* Lawrence, Kan.: University of Kansas, 1995.

Zubok, Vladislav, and Constantine Pleshakov. *Inside the Kremlin's Cold War: From Stalin to Khrushchev.* Cambridge, Mass.: Harvard University Press, 1996.

6. RAPPROCHEMENT AND NORMALIZATION, 1969–1989

Barnds, William J., ed. *China and America: The Search for a New Relationship.* New York: New York University Press, 1977.

Barnett, A. Doak. *China and the Major Powers in East Asia.* Washington, D.C.: Brookings Institution, 1977.

——. *China's Economy in Global Perspective.* Washington, D.C.: Brookings Institution, 1981.

———. *The FX Decision.* Washington, D.C.: Brookings Institution, 1981.

———. *The Making of Foreign Policy in China.* Boulder, Colo.: Westview Press, 1985.

———. *A New US Policy Toward China.* Washington, D.C.: Brookings Institution, 1971.

———. *U.S. Arms Sales: The China–Taiwan Tangle.* Washington, D.C.: Brookings Institution, 1982.

Brown, Harold. *Thinking About Foreign Policy.* Boulder, Colo.: Westview Press, 1983.

Brzezinski, Zbigniew. *Power and Principle: Memoirs of the National Security Adviser, 1977–1981.* New York: Farrar, Straus, Giroux, 1983.

Bundy, William. *A Tangled Web: The Making of Foreign Policy in the Nixon Presidency.* New York: Hill and Wang, 1998.

Burles, Mark, and Abram N. Shulsky. *Patterns in China's Use of Force.* Santa Monica, Cal.: Rand, 2000.

Burr, William, ed. *The Kissinger Transcripts: The Top Secret Talks with Beijing and Moscow.* New York: New Press, 1998.

Carter, Jimmy. *Keeping Faith: Memoirs of a President.* New York: Bantam Books, 1982.

Cohen, Jerome A., ed. *Taiwan and American Foreign Policy: The Dilemma in US–China Relations.* New York: Praeger, 1971.

Cohen, Warren I., ed. *New Frontiers in American–East Asian Relations.* New York: Columbia University Press, l983.

Dai, Qing. *Yangtze! Yangtze!* London: Earthscan, 1989.

Dittmer, Lowell. *Sino–Soviet Normalization and Its International Implications, 1945–1990.* Seattle, Wash.: University of Washington Press, 1992.

Dittmer, Lowell, and Samuel S. Kim, eds. *China's Quest for National Identity.* Ithaca, N.Y.: Cornell University Press, 1993.

Edmonds, Richard Louis, and Steven Goldstein, eds. *Taiwan in the Twentieth Century.* Cambridge, England: Cambridge University Press, 2001.

Evans, Richard. *Deng Xiaoping and the Making of Modern China.* New York: Penguin Books USA, 1993.

Faust, John, and Judith Kornberg. *China in World Politics.* Boulder, Colo.: Lynne Reinner Publishers, 1995.

Fingar, Thomas, ed. *China's Quest for Independence.* Boulder, Colo.: Westview Press, 1980.

Foot, Rosemary. *The Practice of Power: US Relations with China Since 1949.* New York: Oxford University Press, 1997.

Garthoff, Raymond L. *Détente and Confrontation: American–Soviet Relations from Nixon to Reagan.* Washington, D.C.: Brookings Institution, 1985.

Garver, John W. *China's Decision for Rapprochement with the United States, 1968–1971.* Boulder, Colo.: Westview Press, 1982.

———. *Foreign Relations of the People's Republic of China.* Englewood Cliffs, N.J.: Prentice Hall, 1993.

Gilbert, Stephen P., and William M. Carpenter, eds. *America and Island China: A Documentary History.* Lanham, Md.: University Press of America, 1989.

Gong, Li. *Kuayue: 1969–1979 nian Zhong Mei guanxi de yanbian* [Across the Chasm: The Evolution of China–US Relations, 1969–1979]. Henan: Henan People's Press, 1992.

Goodman, David G. *Deng Xiaoping and the Chinese Revolution: A Political Biography.* New York: Routledge, 1994.

Gottlieb, Thomas. *Chinese Foreign Policy Factionalism and the Origins of the Strategic Triangle.* Santa Monica, Cal.: RAND, 1977.

Haig, Alexander Jr. *Caveat: Realism, Reagan, and Foreign Policy.* New York: Macmillan, 1984.

Hamrin, Carol Lee, and Suisheng Zhao, eds. *Decision-Making in Deng's China: Perspectives from Insiders.* Armonk, N.Y.: M.E. Sharpe, 1995.

Hao, Yufan, and Guocang Huan, eds. *The Chinese View of the World.* New York: Pantheon, 1989.

Harding, Harry. *A Fragile Relationship: The US and China Since 1972.* Washington, D.C.: Brookings Institution, 1992.

———. *China's Second Revolution.* Washington, D.C.: Brookings Institution, 1987.

Harding, Harry, ed. *China's Foreign Relations in the 1980s.* New Haven, Conn.: Yale University Press, 1984.

Hellman, Donald C., ed. *China and Japan: A New Balance of Power.* Lexington, Mass.: Lexington, 1976.

Hersh, Seymour. *The Price of Power: Kissinger in the Nixon White House.* New York: Summit Books, 1983.

Holdridge, John H. *Crossing the Divide: An Insider's Account of the Normalization of US–China Relations.* Lanham, Md.: Rowman and Littlefield, 1997.

Holdridge, John, and Marshall Green. *War and Peace with China: Firsthand Experiences in the Foreign Service of the United States.* Bethesda, Md.: Dacor-Bacon House, 1994.

Hsiao, Gene T., ed. *Sino–American Detente and Its Implications.* New York: Praeger, 1974.

Isaacson, Walter. *Kissinger: A Biography.* New York: Simon and Schuster, 1992.

Jiang, Changbin, and Robert S. Ross, eds. *1955–1971 Nian de Zhong Mei Guanxi—Huanhe Zhigian: Lengzhan Chongtu yu Keshi de Cai Tantao* [US–China Relations, 1955–1971—Before Détente: An Examination of Cold War Conflict and Restraint]. Beijing: Shijie Zhishi Chubanshe, 1998.

Kissinger, Henry. *White House Years.* Boston: Little, Brown, 1979.

——. *Years of Upheaval.* Boston: Little, Brown, 1983.

Kusnitz, Leonard. *Public Opinion and Foreign Policy: America's China Policy, 1949–1979.* Westport, Conn.: Greenwood Press, 1984.

Lampton, David M., *A Relationship Restored: Trends in US–China Educational Exchanges, 1978–1984.* Washington, D.C.: National Academy Press, 1986.

Lardy, Nicholas. *Foreign Trade and Economic Reform in China.* New York: Cambridge University Press, 1992.

Lasater, Martin L. *The Taiwan Issue in Sino–American Strategic Relations.* Boulder, Colo.: Westview, 1984.

Lawson, Eugene, ed. *U.S.–China Trade: Problems and Prospects.* New York: Praeger, 1988.

Lee, David Tawei. *The Making of the Taiwan Relations Act.* New York: Oxford University Press, 2000.

Li, Victor. *Derecognizing Taiwan: The Legal Problems.* Washington, D.C.: Carnegie Endowment for International Peace, 1977.

Lin, Qing. *Zhou Enlai zaixiang shengya* [The Career of Prime Minister Zhou Enlai]. Hong Kong: Changcheng Wenhua Chubanshe, 1991.

Lu, Ning. *The Dynamics of Foreign Policy Decision Making in China.* Boulder, Colo.: Westview Press, 1997.

Madsen, Richard. *China and the American Dream: A Moral Inquiry.* Berkeley, Cal.: University of California Press, 1995.

Mann, Jim. *About Face: A History of America's Curious Relationship with China, From Nixon to Clinton.* New York: Knopf, 1999.

Moorstein, Richard, and Morton Abramowitz. *Remaking China Policy.* Cambridge, Mass.: Harvard University Press, 1971.

Myers, Ramon, ed. *A Unique Relationship: The United States and the Republic of China Under the Taiwan Relations Act.* Stanford, Cal.: Hoover Institution, 1989.

Nathan, Andrew J., and Robert S. Ross. *The Great Wall and the Empty Fortress: China's Search for Security.* New York: W. W. Norton, 1997.

Nixon, Richard. *RN: The Memoirs of Richard Nixon.* New York: Grosset and Dunlap, 1978.

Oksenberg, Michel, and Robert B. Oxnam. *Dragon and Eagle: United States–China Relations, Past and Future.* New York: Basic Books, 1978.

Orleans, Leo. *Chinese Students in America: Policies, Issues, and Numbers.* Washington, D.C.: National Academy Press, 1988.

Pei, Jianzhang. *Yanjiu Zhou Enlai: Waijiao sixiang yu shijian* [Researching Zhou Enlai: Diplomatic Thought and Practice]. Beijing: Shijie Zhishi Chubanshe, 1989.

Perkins, Dwight. *China: Asia's Next Economic Giant?* Seattle, Wash.: University of Washington Press, 1986.

Qian, Jiang. *Ping Pong waijiao muhou* [Behind the Ping Pong Diplomacy]. Beijing: Dongfang, 1997.

Robinson, Thomas W., and David Shambaugh, eds. *Chinese Foreign Policy: Theory and Practice.* New York: Clarendon Press, 1997.

Ross, Robert S. *The Indochina Tangle.* New York: Columbia University Press, 1988.

———. *Negotiating Cooperation: The United States and China, 1969–1989.* Stanford, Cal.: Stanford University Press, 1995.

Rostow, Walt W. *The United States and the Regional Organization of Asia and the Pacific, 1965–1985.* Austin, Tex.: University of Texas Press, 1986.

Schulzinger, Robert. *Henry Kissinger: Doctor of Diplomacy.* New York: Columbia University Press, 1989.

———. *A Time for War: The United States and Vietnam, 1941–1975.* New York: Oxford University Press, 1997.

Shambaugh, David. *Beautiful Imperialist: China Perceives America, 1972–1980.* Princeton, N.J.: Princeton University Press, 1991.

Shirk, Susan L. *How China Opened Its Door: The Political Success of the PRC's Foreign Trade and Investment Reforms.* Washington, D.C.: Brookings Institution, 1994.

Shultz, George. *Turmoil and Triumph.* New York: Scribners, 1993.

Smith, Hendrick. *The Power Game: How Washington Works.* New York: Random House, 1988.

Solomon, Richard H. *Chinese Political Negotiating Behavior, 1967–1984: An Interpretive Assessment.* Santa Monica, Cal: RAND, 1995.

Sutter, Robert G. *The China Quandary: Domestic Determinants of US China Policy, 1972–1982.* Boulder, Colo.: Westview Press, 1983.

———. *Taiwan: Entering the 21st Century.* Lanham, Md.: University Press of America, 1988.

Tain, Zengpei, ed. *Gaige kaifang yilai de Zhongguo waijiao* [Chinese Diplomacy Since Reform and Opening]. Beijing: Shijie Zhishi Chubanshe, 1993.

Taylor, Jay. *The Generalissimo's Son: Chiang Ching-kuo and the Revolutions in China and Taiwan.* Cambridge, Mass.: Harvard University Press, 2000.

Topping, Seymour. *Journey Between Two Chinas.* New York: Harper and Row, 1973.

Tucker, Nancy B. *China Confidential: American Diplomats and Sino–American Relations, 1945–1996.* New York: Columbia University Press, 2001.

Tyler, Patrick. *A Great Wall: Six American Presidents and China.* New York: Public Affairs, 1999.

US Congress. House. Committee on Foreign Affairs. *Executive-Legislative Consultations over China Policy, 1978–1979.* Washington, D.C.: US Government Printing Office, 1980.

——. *Implementation of the Taiwan Relations Act.* Hearings, October 23 and November 8, 1979. Washington, D.C.: US Government Printing Office, 1980.

——. *Taiwan Legislation.* Hearings, February 7 and 8, 1979. Washington, D.C.: US Government Printing Office, 1979.

——. *Taiwan Relations Act.* Conference Report, March 24, 1979. Washington, D.C.: US Government Printing Office, 1979.

——. *United States–Taiwan Relations Act.* Report, March 3, 1979. Washington, D.C.: US Government Printing Office, 1979.

US Congress. House. Committee on Foreign Affairs. Subcommittee on Asian and Pacific Affairs. *China and Asia—An Analysis of China's Recent Policy Toward Neighboring States.* Washington, D.C.: US Government Printing Office, 1979.

——. *Playing the China Card: Implications for United States–Soviet–Chinese Relations.* Washington, D.C.: US Government Printing Office, 1979.

——. *Implementation of the Taiwan Relations Act: Issues and Concerns.* Washington, D.C.: US Government Printing Office, 1979.

——. *The United States and the People's Republic of China: Issues for the 1980s.* Hearings, April 1, July 22, August 26, and September 23, 1980. Washington, D.C.: US Government Printing Office, 1980.

——. *Security and Stability in Asia: 1979.* Washington, D.C.: US Government Printing Office, 1979.

US Congress. House. Committee on International Relations. *United States–China Normalization: The Process of Normalization of Relations.* Washington, D.C.: US Government Printing Office, 1976.

——. *United States–Soviet Union–China: The Great Power Triangle.* Washington, D.C.: US Government Printing Office, 1976.

US Congress. House. Committee on International Relations, Subcommittee on Asian and Pacific Affairs. *Normalization of Relations with the People's Republic of China: Practical Implications.* Washington, D.C.: US Government Printing Office, 1977.

US Congress. House. Committee on Ways and Means. *Approving the Extension of Nondiscriminatory Treatment to Products of the PRC.* Washington, D.C.: US Government Printing Office, 1980.

US Congress. Joint Economic Committee. *China Under the Four Modernizations.* Washington, D.C.: US Government Printing Office, 1982.

——. *Chinese Economy Post-Mao.* Washington, D.C.: US Government Printing Office, 1978.

US Congress. Senate Foreign Relations Committee. *Implementation of the Taiwan Relations Act: The First Year.* Washington, D.C.: US Government Printing Office, 1980.

――. *The Implications of U.S.–China Military Cooperation.* Workshop Sponsored by Senate Committee on Foreign Relations and Congressional Research Service. Washington, D.C.: US Government Printing Office, 1981.

――. *Sino–American Relations: A New Turn.* Washington, D.C.: US Government Printing Office, 1979.

――. *Some Recent Developments Related to Human Rights in the People's Republic of China.* Washington, D.C.: US Government Printing Office, 1979.

――. *Taiwan.* Hearings, February 5, 6, 7, 8, 21, and 22, 1979. Washington, D.C.: US Government Printing Office, 1979.

Vance, Cyrus. *Hard Choices.* New York: Simon and Schuster, 1983.

Watts, William, et al. *Japan, Korea and China: American Perceptions and Policies.* Lexington, Mass.: D.C. Heath, 1979.

Wolff, Lester, and David L. Simon. *Legislative History of the Taiwan Relations Act.* Jamaica, N.Y.: American Association for Chinese Studies, 1982.

Xie Xide, and Ni Shixiong. *Quzhe de licheng: Zhong Mei jianji ershi nian* [From Normalization to Renormalization: 20 Years of Sino–US Relations]. Shanghai: Fudan Daxue Chubanshe, 1999.

Yahuda, Michael. *China's Role in World Affairs.* New York: St. Martins, 1978.

――. *The International Politics of the Asia–Pacific, 1945–1995.* New York: Routledge, 1996.

Yang, Benjamin. *Deng: A Political Biography.* Armonk, N.Y.: M.E. Sharpe, 1998.

7. TIANANMEN, TAIWAN, AND POST-COLD WAR REALITIES, 1989–2004

Allen, Kenneth W., and Eric A. McVadon. *China's Foreign Military Relations.* Washington, D.C.: Henry L. Stimson Center, 1999.

Asia Pacific Center for Security Studies. *Asia's China Debate.* Honolulu: Asia Pacific Center for Security Studies, December 2003.

Baker, James A. III. *The Politics of Diplomacy—Revolution, War, and Peace, 1989–1992.* New York: G.P. Putman, 1995.

Barnett, A. Doak. *U.S.–China Relations: Time for a New Beginning—Again.* Washington, D.C.: Johns Hopkins University, School for Advanced International Studies, 1994.

Bernstein, Richard, and Ross H. Munro. *Coming Conflict with China.* New York: Knopf, 1998.

Burles, Mark. *Chinese Policy Toward Russia and the Central Asian Republics.* Santa Monica, Cal.: RAND, 1999.

Burles, Mark, and Abram N. Shulsky. *Patterns in China's Use of Force.* Santa Monica, Cal.: Rand, 2000.

Bush, George H. W. *All the Best: My Life in Letters and Other Writings.* New York: Scribner, 1999.

Bush, George H. W., and Brent Scowcroft. *A World Transformed.* New York: Knopf, 1998.

Callick, Rowman. *Comrades and Capitalists: Hong Kong Since the Handover.* Sydney, Australia: University of New South Wales Press, 1998.

Carter, Ashton B., and William J. Perry. *Preventive Defense: A New Security Strategy for America.* Washington, D.C.: Brookings Institution, 1999.

Chang, Gordon. *The Coming Collapse of China.* New York: Random House, 2001.

Chin, Ko-lin. *Smuggled Chinese: Clandestine Immigration to the United States.* Philadelphia, Penn.: Temple University Press, 1999.

Christensen, Thomas J. "China, the US–Japan alliance, and the Security Dilemma in East Asia." *International Security* 23 no. 4 (Spring 1999): 49–80.

——. *New Challenges and Opportunities in the Taiwan Strait: Defining America's role.* New York: National Committee on US–China Relations, November 2003.

——. "Posing Problems Without Catching Up: China's Rise and Challenges for US Security Policy," *International Security* 25 no. 4 (spring 2001): 5–40.

Christopher, Warren. *In the Stream of History: Shaping Foreign Policy for a New Era.* Stanford, Cal.: Stanford University Press, 1998.

Clough, Ralph. *Cooperation or Conflict in the Taiwan Strait?* Lanham, Md.: Rowman and Littlefield, 1999.

——. *Reaching Across the Taiwan Strait.* Boulder, Colo.: Westview Press, 1993.

Cohen, Warren I., ed. *Pacific Passage: The Study of American–East Asian Relations on the Eve of the Twenty-First Century.* New York: Columbia University Press, 1996.

Cummings, Bruce. *Parallax Visions: Making Sense of American–East Asian Relations at the End of the Century.* Raleigh–Durham, N.C.: Duke University Press, 1999.

Davis, Michael C., ed. *Human Rights and Chinese Values.* New York: Oxford University Press, 1995.

Dickson, Bruce J., and Chien-min Chao, eds. *Assessing the Lee Teng-hui Legacy.* Armonk, N.Y.: M.E. Sharpe, 2002.

Economy, Elizabeth, and Michel Oksenberg, eds. *China Joins the World: Progress and Prospects.* New York: Council on Foreign Relations Press, 1999.

Funabashi, Yoichi, et al. *An Emerging China in a World of Interdependence.* New York: Trilateral Commission, 1994.

Fung, K. C., and Lawrence J. Lau. *The China–United States Bilateral Trade Balance: How Big Is It Really?* Stanford, Cal.: Asia/Pacific Research Center, 1996.

Garver, John W. *Face Off: China, the United States, and Taiwan's Democratization.* Seattle, Wash.: University of Washington, 1997.

Gilley, Bruce. *Tiger on the Brink: Jiang Zemin and China's New Elite.* Berkeley, Cal.: University of California Press, 1998.

Goldstein, Melvyn C. *The Snow Lion and the Dragon.* Berkeley, Cal.: University of California Press, 1997.

Gong, Gerritt, ed. *Taiwan Strait Dilemmas.* Washington, D.C.: Center for Strategic and International Studies, 2000.

Guthrie, Doug. *Dragon in a Three-Piece Suit: The Emergence of Capitalism in China.* Princeton, N.J.: Princeton University Press, 1999.

Hughes, Christopher. *Taiwan and Chinese Nationalism.* New York: Routledge, 1997.

Johnston, Alastair Iain, et al. *The Cox Committee Report: An Assessment.* Stanford, Cal.: Center for International Security and Cooperation, 1999.

Kent, Ann. *China, the United Nations, and Human Rights.* Philadelphia, Penn.: University of Pennsylvania Press, 1999.

Khalilzad, Zalmay M., et al. *The United States and a Rising China: Strategic and Military Implications.* Santa Monica, Cal.: Rand, 1999.

Kim, Samuel S., ed. *China and the World: Chinese Foreign Relations in the Post–Cold War Era.* Boulder, Colo.: Westview Press, 1998.

Klintworth, Gary. *New Taiwan, New China: Taiwan's Changing Role in the Asia–Pacific Region.* New York: St. Martins, 1995.

Knaus, John Kenneth. *Orphans of the Cold War: America and the Tibetan Struggle for Survival.* New York: Public Affairs, 1999.

Lam, Willy-Wo-Lap. *The Era of Jiang Zemin.* Singapore: Prentice Hall, 1999.

Lampton, David M. *Same Bed, Different Dreams: Managing US–China Relations, 1989–2000.* Berkeley, Cal.: University of California, 2001.

Lampton, David M., ed. *The Making of Chinese Foreign and Security Policy.* Stanford, Cal.: Stanford University Press, 2001.

Lampton, David M., and Alfred Wilhelm. eds. *United States and China: Relations at a Crossroads.* Lanham, Md.: University Press of America, 1995.

Lardy, Nicholas. *China's Unfinished Economic Revolution.* Washington, D.C.: Brookings Institution, 1998.

———. *Integrating China Into the Global Economy.* Washington, D.C.: Brookings Institution, 2002.

Lee, Wei-chin, and T.Y. Wang. eds. *Sayonara to the Lee Teng-hui Era: Politics in Taiwan, 1988–2000.* Lanham, Md.: University Press of America, 2003.

Lilley, James R., and Wendell L. Willkie II, eds. *Beyond MFN: Trade with China and American Interests.* Washington, D.C.: American Enterprise Institute, 1994.

Madsen, Richard. *China and the American Dream: A Moral Inquiry.* Berkeley, Cal.: University of California Press, 1995.

Mandelbaum, Michael. *The Strategic Quadrangle.* New York: Council on Foreign Relations Press, 1995.

Mann, Jim. *About Face: A History of America's Curious Relationship with China, From Nixon to Clinton.* New York: Knopf, 1999.

Mosher, Steven. *Hegemon: China's Plan to Dominate Asia and the World.* San Francisco, Cal.: Encounter Books, 2000.

Mulvenon, James C., and Richard H. Yang, eds. *The People's Liberation Army in the Information Age.* Santa Monica, Cal: RAND, 1999.

Nathan, Andrew J., et al., eds. *The Tiananmen Papers: The Chinese Leadership's Decision to Use Force Against Their Own People—in Their Own Words.* New York: Public Affairs, 2001.

Nathan, Andrew J., and Robert S. Ross. *The Great Wall and the Empty Fortress: China's Search for Security.* New York: W. W. Norton, 1997.

Naughton, Barry, ed. *The China Circle: Economics and Technology in the PRC, Taiwan, and Hong Kong.* Washington, D.C.: Brookings Institution, 1997.

Nye, Joseph S., Jr. *Bound to Lead: The Changing Nature of American Power.* New York: Basic Books, 1991.

O'Hanlon, Michael. "Why China Cannot Conquer Taiwan." *International Security* 25 no. 2 (Fall 2000): 51–86.

Patten, Christopher. *East and West.* New York: New York Times Books, 1998.

Pillsbury, Michael. *China Debates the Future Security Environment.* Washington, D.C.: National Defense University, 2000.

———. *Chinese Views of Future Warfare.* Washington, D.C.: National Defense University, 1998.

Pollack, Jonathan D., and Richard H. Yang, eds. *In China's Shadow: Regional Perspectives on Chinese Foreign Policy and Military Developments.* Santa Monica, Cal.: RAND, 1998.

Pollpeter, Kevin. *US–China Security Management: Assessing the Military-to-Military Relationship.* Santa Monica, Cal.: RAND, 2004.

Rigger, Shelley. *From Opposition to Power: Taiwan's Democratic Progressive Party.* Boulder, Colo.: Lynne Rienner Publishers, 2001.

———. *Politics in Taiwan.* New York: Routledge, 1999.

Robinson, Thomas W., and David Shambaugh, eds. *Chinese Foreign Policy: Theory and Practice.* New York: Clarendon Press, 1997.

Romberg, Alan. *Rein In at the Brink of the Precipice.* Washington, D.C.: Henry Stimson Center, 2003.

Ross, Robert S. *After the Cold War: Domestic Factors and US–China Relations.* Armonk, N.Y.: M.E. Sharpe, 1998.

———. "The Geography of Peace: East Asia in the Twenty-First Century." *International Security* 23 no. 4 (Spring 1999): 81–118.

Roy, Denny. *China's Foreign Relations*. Lanham, Md.: Rowman and Little-field, 1998.

——. *Taiwan: A Political History*. Ithaca, N.Y.: Cornell University Press, 2003.

——. *Taiwan's Threat Perceptions: The Enemy Within*. Honolulu: Asia Pacific Center for Security Studies, Occasional Paper, March 2003.

——. "Tensions in the Taiwan Strait." *Survival* 42 no. 1 (Spring 2000): 76–96.

Seymour, James D., and Richard Anderson. *New Ghosts, Old Ghosts: Prisons and Labor Reform Camps in China*. Armonk, N.Y.: M.E. Sharpe, 1998.

Shambaugh, David. "China's Military Views the World." *International Security* 24 no. 3 (Winter 1999): 52–79.

——, ed. *Contemporary Taiwan*. New York: Clarendon Press, 1998.

——. *Is China Unstable?: Assessing the Factors*. Washington, D.C.: Sigur Center for Asian Studies, George Washington University, 1998.

——. *Modernizing China's Military: Progress, Problems, and Prospects*. Berkeley, Cal.: University of California Press, 2002.

——. "Sino–American Strategic Relations: from Partners to Competitors," *Survival* 42 no.1 (Spring 2000): 97–115.

Sheng, Lijun. *China's Dilemma: The Taiwan Issue*. Singapore: Institute of Southeast Asian Studies, 2000.

Shinn, James, ed., *Weaving the Net: Conditional Engagement with China*. New York: Council on Foreign Relations, 1996.

Shlapak, David, David Orletsky, and Barry Wilson. *Dire Strait? Military As-pects of the China–Taiwan Confrontation and Options for US policy*. Santa Monica, Cal.: RAND, 2000.

Smith, Paul J., ed. *Human Smuggling: Chinese Migrant Trafficking and the Challenge to America's Immigration Tradition*. Washington, D.C.: Center for Strategic and International Studies, 1997.

Song, Qiang, Zhang Changchang, and Qiao Bian. *Zhongguo keyi shuo bu: Lengzhanhou shidai de zhengzhi yu qinggan jueze* [China Can Say No: The Decision Between Politics and Sentiment in the Post–Cold War]. Beijing: Zhonghua Gongshang Lianhe Chubanshe, 1996.

Suettinger, Robert L. *Beyond Tiananmen: The Politics of US–China Relations, 1989–2000*. Washington, D.C.: Brookings Institution, 2003.

Su, Ge. *Meiguo: Dui hua Zhengce yu Taiwan wenti* [America: China Policy and the Taiwan Issue]. Beijing: Shijie Zhishi Chubanshe, 1998.

Sutter, Robert G. *Chinese Policy Priorities and Their Implications for the United States*. Lanham, Md.: Rowman and Littlefield, 2000.

——.*US Policy Toward China: An Introduction to the Role of Interest Groups*. Lanham, Md.: Rowman and Littlefield, 1998.

Sutter, Robert, and William Johnson, eds. *Taiwan in World Affairs*. Boulder, Colo.: Westview Press, 1994.

Swaine, Michael D. *China: Domestic Change and Foreign Policy*. Santa Monica, Cal.: RAND, 1995.

———. *Deterring Conflict in the Taiwan Strait: The Successes and Failures of Taiwan's Defense Reform and Modernization Program*. Washington: Carnegie Endowment for International Peace. Carnegie Paper 46, July 2004.

———. *Reverse Course? The Fragile Turnaround in U.S.–China Relations*. Washington, D.C.: Carnegie Endowment for International Peace. Carnegie Endowment Policy Brief No. 22, February 2003.

———. *The Role of the Chinese Military in National Security Policymaking*. Santa Monica, Cal.: RAND, 1998.

Swaine, Michael D., and Ashley J. Tellis. *Interpreting China's Grand Strategy: Past, Present, and Future*. Santa Monica, Cal.: RAND, 2000.

Swaine, Michael, and James Mulvenon. *Taiwan's Foreign and Defense Policies: Features and Determinants*. Santa Monica, Cal.: RAND, 2001.

Tucker, Nancy B. "China–Taiwan: U.S. Debates and Policy Choices," *Survival* 40 no.4 (Winter 1998): 150–167.

———. "If Taiwan Chooses Unification, Should the US Care?" *Washington Quarterly* 25 no. 3 (Summer 2002): 15–28.

Tyler, Patrick. *A Great Wall: Six American Presidents and China*. New York: Public Affairs, 1999.

US Congress. Joint Economic Committee. *China's Economic Future: Challenges to U.S. Policy*. Washington, D.C.: US Government Printing Office, 1996.

US Congress. Senate Foreign Relations Committee. *Sino–Soviet Relations After the Summit*. Workshop Sponsored by the Senate Foreign Relations Committee—Congressional Research Service. Washington, D.C.: US Government Printing Office, 1990.

US–China Economic and Security Review Commission. *Report to Congress, June 2004*. Washington, D.C.: US Government Printing Office, 2004.

US–China Security Review Commission. *Report to Congress, July 2002*. Washington, D.C.: US Government Printing Office, 2002.

US Department of Defense. *Annual Report on the Military Power of the People's Republic of China, 2004*. Washington, D.C.: US Department of Defense, 2004.

US Department of Defense. *Annual Report on the Military Power of the People's Republic of China, 2003*. Washington, D.C.: US Department of Defense, 2003.

US Department of Defense. *Annual Report on the Military Power of the People's Republic of China, 2002*. Washington, D.C.: US Department of Defense, 2002.

Vogel, Ezra., ed. *Living with China: US–China Relations in the Twenty-First Century*. New York: W.W. Norton, 1997.

Wachman, Alan M. *Taiwan: National Identity and Democratization.* Armonk, N.Y.: M.E. Sharpe, 1994.

Wang, Jisi. "The Role of the United States as a Global and Pacific Power: A View from China." *Pacific Review* 10, no. 1 (1997): 1–18.

Watson, James L. *Golden Arches East: McDonald's in East Asia.* Stanford, Cal.: Stanford University Press, 1997.

World Bank, *China 2020: Development Challenges in the New Century.* Volume 1 of *China 2020.* Washington, D.C.: World Bank, 1997.

Xie, Xide, and Ni Shixiong. *Quzhe de licheng: Zhong Mei jianji ershi nian* [From Normalization to Renormalization: 20 Years of Sino–US Relations]. Shanghai: Fudan Daxue Chubanshe, 1999.

Yan, Xuetong. *Zhongguo guojia liyi fenxi* [The Analysis of China's National Interest]. Tianjin: Tianjin Renmin Chubanshe, 1996.

Yan, Xuetong, Wang Zaibang, Li Zhongcheng, and Hou Roushi. *Zhongguo jueqi: Guoji huanjing pinggu* [International Environment for China's Rise]. Tianjin Renmin Chubanshe, 1998.

Zagoria, Donald S. *Breaking the China–Taiwan Impasse.* Westport, Conn.: Praeger, 2003.

Zhang, Ming. *China's Changing Nuclear Posture.* Washington, D.C.: Carnegie Endowment for International Peace, 1999.

Zhang, Yunling, ed. *Hezou haishi duikang: Lengzhanhou de Zhongguo, Meiguo he Riben* [Cooperation or Confrontation: China, the United States, and Japan After the Cold War]. Beijing: Zhongguo Shehui Kexue Chubanshe, 1997.

Zhao, Quansheng. *Interpreting Chinese Foreign Policy.* New York: Oxford University Press, 1996.

Zhao, Suisheng. *Making Sense of Relations Across the Taiwan Strait: The Crisis of 1995–1996.* New York: Routledge, 1999.

About the Author

Robert Sutter has been a visiting professor in the School of Foreign Service at Georgetown University since August 2001.

Dr. Sutter specialized in Asian and Pacific Affairs and US foreign policy in a US government career of more than 30 years. He held a variety of analytical and supervisory positions with the Library of Congress for more than 20 years, and he also worked with the Central Intelligence Agency, the Department of State, and the Senate Foreign Relations Committee. After leaving the Library of Congress, where he was for many years the Senior Specialist in International Politics for the Congressional Research Service, Dr. Sutter served for two years as the National Intelligence Officer for East Asia and the Pacific at the US Government's National Intelligence Council.

He received a Ph.D. in History and East Asian Languages from Harvard University. He has held adjunct faculty positions with Georgetown, George Washington, and Johns Hopkins Universities and the University of Virginia. He has published 14 books, numerous articles, and several hundred government reports dealing with contemporary East Asian and Pacific countries and their relations with the United States. His work has focused often on US policy toward China, China's role in Asian and world affairs, and their implications for US–China relations.

Sutter's first book, *China Watch: Toward Sino-American Reconciliation* (Johns Hopkins University Press, 1978) was based on his Ph.D. dissertation and assessed the origins of the US–China breakthrough in relations in the late 1960s against the background of earlier unsuccessful efforts to improve relations in the 1940s and 1950s. His most recent book, *China's Rise in Asia: Promises and Perils* (Rowman and Littlefield, 2005), assesses the strengths and weaknesses of China's rising influence in Asia and what they mean for US policy and interests.